WARRIOR POLICE

WARRIOR POLICE

Rolling with America's Military Police in the World's Trouble Spots

Lieutenant Colonel (Ret.) Gordon Cucullu
and **Chris Fontana**

St. Martin's Press ✹ New York

www.stmartins.com

Library of Congress Cataloging-in-Publication Data

Cucullu, Gordon.
  Warrior police : rolling with America's military police in the world's trouble
spots / Gordon Cucullu and Chris Fontana.
     p. cm.
  Includes bibliographical references and index.
  ISBN 978-0-312-65855-7
 1. United States—Armed Forces—Military police. 2. Iraq war, 2003—
Campaigns. 3. Iraq War, 2003—Personal narratives, American. 4. Afghan
War, 2001—Campaigns. 5. Afghan War, 2001—Personal narratives, American.
I. Fontana, Chris. II. Title. III. Title: Rolling with America's military police in
the world's trouble spots.
  UB825.U54C84 2011
  956.7044'342—dc23

2011020902

First Edition: September 2011

10 9 8 7 6 5 4 3 2 1

To generations of Americans past and present, who when called by their country said, "Send me!"

For the Valhalla Project and all that it will become.

CONTENTS

PART I

Testing the Regiment

PART II

Gobsmacked: A Downrange Reality Check

WARRIOR POLICE

TESTING THE REGIMENT

1

NOTHING BUT THE FLAG

The windowless Pentagon conference room shuddered with a strange vibration seconds before the deep rumble of an explosion rocked the building. Colonel David Phillips glanced at his watch, noting the time—0937—while springing from his chair, running for the door alongside shocked colleagues.

As if in a slow-motion nightmare Phillips raced down the long Pentagon corridors in the most direct route to his far-side office. He quickly encountered emergency workers who already blocked the way. Without pause Phillips glanced around, desperately looking for a stairwell. He almost tumbled down the wide staircase toward the nearest exit. Pushing his way through crowds of evacuees, he sprinted outside.

He was blinded for a moment in the bright sunlight. As he looked west, his worst fears crashed into the center of his soul—gigantic roiling clouds of oily black smoke gushed from the distant side of the building. All that he had prepared for during his long Army career, yet had never personally experienced, stretched out before his eyes in a kaleidoscope of chaos.

Fire trucks and emergency vehicles were already jumping the curbs and tearing across the lawns as onlookers—witnesses—were driven back from the scorching heat, the stench of jet fuel and flames shooting out from a monstrous crater in the side of the Pentagon's smooth, five-story wall.

His side of the building.

Where are my people? his mind screamed as he struggled to absorb what was clearly a mass-casualty situation and fought against waves of nausea at the realization that every one of his staff could be dead or lying wounded inside.

That fateful morning certainly hadn't started out that way.

Phillips, a lanky military police officer, had only recently been parked in a relatively quiet temporary assignment at the Pentagon, as director of security for the Army staff, while waiting to take command of the 89th Military Police Brigade at Fort Hood, Texas. "We're going to put you in a quiet job, in charge of Army security at the Pentagon for a few months, so that you can focus your energies on prepping up for your new command," his superiors had told him. And it was working out very well.

Life was good for the forty-five-year-old native of Cleveland, Ohio. Things at his current home in Alexandria, Virginia, were humming along, and he had a great staff with an energetic senior noncommissioned officer at his side. His unit ran smoothly without a lot of stress. After almost twenty-one years in the Army his future looked brighter than ever.

Even the commute to the Pentagon had been pleasant that morning. The stifling humid heat of August in Washington had blown away, replaced by the kind of crisp, clear September weather that makes real estate agents salivate. On a day like today you could sell D.C. to anyone. After checking in with his office and grabbing a cup of coffee he'd hiked across the Pentagon complex to attend a meeting.

Phillips had idly wondered how long the building could function without the endless stream of meetings that occupied his days. Meetings, he decided, were a mental treadmill: Run like hell but never really get anywhere.

Everyone in the conference room was dutifully focused on the issues at hand when suddenly a faceless staffer—later on, nobody could recall who it was—erupted through the door shouting, "Quick, turn on the television. An aircraft has just crashed into the World Trade Center in New York!"

Someone snapped on the conference room flat screen and all present gaped at the terrifying sight of the North Tower of the World Trade Center consumed by billowing gray clouds of smoke, debris, and flames against the bright blue New York morning.

"How in the hell did that happen?" someone wondered aloud. "There's not a cloud in the damn sky."

Voices began to chatter. "Look!" someone exclaimed. "There's an airplane." In the background the camera caught a civilian airliner dipping low over the harbor and banking steeply.

"Jesus Christ!" The second plane impacted the South Tower in a fiery billow. Those in the meeting could only imagine the sound as pieces of debris showered downward and flames licked hungrily at the higher floors.

The room erupted with chatter. "This looks deliberate," someone noted. "We're under attack!" By now news crews began to focus long-distance lenses on hapless people crowding openings in broken windows, waving shirts, crying for help.

The tiny distant figures on the flat screen before them began, slowly, individually or while holding hands, to jump from more than eighty stories high to their deaths.

The conference room fell silent. Colonel Phillips struggled to comprehend the images before him.

It was as if time itself stopped, although everyone in that conference room knew that everything—reality itself—had instantly changed in a way that most civilians would not fully recognize.

And then under their own feet the entire building vibrated. A deep explosion resounded through the building. "We've been hit!" someone shouted. They rose simultaneously, moving as one for the door and whatever the future held.

Now outside, Colonel Phillips paused, trying to absorb the magnitude of the disaster that confronted him. It seemed to be a version of the aftermath of a car bomb in Beirut or some other war zone. Somewhere else in the world, certainly not America. He was nauseous with worry. How many of his people had been killed or wounded?

Even from a relatively safe distance he could see furniture, drapery, and plumbing hanging obscenely from broken floors, waving in the heat from roaring flames. Twisted rebar was exposed along jagged concrete edges where American Airlines Flight 77 had hit his office suite. *Where are my people?* The thought screamed again in his head, over the cacophony of shouts, sirens, and roaring engines.

A familiar face darkened by smoke popped out next to him without warning. His acting sergeant major, Sergeant First Class Harry T. Byrd, shouted into his ear over the roar of the fire, "We've got to get any of our people who are still alive out of there!"

Phillips made a quick visual reconnaissance. Before him a gaping hole was ripped in the side of the Pentagon. Where could they enter that gave them the best chance?

Some trucks had already broken out hoses and were beginning to pour streams of water into the inferno, made even more intense by burning jet fuel. Water hitting the flames turned into steam, further clouding the view. Bodies lay on the ground and on stretchers. Wounded military and civilian workers staggered from the wreckage. People— both fellow Pentagon workers and emergency services personnel— rushed to assist.

Phillips snapped into warrior mode, connecting with Byrd's eyes. "Let's go!" Ignoring emergency workers who were waving and shouting at them to get back they both swiftly moved into the flaming wreckage. They felt the flames burn their exposed skin.

Phillips smelled the singe of burning hair and recoiled at the stinging on his face and arms. Oily smoke blackened their uniforms. Stumbling through the debris they made their way to the destroyed offices.

There was no one left alive to help. Frantically running from office to office they shouted into the roar of the flames. With ceilings crashing down and flames erupting around them they realized that everyone was either dead or had escaped.

Phillips made it to his own destroyed office. He glanced at the wreckage and found one object that meant more to him than anything else in the room: an American flag, sheathed in a protective thick cloth case, damaged by flames but intact. Grabbing the flag, Phillips yelled for Byrd. "Let's get out of here! There's nothing more we can do."

Together they stumbled coughing and choking from the ruined wing of the Pentagon, gasping for clean air to clear the smoke from burning lungs. As emergency workers surged past Phillips grasped the flag tight to his body. It was all he could save from the deadly attack.

Phillips was lucky. He survived the 9/11 attack without undue physical damage. Sergeant Byrd suffered lingering damage from smoke inhalation and would ultimately be medically retired from the Army.

2

MILITARY POLICE SOLDIERS' 9/11 AWAKENING

It was a nice early fall morning when Donald Lowery woke that September 11th in Centralia, Illinois, not far from his hometown of Salem. Lowery, a landscaper working hard to establish a steady business, was struggling along on two to three hundred dollars per week and had his fair share of challenges. He was preparing to head out to the latest job when the phone rang. It was a message being repeated millions of times over that morning: "Turn on the TV!"

He watched smoke pour from the North Tower of the World Trade Center and heard the hysterical voices of commentators as they spotted the second airliner banking in from the south across the broad expanse of New York Harbor. Lowery was stunned as the fireball erupted in the second tower. Over the following days, as he watched repeats of the attack and solemn presidential addresses to Congress and the American people, Don Lowery was determined that he would revenge the attack. He decided to join the Army and get into the fight.

Staring into an unknown future, Lowery could never imagine that one day in a firefight in a gritty faraway town in Afghanistan he would be forced to make a decision to shoot grenades at Taliban fighters—a decision that his Army career would hinge upon.

•   •   •

Staff Sergeant Andrew J. Chesser was watching *Sponge Bob Square Pants* with his two children, Austin and Ashlynn, when the phone rang. He flipped to a cable news channel, and like most of America, he was immediately transfixed. *This can't be real, this is like a Hollywood disaster movie,* Chesser thought. *It must be a hoax of some kind.* Yet when the news of a third aircraft hitting the Pentagon came up, the reality immediately sank in: He was a soldier, and his country was now at war.

For the Lake Worth, Florida, native it was not his first rodeo, having served in Kosovo, Somalia, Bosnia, and Desert Storm. He knew war and that he would shortly become involved. However, not even Chesser, who was on leave that day, would have been able to predict how quickly. Within two days he was told to report to his MP unit in Hawaii. "Get ready to deploy," were his orders.

It seemed a fairly cut-and-dried proposition at the time. No one could predict, least of all Chesser, that he would spend five of the next nine years in the seemingly endless dusty plains of both Iraq and Afghanistan.

While Jennifer Manning sat in sixth-grade history class in Greenfield, Indiana, the morning was suddenly interrupted by an announcement from the principal. "All classes are to cease immediately," the voice on the PA system intoned. "Turn all classroom televisions to CNN now."

It was the morning of September 11 and Jennifer—along with millions of American children in class—watched the second hijacked flight crash into the South Tower of the World Trade Center, heard the frantic news of a hijacked flight hitting the Pentagon, and one crashing into a Pennsylvania farm field. Students were stunned.

The scene definitely affected Manning. On the spot, she pledged that, when she was old enough, she would do something to somehow help her country.

On that day Manning may have imagined herself in a starched uniform, standing proudly before an admiring group of friends—yet not even in her dreams could she have ever envisioned herself balanced in the lurching turret of an MRAP gripping a .50 caliber heavy machine gun in her gloved fists, goggles down against the swirling dust, preparing to help search for Taliban fighters in a dirty Afghan qalat.

As a female MP, Manning would become one of those responsible for frisking burqa-clad women, with full knowledge that burqas had occasionally been used to hide suicide vests or even to hide fully armed men in disguise. Neither the smell, the dirt, nor the danger would stop her. The little pixie-faced schoolgirl would indeed become fully prepared to fight in some of the harshest conditions experienced by humankind.

Sergeant Tony Rosado was in the Basic NCO Course at Fort Leonard Wood, Missouri, training at the MOUT (Military Operations in Urban Terrain) site, where a collection of nondescript buildings provides trainees with simulated combat scenarios in streets, alleyways, and inside mock-up banks, stores, houses, and apartment complexes. They were given the word at the field training site and were uniformly shocked and confused by the news. Most of the soldiers there realized that war had been thrust upon them, and believed combat was imminent.

Rosado's developmental training course requirements were part of a set of orders that would move him from his previous duty station in Hawaii to his receiving unit at Fort Hood, Texas. *When I get to Hood,* he thought, *I'd better be really ready to go.*

Within months Rosado would find himself deep into the country and people of Afghanistan, a place few Americans thought of or could even locate accurately on a map. He had no way of knowing that much of his future in the Army would revolve around that blood-soaked geographical anomaly or that he would hold several score soldiers' lives in his hands, dependent on his sound judgment.

•   •   •

At about 11 P.M. in Taegu, South Korea, Buck Sergeant Gary Watford and some buddies were leisurely working on their third case of beer and watching an Armed Forces Network Korea baseball game when their platoon sergeant abruptly stormed in, ordering them to get their gear on and report to headquarters immediately. The United States was under attack.

They threw their stuff on, stumbled over to headquarters, and began calling in their units.

For seven straight days after that, the base was completely locked down, everyone sleeping on cots, sofas, or the floors. Nobody knew what was going to happen next or if a global attack was imminent. *Bet it's Saddam behind this,* Watford and many others in his unit thought. *Taking revenge for unfinished business after Desert Storm.*

Watford never imagined that one day he would be standing outside the gates of the Afghani presidential palace—knowing that the president of the United States was behind a locked gate   and hearing a Navy SEAL whisper in his ear: "Kill that guard!"

In the small Upstate New York town of Keeseville, Jesse James Shambo, son of a logger, was in shop class at AuSable Valley Central High. He was doing some engineering drawings, making a blueprint for a residence. A messenger ducked in and whispered something to his shop instructor, who hurriedly flipped on the television. There the frightful scenes unfolded.

Shambo watched the images before him with growing fury. His two older brothers, Alan and Corey, had already joined the military. Determined to leave the logging business and train for some other trade, he now felt the pull to follow his brothers' example in defending the United States.

About eighteen months later, on July 14, 2003, Shambo signed enlistment papers to be a military policeman. After two months he graduated from basic and advanced individual training and pinned the crossed pistols of the MP Corps on his collar. By November 2003 he was running missions in Iraq.

What is the Army Military Police Corps—who makes up its ranks, what makes the regiment distinct and unique among the many branches and specialties that comprise the United States Army? Perhaps the singular characteristic that captures the ethos of the regiment is the name bestowed upon its soldiers by one of the famed contemporary leaders, Major General David Quantock: Warrior Police. The Norwich University graduate is one of the legendary leaders of the MP Regiment, who came into the fullness of his career in the cauldron of multiple wars in Iraq, Afghanistan, and remote, mysterious places around the world to which MPs are sent in times of trouble.

Defining MP soldiers as Warrior Police effectively describes the scope and breadth of their role in these current wars. They are infantry and cops, destroyers and builders, eliminators and facilitators. And they have to be able to turn from one role to the next—and back—on a dime. In this aspect they are unique among America's fighting forces.

From their very first days in training at Fort Leonard Wood all MPs are taught that they will be called upon to perform a dual role. They deploy into combat realizing that one day they will be called upon to shoot, the next to extend a helping hand. Only the Army's Special Forces, in its dual role as warriors and teachers, includes such a diversity of missions. Unlike the famed Green Berets, who draw a limited number of experienced NCOs and officers into their ranks annually, the MPs include green soldiers on their first tours of duty and rely heavily upon the imagination, bravery, and innovation these men and women provide.

These Warrior Police are routinely deployed to troubled areas of the world—places like Haiti, Kosovo, Somalia, Bosnia, and Panama, as well as war-torn Afghanistan and Iraq. When they get there they often have to fight first, then take some degree of control within chaotic locations in order to instill a law-and-order environment as quickly as possible. That means, more often than not, helping the same people today that were shooting at them just yesterday. It means learning personal relationship skills that can't come from a classroom—how to handle a corrupt policeman, a distraught citizen, a mob of looters, or a population out of its mind with drugs and heading your way—all the while having to find ways to work around often extreme language and cultural barriers.

The remarkable quality of MPs is that they demand these qualifications from all ranks from private to general—and they are able to produce quality year after year under the most stressful circumstances. As good as the training is at the "Schoolhouse"—the military police school at Fort Leonard Wood, Missouri—there are limits to what can be taught on the ranges and in the classroom. For most new soldiers their real training begins after they are assigned to a unit and come in contact with the noncommissioned officers (NCOs) who comprise the backbone of the Military Police Regiment.

Starting at the level of sergeant, the NCO corps within MP branch is one of the tightest in the business. Given the unusually small size of the regiment compared to other branches, most NCOs serve with each other at some point in their careers. In more than a few cases senior NCOs groom and prepare their juniors for higher levels of responsibility, while the juniors focus on taking the best care of the soldiers under their supervision that they are able.

As a result, the MPs consistently produce good NCOs, and these train their officers and their soldiers in equal portion. Do some less competent slip through the net? Occasionally; for MPs, as all humans, are imperfect. As with individuals in any other occupation—from top football or basketball players, to schoolteachers and movie stars, to doctors and truck drivers—there have even been a tiny number of rogue units who went bad in the absence of skilled leadership, with disastrous results. However, overall the NCO corps is a demanding group and consistently weeds from its ranks those it thinks either cannot fill the requirements of the mission, or will place personal interests above the welfare of their soldiers.

Such facts about the MPs will be news to many. It certainly was for me and my coauthor. My previous experience with MPs while on active duty in the 1960s through '80s was less than awe-inspiring. In those days MPs primarily carried out the necessary but prosaic tasks of policing bases, conducting rear-area security, handling POWs, and other jobs that seemed dull, boring, and painfully routine (at least to an outsider). But times have changed.

In Vietnam, the Tet Offensive in 1968 thrust MPs sharply into combat environments, not for the first time in the corps' history, but on a large scale. As missions changed, the MP Corps changed with them. Intervention in Haiti, active fighting in Panama, and all-consuming missions in the disturbed Balkans gradually modified the MP Corps— not so much in capability as in mind-set of its leaders—from a rear-area-based combat service support unit to one with a skill set that was of primary importance in counterinsurgency and nation building, the two missions that the original Global War on Terror has become.

Today the evolving tempo of the two major wars that America is engaged in at present—Iraq and Afghanistan—has emphasized the need for and role of the MPs to larger and larger measure. While they certainly were necessary in the early days of Operation Iraqi Freedom (to this day General David Phillips and others rue the Pentagon planners who pulled the brigade out of the original force mixture) they have only become more vital over time. Though they were once handled as mere reinforcements for the major U.S. elements that led the charge in Iraq, a new realization developed regarding the MPs' potentially most important role: In order to establish a law-and-order environment necessary for continued peace and relative security for the population, a local police presence *had* to be established. And that mission fell squarely and also exclusively into the province of the MP Corps.

Not that Iraqi or Afghani police development, training, and mentoring was the only mission taken on by the MP Corps post–9/11. The stories thrust into public awareness most directly were about the lawless behavior of guards at the Abu Ghraib prison in Iraq and of maltreatment of detainees at the Guantánamo detention facility. We don't intend to dwell extensively here on Abu Ghraib—this has been done in the heat of the event, and someday will be done objectively, but not here, not now. In that regard we will convey only the perceptions of soldiers who are acutely aware of the damage caused to the image of the MP Corps by scurrilous reporting. Their comments are particularly germane to understanding the present-day mind-set of MPs.

Most of all, this book seeks to recount the experiences of MPs who do it right, to serve as an inspiration to those who aspire to become the best individuals that they can be—no matter what the career choice— and to honor the sacrifices made by ordinary people who ended up becoming simply extraordinary through their work.

That said, *Warrior Police* is also in fact an exposé in its own right since it contains the sometimes painful, often routine, and occasionally hilarious experiences of MPs that have never been published elsewhere.

We also realize that significant stories have been missed, as we did not meet many of the soldiers who deserved to be interviewed, and that this work is painfully incomplete. For this reason we apologize to all involved. Circumstances dictated such an outcome and we were aware of the shortcomings from the start. At any given time thousands of soldiers are serving in military police units worldwide in active, Reserve, and Guard units. Each has a story worth recounting, but the sheer magnitude of attempting a thorough screening of that enormous pool left us no alternative but to interview soldiers we met or were indirectly linked to through those who we met.

Many of our interviews arose by chance: who we met while roaming around, where we were, which unit we were embedded with at the time, when in the long continuum of a decade-long war we appeared on scene. All these factored into the end results herein.

History is about people, and people are interesting. People at war are tested to their most extreme at multiple levels and thereby become more so. People also are fallible individuals. Soldiers in the same action, riding the same truck, fighting the same enemy can emerge post-combat with widely varying accounts of what happened. Because we are thinking creatures we filter our experiences and process stressful events differently even in terms of time and space.

Even in the case of a civilian fender-bender witnessed by seven individuals there will be wildly different reports on what they saw.

Knowing this frailty, we have made great efforts to get facts aligned, tell what actually happened, and, if possible, what individuals thought at the time. Others who were present at some of these actions may have differing memories. To them we can only say that we told the stories as best as they were recounted to us and to the extent that research verified them. Errors, of course, are ultimately our sole responsibility and we accept that.

Come along with us and ride into combat with some of America's finest soldiers: the Warrior Police of the modern MP Regiment.

3

FINDING A ROLE FOR THE MILITARY POLICE: OPERATION ENDURING FREEDOM

The pilot wrenched the monstrous C-130 Hercules aircraft through a series of tight turns and dizzying random changes of altitude in the black, icy November sky over Bagram, Afghanistan. Fifty-plus passengers, strapped tightly to aluminum and nylon bucket seats, gripped their weapons and reflexively tightened straps on their Kevlar helmets.

Sergeant Tony Rosado's stomach flipped as he listened to the four propeller-driven engines straining in the thin air to keep the plane aloft as the pilot jinxed from side to side in tight turns. It seemed to the tense soldiers on board that they were dropping like a rock.

"Keeps anyone from getting a good shot at us," someone shouted over the roar. The enemy below still had some Soviet SA-7 portable missiles that could reach up and hit low, incoming aircraft. And there were always conventional machine guns. *Don't make yourself an easy target!* The axiom was drummed into the heads of the pilots. They took it very seriously.

Whining hydraulic motors sounded throughout the darkened cabin as the Herky Bird dropped giant landing gear with specialized shock absorbers. Speed suddenly increased. A sensation of falling brought hearts into throats.

Rosado glanced at the Air Force loadmaster, who had a death grip on a wall stanchion and a booted foot braced against a tightly strapped-in cargo pallet. *Here we go!*

The force of the combat landing—also dubbed for a reason by the Air Force as a "controlled crash"—resonated throughout the cabin, jolting passengers and crew. It was like being inside a sack of bricks falling from a rooftop. A huge roar from reversed props stifled any conversation as the aircraft slowed noticeably. Abruptly all motion ceased except a slight forward roll. Spontaneously, passengers who'd been unconsciously holding their breath collectively exhaled and relaxed.

Around the aircraft soldiers pulled the quick releases on the seat belts they had been grateful for in the final tense minutes of the inbound flight and began securing their gear. Faces that had run from pale to green now broke into insouciant grins as if to say, *No problem. I do this every day!*

The loadmaster was busily working hydraulic controls to lower the rear ramp on the still-rolling C-130 as it taxied up to a parking space. Rosado was immediately struck by the blackness of the world outside and the bitter cold that swept through the aircraft. Men gasped at the shock of the frigid air as the first forklifts pulled up and rapidly removed large pallets of cargo strapped to the rear and ramp area. Grunting and shoving, loadmasters and ground crews strained to push the pallets over the floor rollers onto the blades of the waiting forklifts.

Once clear, a parka-clad airman—Rosado noticed the parka was fur-lined—stuck his head in the cavernous space and waved a blue chemlight in a "come here" motion. Everybody grabbed up their weapons and gear, and stumbled out the back of the plane while straining to hear what their guide was shouting, unintelligible because of the still-roaring engines. As they trudged along in single file and got farther from the plane Rosado finally heard what the airman was repeating over and over: "Stay directly behind me because there's mines and unexploded munitions on both sides of us." The newly landed soldiers all tightened on the path and stayed close.

It was the first week of November and at that point Sergeant Rosado hadn't expected to land in Afghanistan at all. Of course, before the smoke and debris cleared on 9/11, Rosado, who'd been at Fort Leonard Wood, Missouri, at the time, had known right away that his unit would be among the first to deploy, presumably to wherever Osama bin Laden and his al-Qaeda ilk were hiding.

By October the scuttlebutt around his MP unit, not to mention headlines and speculation internationally, all pointed to the near certainty of a war in Iraq.

Exactly who to attack had quickly become a muddled and confusing question when someone began mailing letters laced with anthrax in the United States. The first five letters were mailed on September 18 or 19, just a week after the planes hit the World Trade Center, the Pentagon, and the grassy field in Pennsylvania. They were sent to ABC News, CBS News, NBC News, the *New York Post,* and a tabloid newspaper run by American Media in Boca Raton, Florida. By the end of September American Media photo editor Robert Stevens became gravely ill in Florida, and on October 5 became the first of five people to die of anthrax poisoning.

The letters sent to NBC News and the *New York Post* further contained the following note:

"09-11-01 THIS IS NEXT / TAKE PENACILIN NOW / DEATH TO AMERICA / DEATH TO ISRAEL / ALLAH IS GREAT."

The mainstream media, who appeared to be the primary targets, naturally went crazy. Sensational, hysterical articles speculating on motive and particularly who the perpetrators might be overran almost all other news. As William Safire wrote in a *New York Times* op-ed at that time, "Veteran reporters and creaking commentators have a single goal in writing about great events: advance the story. Unearth facts that policy makers do not know, do not want to know, or do not want the public to know they know . . ."

Virtually every news outlet was therefore running profiles and exposés on what many reporters and commentators assumed to be the most likely culprit: Iraq, Iraqi chemists, and their president, Saddam Hussein. That madman Saddam, who was known to have produced stocks of weaponized biological agents, and had a history of using chemicals against Iran and his own Kurdish peoples.

Hysteria understandably worsened when two more letters were sent on October 9 addressed to two Democratic senators, Tom Daschle of South Dakota and Patrick Leahy of Vermont, with this note:

"09-11-01 / YOU CAN NOT STOP US / WE HAVE THIS AN-THRAX / YOU DIE NOW / ARE YOU AFRAID? / DEATH TO AMERICA / DEATH TO ISRAEL / ALLAH IS GREAT."

By October 17 over thirty Capitol Hill employees had tested positive. The House of Representatives shut down. The following week, two postal employees in the D.C. area died, and on October 31 a nurse in New York City mysteriously died of inhalational anthrax.

By that time the BBC and many other media outlets were trumpeting news that the anthrax was "weapons-grade." And the vast majority of journalists, as well as government sources, were pointing fingers at Iraq.

This was the climate when Rosado and his unit shipped out to Kuwait, fully expecting that they were gearing up to invade Iraq. Besides, Rosado later recalled, "All of us thought that Desert Storm—that 1991, one-hundred-hour war with Iraq—had only partially completed the job. We figured that somehow, some way, Saddam Hussein was involved with the World Trade Center attack and that we'd be going in to get him."

While waiting in Kuwait, a lot of the guys in his unit had nonetheless been woofing a good line about how eager they would be to get to kicking some ass on the front lines in Afghanistan, instead of getting shuttled off to Iraq. After all, the Taliban government there was harboring al-Qaeda and refused to give up Osama bin Laden. In officially responding to U.S. demands, the Taliban, communicating through their embassy in Pakistan, took the position that there was no evidence that bin Laden was responsible for the 9/11 attacks and they therefore weren't going to hand him over.

Then in an attempt to stop U.S. military action they whipped around and offered to bring bin Laden to trial in their own Islamic court, but that feeble attempt was dismissed by the first U.S. bombs falling on their heads on October 7.

Maybe Iraq and Saddam had something to do with killing Americans, maybe not, but every MP there knew there wasn't any doubt that the bad guys were definitely in Afghanistan.

But then came the night they were startled awake in the wee hours with the final order: "Get your shit on, we're going to . . . Afghanistan!"

"That was definitely the end of a lot of cheap talk," Rosado noticed.

As they walked through the dark on the tarmac that first night, Afghanistan was in fact a month-old experimental war: one fought almost exclusively by special operators rather than conventional forces in an aggressive effort to minimize both American military and Afghan civilian casualties. General Tommy Franks's Central Command in Tampa, Florida, had formulated the plan to fight a war "on the cheap," using a combination of special operators from CIA, Army Special Forces, Air Force Combat Controllers, and Navy SEALs augmented by all the airpower the U.S. could throw in theater, both land-based Air Force and carrier-based Navy, to defeat the Taliban government and destroy al-Qaeda.

This on-the-cheap concept of operations had been run up Pentagon and White House flagpoles; political leaders saluted, and ordered Operation Enduring Freedom to proceed as planned.

If this approach worked—and there was serious concern among many political and senior military officials that it would be an embarrassing failure—then the immediate objective of achieving justice for 9/11 would be accomplished. If the special operators got bogged down, plans were already being formulated to reinforce the effort with quick reaction forces from the 18th Airborne Corps assets of paratroopers and air assaulters and with Marine rapid deployment units.

Combat support units like military police were initially pushed to the side for the moment. At first there was not a readily apparent role for their expertise and specialized policing abilities, other than to stand guard over any enemy combatants that might be captured.

Bagram was definitely a war zone. Only shortly before, the Taliban had defended Bagram field. It was littered with debris from the Soviet days as well as more recent war wreckage. Unmarked minefields checkerboarded the area. Munitions from both U.S. and Taliban fighters that had not exploded (UXO or "unexploded ordinance" in military terms) were littered everywhere, like Mardi Gras debris on Bourbon Street on a hungover Wednesday morning.

Just a few weeks after their arrival, on December 18, the MPs saw a soldier specializing in bomb disposal (from a branch known as explosive ordinance disposal, or EOD) at work near where they were bunking. As he carefully crossed the field an antipersonnel mine detonated, traumatically amputating his foot.[1] Medics from the nearby Special Forces unit worked their way through the field, treated him on the spot, and evacuated him.

"Stay right here! Don't any of you walk anywhere but close to this building!" Rosado's platoon sergeant ordered. They didn't need to be told twice.

Almost immediately Rosado's MP unit was tasked with guarding and maintaining a facility for the increasingly large number of battlefield captures who were swept up in the fighting.

Unfortunately, modern prisons are not available in quick-construction, pop-up kits of any kind. Nor did Bagram, only recently wrenched from Taliban control, have adequate detention facilities conveniently in place.

The MPs therefore helped establish a temporary compound that included four concertina wire enclosures, covered facilities, latrines, medical stations, and other necessities. Armed guards in makeshift towers looked down upon detainees while those MPs who worked among them carried batons. Control was essential and was implemented immediately.

"We followed strict guidance about treatment," Rosado later recalled. "When detainees were delivered—and in the early days, most were high-value target [HVT] personnel marked for eventual evacuation to Guantánamo—they were given a preliminary search in a small holding area adjacent to the main compound. We found grenades and small arms on them sometimes. Then they were flex-cuffed and moved to a private search area in the main compound where they removed all clothing and were thoroughly searched. We had a doctor or Special Forces medic who gave them a physical and, if necessary, initiated treatment for injuries, wounds, or obvious disease. Many of them were brought off the battlefield and had wounds of some type. A lot of them were sick."

In the early days they received from one to fifteen detainees a day, primarily HVTs and other key fighters. As the war progressed and numbers of detainees became mind boggling (there are reports of total numbers of Taliban, al-Qaeda, and others ranging from fifty thousand to seventy thousand total captured) the number quickly increased and the facility expanded to accommodate them.

After first placing detainees in orange jumpsuits, soldiers, with the help of interpreters, briefed them on the rules. "It is absolutely essential that they are made fully aware of what they may and may not do. The guidance for safe, humane treatment is for the detainee to know the limits," Rosado explained. "They know, we know, and everyone behaves accordingly."

Detainees were originally placed in four large holding pens surrounded by concertina wire, with instructions that they must sit down or lie down at all times. Only by raising their hands and being escorted to the latrine, for example, or to seek medical attention, were they allowed to stand. Violators would be removed by guards and segregated in different cells.

At first everyone ate "Meals, Ready to Eat"—MREs—although any pork products were removed from those given to the detainees. Civil affairs personnel were eventually able to obtain food locally so they could have more traditional halal meals. After the combat situation moved southward and away from the immediate vicinity, conditions steadily continued to improve. International Red Cross visits began and some of the strict standards were relaxed to allow exercise periods and interaction.

Just weeks after Rosado and his unit began to process detainees at Bagram, the November 25 prisoner revolt at Qala-i-Jangi near

Mazar-i-Sharif in the north shocked coalition authorities into recognizing that the old traditional ways of Afghanistan would not work in this new campaign.

Among the American media and some military and political leadership a myth was widespread that Afghanis had a cultural imperative of crude chivalry: that once surrendered a fighter would not take up arms again. As with many legends about the people of Central Asia, it did not take long to dispel this one.

The Northern Alliance, a force that united members of many different Afghan ethnic groups to fight against the Taliban and al-Qaeda, were collaborating with American and other coalition forces. They ran the Qala-i-Jangi prison while allowing CIA, Special Forces, and other coalition interrogators inside the walls to question detainees. What happened there that November was not a prison riot (as horrific as that might have been), but, in the words of a Special Forces captain present, "a full-scale battle." CIA officer Mike Spann was the first to die when the detainees attacked, thus tragically becoming the first American killed in the fighting in Afghanistan. After several days of intense fighting the butcher's bill was tallied: Several hundred enemy fighters had been killed and scores more wounded, a few holdouts surrendered, and many Northern Alliance soldiers had died or were wounded.

The Qala-i-Jangi fight was a catalyst, in some measure, for two immediate U.S. reactions: First, it was painfully apparent that captured enemy combatants would have to be handled more professionally. Interrogation was obviously impossible under such circumstances and information was sorely needed on the movements of high-value al-Qaeda targets and possible future terror attacks. This could not be done successfully in-country to the extent necessary. Nor was it realistic to expect that surrendered fighters would remain quiescent, cooperative prisoners. Secondly, the leadership realized that slapdash prisoner handling like at Qala-i-Jangi was unacceptable: It led to unnecessary casualties on both sides.

The solution was patently obvious: expand the military police footprint on the ground. Get them in theater and put them to work. Ultimately two decisions resulted: enlarge the existing detainee-handling facility at Bagram, and prepare a remote, secure site to handle the especially serious al-Qaeda and Taliban operatives who were captured. In a few short weeks the MPs were tasked to deploy more units to Afghanistan, and Navy Seabee units began preparation for receiving the high-value detainees at Guantanamo Bay in southeast Cuba.

Because of strict procedures instituted by the Americans from the beginning, as opposed to slipshod handling by the Northern Alliance fighters, prisoner revolts were not an issue at Bagram. Eventually the Bagram facility was relocated into a two-story aircraft hangar. The second story was converted into individual cells to hold HVTs.

Sergeant Rosado's unit remained on the ground for approximately six months before being replaced by another unit. "I heard rumors about a beating death of a detainee after we left. Don't know the circumstances. All I'm sure of is that during our period we had no serious incidents and ran a very humane, but tightly controlled operation."[2]

Staff Sergeant Andrew Chesser soon arrived in Bagram. He had been rushed into theater as an individual augmentee and was assigned as operations sergeant in the provost marshall section at the base. "We had three cages with about sixty-three detainees in them at the time. Ultimately they would be processed and sent to Guantanamo. It was a very rough time. We had to deal with the detainees right after the September 11 attack. It was really not pleasant duty.

"It was a difficult period to try to figure out," recalled Chesser. "We were in Afghanistan, but were not all that sure what we were supposed to be doing there." Chesser saw MPs primarily focusing on the detention side of their skill set in Bagram. "Not that many MPs have the occupational specialty for detainee handling. All of us have some training along those lines, but only a very small group are actually designated for that duty."

4

MILITARY POLICE IN THE SHADOWS

In January 2002 Colonel Dave Phillips was working out of temporary offices in the Pentagon. Construction work had begun as soon as investigators cleared the site of the 9/11 attack, but damage was extensive and repairs would take time. And just four months after that terrible day, many Pentagon drones had already returned to the prewar "paint rocks and stack paper clips" mentality.

While firefights raged and other MPs struggled with properly securing detainees on the other side of the planet in Afghanistan, chief of Pentagon security Phillips was charged with overseeing battles over parking spaces.

Since rank at the building is an inverted pyramid, only the most senior, multistar generals and rarified-air civilians have reserved spaces. Everybody else wrestles with the unwashed mob for a place to park. Like most unimportant issues, this one was capable of eliciting high emotion and road rage from even the mildest pencil pushers. Phillips was frequently caught in the middle.

Phillips continually had bureaucratic tiffs with the parking-space barons to secure a temporary space for visiting VIPs. It was one of those tasks that normally fell in the "I wish someone else would deal with this crap" pile. One day that January he was summoned to the office of the director of the army staff (DAS), Lieutenant General Kevin P. Byrnes, over a new parking problem. That something like parking place assignments landed on the desk of a three-star general reflects the high emotion associated with the issue. Phillips was called to his office frequently.

On this day Byrnes was especially concerned. There had been a recent parking problem involving a visiting VIP. With another very important visitor scheduled for the next day, Byrnes wanted to make sure Phillips guaranteed a smooth visit. "We've got a space locked in, General," Phillips told him. "The 503rd MP Battalion is here pulling additional security and they can hold it for me, no problems."

"I hope not. We have some rock star coming and I don't need any issues with her access to the building or parking," Byrnes cautioned with a dire look.

"Who's the rocker?" asked Phillips.

Byrnes waved a hand dismissively. "Oh, someone named Jett."

Shock splashed over Phillips's face. "Joan Jett!" he blurted out. "Wow. I'll definitely ensure that *she* has a parking space." Like many soldiers, Phillips appreciated the star's genuine devotion to the military and the time she had donated to war-zone appearances. Jett had recently become the first non-combatant to entertain the troops in Afghanistan. Phillips had attended several concerts over the years and was a huge fan.

The DAS gave him a strange look and waved him out of the office.

Phillips had no sooner finished the long trek back to his temporary office when his administrative assistant, Staff Sergeant O'Brien, told him that Byrnes wanted him back in his office. *Now what's the problem?* Phillips wondered as he strode back.

Byrnes's secretary gave him the news: "Colonel, General Byrnes said that he doesn't know Ms. Jett, but you apparently do. He would therefore like you to meet her and be her escort." Happily, Phillips burst out, "You're kidding! That's fantastic." She smiled and then gave him the schedule. He was so excited that he practically ran back to his office.

Reviewing the schedule, Phillips saw that he was to escort Joan Jett around damaged areas of the Pentagon and then take her to a luncheon at the General Officers' Mess. He immediately coordinated with his friend Lieutenant Colonel Wade Dennis, who commanded the 503rd MP Battalion at the time. "Everything's good to go," he was told.

After calming down a bit, Phillips had a troubling thought. He called his oldest daughter, Noelle, to discuss it with her. "How am I going to explain this to Mom? It's not every day I get to escort a female rock star and she might be bothered by that." Noelle, the consummate problem-solver, replied easily: "Dad, just let Mom know that when Mel Gibson comes to the Pentagon, you'll bring her in to meet him." Phillips said that Mel Gibson wasn't scheduled to visit the Pentagon, at least not that he knew of. "That's irrelevant. If he does come and visit, you'll just have to ensure that you bring Mom in to meet him." Problem solved.

Early the next morning Phillips made a last-minute double-check of all arrangements, and of course, ensured that the precious parking space remained unoccupied. Everything was set! At the appointed hour a purple Jaguar pulled up, was waved through, and Phillips personally directed the car to the pristine reserved parking slot. Joan Jett emerged exactly as he remembered her from her album covers, black leather jacket and all. "Hi, I'm Joan." That set the tone for the visit.

Phillips remembers her as "very relaxed and laid-back. Easy to talk to, like someone I'd known for years." At the MP checkpoint leading into the Pentagon the young soldiers were all grins. Phillips wondered idly if they knew her and her songs. They were polite and professional and Phillips beamed with pride. "Put your jacket through the screening device," he requested. "Then please step through the metal detector."

Beep, beep. "No problem, ma'am," a young MP said. "I'll just wand you." He passed the wand over the front of her blouse. Beep, beep. Uh-oh.

"That's my nipple rings," Jett said casually, turning to a thoroughly shocked Phillips. The MP was frozen in place with a plaintive "what do I do now?" look on his face.

"Do you need to see them?" Jett offered.

"No, no," Phillips said quickly. The MP looked relieved. Jett smiled, clearly having fun with her escorts. By the time they got to the second checkpoint the word had already spread throughout the entire 503rd MP Battalion: Joan Jett flashed Colonel Phillips! "I never did anything to dispel the rumor," Phillips later recounted with a sly grin.

During the tour of the damaged corridors, Jett was very serious, sincerely interested in details of the attack. As the tour progressed, Phillips realized, *She is really a super supporter of soldiers.* By the time they got to the General Officers' Mess, Byrnes and several others had already arrived to greet her. After a pleasant meal she happily signed autographs for the senior officers and then turned to Phillips, asking if he would like her to sign something. "No, thank you," he replied in his best Rhett Butler fashion. "The memory of escorting you is more than enough." She came over and hugged him. All of the general officers in the mess watched in envy. Phillips was elated. "It was one of the best days I'd had as the director of security since nine-eleven."

Dawn Phillips occasionally reminds him of the visit, adding playfully, "I'm still waiting for that visit from Mel Gibson!"

Despite some entertaining situations David Phillips remained extremely frustrated by what seemed like the endless trivialities at the Pentagon during a time of war. Although he was physically stuck in D.C., his thoughts often turned to the realities in Afghanistan and Guantánamo Bay. He knew there was now an extremely critical need for an MP specialty position that had nearly been eliminated a couple of years before: the specially trained prison guards identified by 31E designator, officially known as internment/resettlement specialists in the military occupational specialty (MOS) listings. And there weren't nearly enough 31-Echos to handle the flood of detainees.

Given a shortage of detention specialists, the task of guarding detainees fell increasingly on the law-enforcement side of the MP Corps. It was true that every MP had received introductory training in detention operations while learning basic soldier skills, but the daunting task at hand could not be satisfactorily accomplished by soldiers with *only* basic instruction in a complex specialty, or even those with on-the-job training. As a consequence, lesson planners at the MP Schoolhouse at Fort Leonard Wood scrambled to beef up the 31E skill set with techniques relevant to the current situations.

Most military jobs have nicknames that might seem pejorative to outsiders but are used as a clubby kind of term of affection. Infantrymen are "grunts," artillerymen "cannon-cockers," tankers "treadheads," and 31E prison guards ended up getting labeled as "cage-kickers."

Sergeant Clifton Stillwell, originally from Louisville, Kentucky, is one of the soldiers who went through the training and the designation change. A medic for the first five years or so of active duty, he'd switched to being a corrections specialist in 2002 because he thought it would be an effective way to get more involved in responding to the aftermath of the September 11 attacks.

Stillwell was dispatched that same year as part of a small team of about ten men, with the specific mission of evaluating the existing facilities for detainee holding at Bagram Collection Point (BCP). There were a lot of rumors flying around the press about how terrible conditions were there. Stories of beating deaths, torture, and abusive policies hit worldwide media. Some reporters tried to portray American soldiers as a vicious army, out of control. Stillwell's assignment was simple: Get over there, find out the facts. If you find anything wrong, make it right.

While his team didn't observe any abuse or mistreatment, and saw the guards were properly handling the detainees, they did see plenty of things that needed to be fixed. Stillwell and his Echos imported the latest doctrine from the Fort Leonard Wood Schoolhouse to set up new standard operating procedures, such as running checks on detainees who were under suicide watch every fifteen minutes instead of twice an hour. MPs at Bagram were also advised on ways to obtain special items for the detainees like recreational equipment, uniforms, shower facilities, and other comfort gear. It was also necessary to square them away on essential administrative tasks such as properly recording detainee actions, handling paperwork, and working with the many different forms that were required.

While at Bagram, Stillwell's team supervised bringing in large, prefabricated fenced units that were normally used to secure supplies and equipment supply cages. These units were modified to be used as communal recreation areas. The team invited the International Red Cross in to visit and inspect the facility. Finally, after all necessary control measures were put into place, they established visitation procedures for the detainees so that families could visit and bring them small items.

By this time the detention area had been formally designated the Bagram Personnel Control Facility and located in a larger, permanent home on the sprawling grounds of what eventually would become Bagram Airfield, or simply "BAF" in military colloquialism. The facility itself was located adjacent to the exterior wire, distant from increasingly busy airfield operations.

Meanwhile, the flow of detainees into the Bagram facility, while nowhere near the staggeringly high levels of the early months of the war, continued apace. Specialized military intelligence units with augmentation from the Department of Defense supervised detainee interrogation, often under the watchful eye—or baleful glare depending on circumstances—of several other government agencies. Of particular note were the ubiquitous CIA operators, who had a legitimate claim to partnership if not ownership over the war. After all, it was their teams that deployed first, opening the path for Special Forces to follow.

An additional presence, of no surprise, was the Federal Bureau of Investigation. In their eyes—a point of view shared by many politicians and a segment of Americans—the 9/11 attack was foremost a monstrous crime. In the institutionally reactive manner taught to FBI agents, they had come to Afghanistan to collect evidence, conduct interrogations of suspects, and assemble a prosecutable case capable of being presented successfully in a U.S. court of law.

Also among the players at the Bagram facility were Drug Enforcement Agency operators. Under the Taliban, and indeed for decades, Afghanistan had been a serious producer of raw opium and derivatives like morphine and heroin, principally for Chinese buyers in the Golden Triangle of northern Thailand, Laos, and Burma. Ultimately, refined drugs were marked for distribution through Turkey, Syria, and the Middle East to Europe, or, increasingly, for the insatiable U.S. market. DEA was after connections and links that they could trace to break up these enormously profitable global enterprises.

Detention operations at Bagram in 2002 remained what a Wall Street investment banker might term a growth industry with plenty of topside potential.

Pressure was thus enormous on the CIA and DEA to uncover any future plots so that they could be thwarted before thousands more lives might be lost—some feared tens of thousands, or higher numbers. September 11 was already being condemned widely as an "intelligence failure" of the highest order. No more mistakes were to be allowed. Find out what we need to know, agents were ordered. *Now!*

While MPs in Afghanistan continued to have control over the detention facility at Bagram, a second major facility was opened in Kandahar—the birthplace of and headquarters for the Taliban, which had fallen to coalition forces on the anniversary of the Pearl Harbor attack, December 7. Additional MP units were rushed into the country to staff the facility. They had a much faster learning curve because of the Bagram experience, and from the start they included Afghani guards under the Ministry of the Interior. The plan was to revitalize and reorganize the key ministries first, with an eye to ultimately turning detention facilities and as many security related tasks as possible over to Afghani ownership at the earliest opportunity.

Military policemen were to work side by side with their local counterparts and train them on the job. From the start it was clear to see that what was considered satisfactory prison management in Afghanistan was woefully inadequate and borderline inhumane by Western standards. Also, in this new war, not only was the possibility of attack or revolt by detainees a legitimate threat, but in the chaotic atmosphere of Afghanistan, jailbreaks—initiated both inside the wire and from outside sources—were a constant concern.

Eventually MPs found that they could most effectively train Afghanis by beginning at the most basic level and moving up, and that the best way to train them was by use of extensive hands-on-type classes. Want to teach a guard how to search a detainee? Then demonstrate the process in great detail, have the students practice under corrective eyes, and repeat as necessary.

"At first they don't pay much attention or put much faith in training," Sergeant Stillwell later recalled. "Honestly, they don't see value in it. But once you can get them to appreciate what can come from it—maybe they search a detainee the way we showed them and find a weapon—then suddenly the light goes on and they get more involved and enthusiastic. They can learn, and we can teach them. They just have to want to do it."

As Sergeant Andrew Chesser remembers those days, it was all a matter of fits and starts. "We were given a mission to train the police, and began unit training wherever the MPs were posted. But there were no centralized plans to standardize training, and not much follow-on after units rotated. Frankly, no one seemed to pay much attention to police at that stage while active fighting was going on around the country."

Most agreed that rebuilding the police force was a back-burner priority for Afghanistan despite obvious local security issues. "The emphasis in those days was highly kinetic," Chesser observed. "We were pulling route security, getting involved in firefights, and operating more like a reinforced infantry unit than pulling strictly law-enforcement missions."

Rebuilding the Afghani Army was a top priority, police a distant second, or lower. With active Taliban fighters operating around the country, even in supposedly "secure" areas, top-level planners considered it necessary to have a force in place that could take the fight to the enemy, push him out of Afghanistan, and restore order to large regions. The goal of secure neighborhoods and villages was desirable, but could wait till the main task was accomplished.

So, route security—always a major Military Police Corps mission— assumed a critically high priority. By late 2002 and into 2003 most of the danger was from fighters engaging convoys that were attempting to bring vital supplies up from Pakistan through some of the world's most treacherous routes. With no access to the sea, options for transporting heavy, bulky, or unstable supplies into theater were limited. Much of the light stuff—personnel and electronic gear, for example—could be flown in successfully. But stringent cuts in DOD beginning with the George H. W. Bush administration and accelerated under Bill Clinton had left the Air Force with severely limited airlift capability. Already the fleet was beginning to show signs of wear and stress from delivering cargo into Afghanistan's high-altitude, crude airstrips.

The only other option was to take cargo by ship into a nearby friendly port and truck it in. The problem was that the ports were distant, the Pakistani hosts irascible, and the roads unimaginably difficult. Anything heavy—fuel, ammunition, containers of supplies—all had to be seaborne, then delivered by truck. This meant landing at a port such as Karachi on the northern end of the Arabian Sea, transferring cargo to contract trucking firms (less the large amounts that were skillfully pilfered from the dock area, an uninvestigated issue that from anecdotal evidence must run into the tens of millions of dollars lost), then forming convoys.

From there the convoys would head north and a bit west, up the length of Pakistan where local police or bandits may extort "tolls" for passage, roughly to Quetta, where the road forks. The western route will cross the Afghanistan border near Chaman and head straight up into Kandahar. The eastern route traverses northward to Islamabad then west through the fabled Khyber Pass to Jalalabad and Kabul. After supplies arrived at major destinations they were then broken down and redistributed around the country, again primarily over treacherous roads.

Gunfights could start at any point from the time the MPs picked up a convoy at the Afghanistan border, and potential for trouble lasted until the convoy cleared the gates at the destination. Kandahar and Helmand Province are hotbeds of Taliban, many of whom drift across the southern border at will. In the eastern part of the country the Khyber Pass has been a caravan route and fighting gauntlet since Silk Route times. Roads in Afghanistan are easily categorized: they are either poorly surfaced, littered with potholes and cracks, or are unimproved dirt, frequently riven by flash floods or erosion.

MPs picked up convoys—sometimes numbering fifty to a hundred trucks or more—at the border and crept across Afghanistan's crumbling roads, always under the looming guns of a hidden enemy. Fuel trucks were especially tempting targets for Taliban for obvious reasons. Hit the side of a fuel truck with an RPG or with multiple tracer rounds and it will catch fire. If the enemy is having a good day, the truck will billow smoke then explode, splashing flames on anyone and anything nearby. Blowing a fuel truck not only had the potential of initiating secondary explosions or causing collateral casualties, but also struck at the Achilles' heel of a road-bound, air-dependent coalition. You can't run the roads without fuel.

5

TOPPLING SADDAM: OPERATION IRAQI FREEDOM BEGINS

With one hot war going on in Afghanistan, pressure was building in Washington and other capitals to take firm action against Saddam Hussein's Iraq. Some sources, such as the Czech Republic ambassador to the United Nations, cited strong evidence that Iraqi intelligence had been linked to the 9/11 terrorists. Since CIA analysts were unable—or unmotivated—to confirm such ties, any connections remained disputed. Nevertheless, the Bush administration had it sights set on removing Saddam or neutering his behavior.

On October 20, 2002, Saddam then completely shocked the world by declaring amnesty for all Iraqi convicts held in Iraq:[1] not just political prisoners who had dared to disagree with his regime, but also thousands of convicted murderers, rapists, thieves, and thugs of every variety. It was an act that revealed his realization that the United States would indeed invade Iraq very soon. By releasing thousands of violent and often mentally ill convicts from prisons all over the country, Saddam was ensuring that coalition forces would be met by not just his own military forces, but also by the most unpredictable, brutal, and agitated criminals, who were capable of reaping chaos on a scale never unleashed before and bestowing it onto the heads of a law-abiding modern Army.

An estimated one hundred thousand prisoners were freed.[2] It would have a profound impact on coalition forces, and U.S. MPs in particular, for years to come.

Members of the Western media were allowed by Saddam to witness the mass exodus of prisoners fleeing and to also see inside Abu Ghraib, one of his now mostly emptied prisons. What they reported was beyond horrifying.

The *Christian Science Monitor* noted "The bodies of the two men, dead that day from tuberculosis, lay in the prison hospital." *New York Times* photographer Tyler Hicks managed to capture the images of prisoners dying in the crush to get out of the gates and corpses sprawled on the ground inside.

John F. Burns from *The New York Times* wrote about "rust-colored butchers' hooks, twenty or more, each four or five feet long, aligned in rows along the ceiling of a large hangar-like building . . . the place of mass hangings that have been a documented part of life under Saddam Hussein . . ." The article went on to describe "fingernail-extracting, eye-gouging, genital shocking and bucket-drowning. Secret police rape prisoners' wives and daughters to force confessions and denunciations. . . ."[3]

U.S. MPs gearing up for an inevitable deployment to Iraq took note. Atrocities such as this had to be remedied and must never happen again.

Members of the military are pledged to obey orders from their commander in chief regardless of their personal views. Like most American citizens they each have opinions of their own. Many who would later put their lives on the line in combat in fact had very strong views about U.S. involvement in Iraq.

Officer students at the Command and General Staff College at Fort Leavenworth, Kansas, are encouraged to indulge in "spirited debate" during seminars and when discussing pressing issues of the day. "Arguments over whether we ought to go into Iraq or not got pretty heated in early 2003," Lieutenant Colonel Duane Miller later recalled. He grinned. "It didn't come to fistfights or name-calling, but got close at times."

For one of the few times in an officer's career, he or she is offered the chance to express opinions freely. The only thing the faculty requires is that logic, good judgment, and sound reasoning apply. After all, these are highly competitive officer students who have been selected from a much larger pool of qualified contemporaries to be trained for assignments including command positions and higher staff slots.

Nor is it a cloistered environment. In addition to officers of every branch in the Army attending, sister services, allies, and other government agencies send students. Quite often the faculty invites particularly "stimulating" speakers to address the group; deep thinkers, like former military intelligence officer and prominent author Ralph Peters, for example, who they know will throw ideas and concepts into the audience that often have the effect of a live grenade.

It was, therefore, totally appropriate and seemly that prior to the final decision being announced from the White House, students would analyze the world situation and voice their opinions. Some hearing them may have been surprised.

"We were mostly against going into Iraq at the time," Miller noted. Not necessarily because sufficient cassus belli might not exist—few were of a mind to defend Saddam Hussein and his brutal regime—but primarily because of external issues. "We were worried that the war in Afghanistan might be marginalized if we had to concentrate on fighting in Iraq simultaneously. We all knew how thin the services had become since the Gulf War. We just weren't certain we had the necessary assets to fight both at once, and [were concerned] that one theater might be neglected."

"Better prepare your unit to go into Iraq." Dave Phillips had been in command of the 89th MP Brigade at Fort Hood for several months when a senior officer phoned him in early 2003.

"Know something I don't?" Phillips queried.

"No, but I can read the papers. Dave, if this thing goes down, and a lot of us hope it doesn't, then MPs are going to be critical to success. From where I sit it looks like the Eighty-ninth is in prime position for deployment."

That January it became particularly obvious that a war in Iraq was absolutely imminent. The Pentagon had already set up the Office for Reconstruction and Humanitarian Assistance (ORHA) to help coordinate civil affairs in Iraq until a democratically elected civilian government could be established.[4] Retired Army Lieutenant General Jay Garner, who had been in Operation Desert Storm in Iraq back in 1991, was appointed as the director of ORHA alongside Britain's Major General Timothy Cross. Allied forces hadn't even invaded yet when this structure for an interim government was created.

It made sense to Phillips and other planners to send the MPs in quickly when the United States entered Iraq. In the Gulf War, following Iraq's 1990 invasion into Kuwait, Iraqis had surrendered by scores that became hundreds and then thousands. Coalition forces led by U.S. combat units sent to drive them out in the early months of 1991 had to detour around mobs of Iraqi soldiers who had walked with their hands in the air, waving anything white they could grab, literally begging to surrender. Everyone in uniform therefore expected the same situation if U.S. boots were to march into the heart of Iraq.

Despite Saddam Hussein's bluff and bluster, the Iraqi Army was still the Iraqi Army: poorly paid if at all, with lousy training, venal high-level officers who owed their positions to Saddam's benevolence, corrupt lower-level officers, a total lack of a noncommissioned corps, and unmotivated draftee foot soldiers. Most U.S. officers expected them to abandon equipment in the desert and flee for their lives.

So Phillips and his staff began with the assumption that any of the several plans offered by the Joint Chiefs of Staff for approval by the secretary of defense, and ultimately the president, would include an MP brigade. While most MPs in Afghanistan had been initially concentrating on guarding detainees behind the wire inside military bases, in Iraq it would make sense to send more MPs to go out with the forward units and provide route security.

It was a certainty among the MPs based at Fort Hood that there would be a big push to get them—along with thousands of other coalition troops—into Kuwait, using that country as a major staging area. The Kuwaitis welcomed the U.S. presence. They were game for more payback for Saddam's 1991 invasion. Vast expanses of empty desert were available for basing and staging, and were sufficiently remote to keep "infidel" presence distant from the population. Good ports were close and the Kuwait road net was sound enough to handle the enormous load. Meanwhile, Kuwait also shared a long border with Iraq; a major north-south highway connected the two.

Phillips and his staff therefore anticipated being part of the larger troop unit list that would land in Kuwait and make the long run north to Baghdad and beyond. MPs were mission-essential to perform route security and protect convoys, and the highways north were long and dangerous. The likelihood of having to process significant numbers of enemy POWs was also on everyone's mind. Plans and equipment were assembled in anticipation of these contingencies.

Another key issue would be traffic control: Iraq's road net was far superior to that of Afghanistan but was still limited. The potential for truckers and support vehicles breaking down or getting lost was not just high: it was 100 percent. "It's going to be one huge traffic jam," one planner predicted. Another was more blunt: "It'll be a giant cluster fuck of broken-down vehicles, ambushes from stay-behinds, and rear-area troops getting lost."

"That road is going to be one helluva mess," Phillips agreed, about summing up what MPs expected to confront on the march north.

And at the very top of the commander's list of concerns towered the need to achieve law and order and civil control, especially in the cities. Once the maneuver units' gunfighters moved through chasing the Iraqi military, cities were going to be left in a vacuum. Vital supplies like water and power would probably be destroyed. The police and army would be either defeated or in hiding. Given the nature of the enemy, it was likely that holdouts or guerrilla fighters would remain hidden and try to attack more lightly armed support units. Looting and crime were definite possibilities if an adequate number of MPs were not inserted from the very beginning.

In past wars, once a city or town was liberated it was normal for Military Police to establish an immediate, visible presence to maintain order and keep the peace until local institutions could be restored. Most recently they had quickly assumed this role in Panama and the Balkans. It was a proven system that worked well.

Considering that the Shi'a tribes in the south had suffered enormously under Saddam, losing tens of thousands of their best people after the Gulf War when the United States urged them to revolt then abandoned them to their fate, it was probable that cities like Najaf, Nasiriyah, and others would be especially prone to violent reaction postliberation. Planners were also hyperaware of all the criminals Saddam had released the previous October, including death-row inmates. Those boys would be very serious trouble for both invading coalition forces and local Iraqi citizens.

"We've got to be prepared to step in quickly and restore order," Phillips charged his staff. "If anything is going to happen in these places we have to be ready to nip it in the bud before it gets started."

Like so many other observers and planners, Phillips fully expected that this was going to be a repeat of the very short 1991 Gulf War—that major combat operations would be over in a matter of days. For this reason he stacked one of his units that had already been selected for deployment, the 720th MP Battalion, with his very best soldiers. The 720th—informally known by their unit motto, "Soldiers of the Gauntlet"—now stood by waiting for orders at Fort Hood, with 1,100 soldiers that included the cream of the crop plucked from Phillips's own 89th MP Brigade.

In effect, by deliberately overstaffing the unit, he front-loaded the battalion and made it "heavy" with talent. Phillips took his best two field grade officers along with many of the best NCOs and assigned and attached them to the 720th so they would have a powerhouse of a battalion, especially anticipating mass surrenders of Iraqi troops.

Another large unit of MPs, the 18th MP Brigade based out of Mannheim, Germany, arrived in Kuwait on February 21, 2003. The overall Iraq invasion plan was fairly simple: The 18th MPs along with a huge wave of other allied forces would enter into Iraq from Kuwait at the southern border, while the 4th Infantry Division would attack simultaneously from the north by entering Iraq from Turkey. Coalition forces could thereby engage Saddam's army and his reportedly elite troops from two different directions, essentially forcing the Iraqis to fight on two different fronts and thus diluting their combat power.

That was the original plan.

Unfortunately, at the very last minute the Turkish government unexpectedly refused to allow the U.S. 4th Infantry Division into their territory as had been previously arranged. The 4th ID therefore found itself floating aimlessly on ships in the Mediterranean off the coast of Turkey. They were then ordered to abandon the northern attack plan altogether and instead join with the troops positioned in Kuwait. That meant they had to steam south through Egypt's Suez Canal, into the Red Sea, around Saudi Arabia into the Persian Gulf, and finally dock at the ports of Kuwait and unload. Since the trip would take two weeks, it meant that desperately needed extra combat power would be late to the fight.

Phillips's own 720th finally left Fort Hood on March 18 for its own long journey to Kuwait.[5]

The very next day the War against Iraq exploded onto television sets around the world with what the administration called a display of "shock and awe." Official combat was initiated on March 19 with an intensive campaign of precision bombing and cruise missile attacks. While the aerial attack progressed on a tight schedule, engineer units rolled teams of earthmovers and bulldozers into position along the large dirt dike that marked the Iraq-Kuwait border. The massive equipment began opening pathways in the berm at preselected locations, creating laneways for the ground forces to enter Iraq.

At dawn on March 21 the order to commence offensive operations crackled over the radios of units poised like racehorses in the starting gate. U.S. Army and Marine units, along with British ground forces, crossed the berm and began pouring into Iraq. Special Operations teams designed for long-range reconnaissance, SCUD missile detection, and direct-action missions had been infiltrated days prior by helicopter and continued to feed intelligence information into headquarters.

The 3rd Infantry Division, 101st Airborne, Marine Expeditionary Force, and British 1st Armour and 3 Commando began their four-division sweep north from Kuwait into Iraq, taking some of the MPs from the 18th with them.

Yet then came the news that a simultaneous assault from Turkey would not take place after all. New orders: Most of the MPs from the 18th and other support units were ordered to freeze in place there in Kuwait.

The MPs of the 18th, all decked out in full battle-rattle and raring to go, collectively gnashed their teeth in disbelief. *That will take weeks and we're needed right now!*

The hole created by the lack of adequate MP numbers was tragically demonstrated on March 23, when a convoy following the initial invading forces into Iraq with vital supplies had taken a wrong road off the main supply route and stumbled into a brutal ambush. The convoy soldiers—all rear-echelon types, drivers, maintenance personnel, and clerks who would ordinarily have been escorted by MPs—were ill prepared to defend themselves. They were easy prey for the fanatical Saddam supporters.

Eleven soldiers were killed during the ambush, and later as a result of it six more were captured, including Private First Class Jessica Lynch and her best friend Lori Piestewa. Lynch would eventually be rescued from a hospital nine days later in a dramatic raid by Special Operations soldiers assisted by friendly Iraqis;[6] Piestewa, who had been in the hospital with her, had already succumbed to her injuries and thus became the first female soldier and also the first Native American to die in the Iraqi war. The shallow graves adjacent to the hospital that concealed the tortured bodies of her comrades received scant press attention.[7]

Frustrated MPs in Kuwait groused aloud about the fact that their mission was convoy security and traffic control. "We could stop shit like that from happening!" MPs complained, kicking rocks in the sand. Keeping MPs out of the fight had already cost American soldiers' lives.

A Marine intelligence officer had an entirely different experience that further showed the dire consequences of having inadequate security forces immediately after the invasion. He and a small team were ordered to occupy Kirkuk, north of Baghdad. When they arrived they were stunned to realize that their small unit was the only coalition force in the large city. Anxious to give the locals the idea that their presence was larger, the Marine ordered his unit to keep vehicles driving around the town continually.

Soon, in searching for anything of military or intelligence value, they stumbled on a vast, multiacre ammunition and weapons storage area just outside of the city. It was surrounded by a double chain-link fence topped with barbed wire. "The size of the place knocked our socks off." Inside were hundreds of bunkers. Highly concerned, the officer radioed higher headquarters to report his find and request a guard unit. His force was far too small to do anything themselves.

"It's just too big," he reported up the chain. "Way too extensive for our small team to guard it, let alone search it. We need help."

Told that there simply were not forces available, he and the team watched in daily growing frustration as first the fences were removed—"just disassembled and stolen in the night"—and then bunker after bunker was broken open and cleaned out.

"We begged for help. This is big, we said, and potentially super-dangerous. Who knew what was in those bunkers?" After the fences disappeared the team broke into a couple of bunkers and found AK-47s and small arms "stacked to the ceilings," along with literally tons of ammunition. The question lingered: What was stored in the rest of those bunkers. We will never know, because within weeks the site had been systematically looted.

"It's anyone's guess what was in some of those bunkers, but you can be certain a lot of Americans died from weapons looted there." This scenario was repeated around the country for weeks.

The MPs fretted on the docks in Kuwait, knowing how much they were needed inside Iraq.

On April 4, Phillips's 720th MP Battalion that had been stacked with his best people crossed the berm from Kuwait, headed north to join the rest of the coalition effort.

Rampant looting was already a big problem. By April 8 reports indicated that it had already been going on for some days. A CBS News journalist saw an elated Iraqi traveling through East Baghdad with an armful of stolen AK-47s as citizens ran in the streets with TVs, VCRs, and computers.[8] Reuters quoted a local resident in Basra angrily asking, "They are terrorizing our neighborhoods. At night, during the day, they steal everything. What kind of liberation is this?"[9]

Meanwhile, on April 9, the Marines used blowtorches to cut through the ankles of the giant bronze statue of Saddam in Baghdad's Firdos Square and drag it down to the ground;[10] the dictator officially had fallen from power on April 9 and, as Osama bin Laden before him, fled into hiding.

By April 12 Iraq's National Museum—the previous home to ancient Islamic texts as well as irreplaceable collections of Babylonian, Sumerian, and Assyrian artifacts—had been completely stripped clean of an estimated 170,000 treasures, prompting calls for an immediate international moratorium on the purchase of Iraqi antiquities.[11]

Looters swarmed Saddam's Al-Salam Presidential Palace, carting off everything they could carry, including fish from his garden pond. Everything was stolen from government buildings, from furniture and office supplies down to electrical wiring, Sheetrock, and plumbing fixtures.[12]

The Chinese embassy was ransacked, with armed men seen carting away refrigerators, computers, and air conditioners, perhaps using the eleven vehicles that vanished from the courtyard to haul away their loot. International law says parties at war are responsible for securing property and personnel of foreign missions, so the Chinese government issued harsh demands for U.S. troops to protect their property.[13]

But it was not until April 12 that the 4th Infantry Division that had previously been positioned near Turkey finally arrived in Kuwait, cleared the berm, and stormed into Iraq. At long last the MPs of the 18th were cleared to start their journey. They were badly needed many miles away.

•   •   •

By the time soldiers attached to the 18th MP Brigade finally were allowed to deploy forward, much of the damage had been done. Leaders were immediately forced to play catch-up in a game that had already been lost.

But finally, they were rolling north! Sergeant Abigail Vantichelt was tired, dirty, and hungry. After weeks training in the blistering Kuwaiti desert, surviving on MREs, and without shower facilities, she was—happy! At long last her 615th MP Company (Bloodhounds) was doing the job they had all worked hard to learn.

Vantichelt had been in the Army since age seventeen when she persuaded her reluctant parents to sign papers allowing her to enlist. It was not an easy decision for them. She grew up in Bath, New Hampshire, a small New England town that draws few visitors. She was the first one in her family to join the military.

When she talks about her childhood and military background, her blue eyes flash with laughter. She finds it amusing that in contrast to some of her fellow soldiers who "bleed olive drab" from their military heritage, she could not find anyone in her lineage who had ever served. She is not certain where the motivation originated, but knows for sure that it wasn't in her inherited DNA.

When at age seven she dreamed of Santa Claus, her Christmas list didn't include Barbie and Ken but was drawn from the Ranger Joe's catalogues stacked in her room. Now she was a soldier and had never looked back. With a tour in Bosnia under her belt she was finally in a real war.

The southern desert that connects Kuwait to Iraq is notorious. Dust—not the romantic wavy sand dunes of movies like *Lawrence of Arabia*, but nasty, scratchy, and invasive grit—is everywhere. Adding to the filth were roads and a landscape strewn with unimaginable amounts of garbage, trash, human feces, and unburied bodies of animals and humans. After weeks of this she was disgusted by her own dirty body. After a few days she and other soldiers came to accept the filth but longed for a shower. A bath? She would have killed for one.

On the march to war even the simplest of bodily functions require a plan. When you have to go, you have to go, but without a gas station or convenience store bathroom to duck into, you have to pick a time and place. One day she decided, as the convoy was in yet another long halt, to avail herself of a nearby truck tire as an "aiming point." She snuggled up beside the tire, but before she began, an amazing racket and clatter came from the sky. Looking up she saw a bizarre sight. A Navy helicopter—for a long moment the thought intruded, *What in hell is a Navy helicopter doing out here?*—obviously having mechanical problems, was struggling to maintain a hover. Right over where she squatted!

The chopper apparently was auto-rotating down—what pilots cynically refer to as a "semi-controlled crash." Desperately trying to stem the flow while pulling up her trousers she stumbled away, clearing the area as the helicopter smacked into the desert. It missed Vantichelt, but not by much. The thought came to mind: *Can't I even pee out here without a Navy helicopter of all things crashing down on top of me? What's next?*

Luckily everybody on the chopper and on the ground survived. Then it was back on the road and continue the march to Baghdad. The 615th had been ordered to the western Baghdad district of Abu Ghraib. "There are a lot of holdouts there," the unit was told. "You're going in to clean them up."

As Vantichelt and the 18th MPs were making their way through Iraq to their assignments, the looting and international outrage continued unabated.

Virtually nothing was spared, from rampaging citizens and criminals alike. On April 17 more than three hundred animals—including monkeys, bears, horses, birds, and even camels—disappeared from the Baghdad Zoo.[14] In some cases infantry units watched in helpless frustration. They were trained to fight organized resistance, not quell civil disorder. Commanders on the spot had no choice—keep pushing north, they ordered troops; others will have to sort this out. On the other hand, some units actually condoned the initial looting, particularly at facilities previously run by Saddam's Ba'ath Party.

Back in the States, David Phillips, like most Americans, watched the images on television and gritted his teeth in frustration. He knew he was watching the direct consequences of a war initially designed by Pentagon and White House planners to be "fought on the cheap." He was aware that a military police brigade—the 18th, which was now pushing as fast as they could at a painfully slow speed through the deserts toward Baghdad—should have accompanied the first invasion forces as originally planned before the Turkish political snafus had stopped them.

Crowd control, civil order, and protection of key installations was exactly the mission that MPs were prepared to deal with to prevent the chaos now being broadcast into all corners of the planet. The "kinetic" units that specialized in warfighting, like the Marine Corps and Army infantry, whose skills were unsurpassed, simply did not have the training to deal with looting, civil unrest, and other law-and-order emergencies.

Although the MPs from the 720th and the 18th MP Brigade had finally entered Iraq, Phillips knew it was a case of "too little, too late." The situation had already begun to tear to shreds what was left of the fragile fabric of a dictatorial Iraq. It was clear that only brutal repression had held the society together for decades. With the removal of Saddam Hussein, pent-up emotions, suppressed for more than thirty years, exploded in an orgy of mass lawlessness. The chaos caught coalition leaders by surprise; most could only watch the frenzied crowds, slack-jawed, and try to pick up the pieces.

The media joined the frenzy and unleashed unbridled fury on the U.S. military and political leadership for not having the foresight to see it coming.[15] Uncontrolled looting brought out worldwide criticism for U.S. incompetence and failed planning. The administration was lampooned with endless sarcastic comments about "being welcomed by cheering crowds,"[16] while video rolled in the background of riots and fires. Though in the first few days Iraqis welcomed coalition forces,[17] the bitter aftermath dominated news cycles and gave new life to a growing legion of war critics.

Yet the tide was turning. On April 16 an *LA Times* headline read: "Reluctant Pentagon Steps up Police Role: U.S. Sending in More Peacekeeping Forces," and later in the month it was announced that an additional four thousand U.S. troops, mostly MPs, were being sent into Baghdad and other key areas to restore order.[18]

In anticipation of having to secure, house, and process literally thousands of people detained during combat operations, the MPs took over Saddam's Abu Ghraib prison complex. What they found there shocked them: body parts slung around like offal in a mad butcher's shop, clear evidence of mass executions, and an estimated one thousand corpses in a mass grave.[19] Saddam released tens of thousands of criminals in October but still had kept political prisoners confined; when he fled some weeks earlier he had ordered them executed before coalition forces arrived.[20]

No amount of training or education could fully prepare these MPs—or anyone else—for the full scope of the horrors found inside that prison and elsewhere in Iraq.

6

CUL-DE-SAC OF DEATH

From darkened windows in the three-story, stone-and-mud buildings that lined the narrow street, AK-47s sprayed fire everywhere. Green tracers whined overhead, ricocheting off vehicles and pavement then spinning into the black sky. The explosion of RPGs slashed through the night, tearing up walls, roads, vehicles, and flesh with bursting warheads. Soldiers were bleeding, crying, and yelling for medics. Vehicles were hit. The noise rose to deafening levels as MPs fired back with .50 caliber machine guns and M-4 rifles. Smoke blinded soldiers, hiding their attackers. Surprise was quickly deteriorating into chaos. For a long instant Sergeant Abigail Vantichelt froze.

It wasn't quite the birthday party that Vantichelt would have wished for. She is of medium height and wears her dark brown hair pulled back tightly in a bun to fit snugly under a helmet. It's a practical style many women in the Army adopt that also complies with regulations. Vantichelt's eyes reflect a distant sadness, the result of too many months of urban combat in Iraq.

"You're bait," she'd been told bluntly when told to run her squad from the 615th MP Company through dangerous roads at night. "Lure Iraqi Army and Fedayeen Saddam holdouts into a firefight. We'll then send a reaction force to smash them." They had done it before many times. It always sounded better in the telling than the actual doing. But this night she thought: *Sometimes the sharks eat the bait!*

It all looked neat and clean when drawn up on the maps back at the tactical operations center. But on the filthy, narrow streets of the Abu Ghraib district west of Baghdad, with enemy fighters spitting fire at her and her squad, Vantichelt wondered if the cavalry would come to the rescue in time. Or would she and her soldiers be lost?

Already one of her trucks was knocked out, having gone nose-first into an adjacent canal at the outset of explosions. Others were disorganized, returning fire sporadically.

On that birthday night, the plan had worked more violently than they had anticipated. The patrol had run into a series of IEDs (improvised explosive devices). Explosions stopped them in their tracks. Then amidst the all-too-familiar cacophony of small-arms fire, a sound new to the battlefield echoed through the night: It was the sharp, ear-splitting crack of recoilless rifle fire. Vantichelt was stunned. This was the first time she had heard these weapons used against her. Recoilless rifles are pinpoint-accurate antiarmor weapons that pack a deadly punch. A recoilless rifle round—a shaped-charge explosive round resembling an oversized bullet—travels at lightning speed and can punch through the side of an armored vehicle. It turns a Humvee into Swiss cheese.

The well-laid plans of the night were falling apart under enemy fire. Vehicles and soldiers were put out of action. Her convoy was trapped in a cul-de-sac of death, stuck alongside a canal with only two ways out—back the way they'd come, into the jaws of the ambush and deadly fire, or a suicidal left turn over a bridge, and that was blocked by the truck that had tumbled face-first into the canal.

With two vehicles burning, the wounded needing assistance, soldiers shouting, weapons firing, and one truck hanging precariously off the side of the road into the canal, Vantichelt wondered for a moment if she was going to lose her entire squad.

She shook off the momentary shock. There would be time for introspection later—if she survived. Right at this very moment—with bullets and high-explosive rounds flying at them—her squad needed her leadership. Now! She got her head back in the fight. It was a situation that called for quick decision and deadly action. Training and experience—the qualities of a good noncommissioned officer—took over.

Vantichelt moved from truck to truck under deadly fire. Yelling to make herself heard over the din, she positioned squad members to direct their fire at the most dangerous targets—*Knock out that recoilless rifle and those machine guns!* Then she ran the lines, ducking past obstacles and vicious small-arms fire intended to kill her, and made sure that all soldiers capable of returning fire were behind cover that was as good as they could get and shooting as fast as they could find targets. "Pour it on them!" she ordered. Their survival depended on them outshooting the enemy—the MPs had to gain fire superiority or risk being overrun and killed.

She counted noses—everyone was accounted for, including the wounded—and reached for her radio handset. As calmly as possible Vantichelt told higher headquarters that her squad was in deep trouble—fighting back but outnumbered and, at the moment, outgunned. Weapons blasted and roared. The MP squad, now given direction, was sending withering fire back at the Iraqi ambushers. Vantichelt's senses were tuned to the fight.

As the fight progressed she sensed the tenor slowly changing. For the first time it sounded like the MPs were giving back more than they were receiving. Her machine gunners were pounding enemy positions. Heavy brass cartridge cases fell like hot rain on the deck of the Humvee and rattled down on the street. Suddenly she noticed that the deadly recoilless rifle was silent. Had they knocked it out? The volume of incoming fire from rocket-propelled grenades and machine guns had slackened. Maybe they would get through this alive after all. Her soldiers had been shocked and surprised by the initial attack. Now they were fighting back. Hard.

The center of gravity of the fight had tilted. Now it was the enemy who began to wilt under the intense fire from the trapped MPs. Vantichelt shouted for medics to drag wounded soldiers to cover, and treat them. She flipped channels on her radio and called for a casualty evacuation. Some of her squad were wounded seriously. She needed them to be flown to a hospital as soon as she could get a bird in to land.

She pulled a few of the squad off the line. Hauling out the truck that was stuck halfway into the canal by rigging tow cables to a working truck, she had them drag it back onto the road, adding its weapons to the fight. By that time the enemy—battered and defeated for the moment by the small unit they hoped to destroy—pulled out.

Shortly thereafter lead elements from the maneuver unit appeared on the scene. Vantichelt reported a brief summary of the ambush and directed them to locations where the enemy may have withdrawn. The fight was won. A single MP squad had prevailed against a superior enemy force with bravery and strong leadership.

That was one night's fight that spring. It was a harbinger of more to come.

On May 1, 2003, President Bush claimed the official end to combat operations in Iraq while standing on the deck of the USS *Abraham Lincoln* under an enormous banner declaring MISSION ACCOMPLISHED.[1] As many Americans and war planners had hoped, it had been a short war and everybody involved just wanted to get on with the business of standing Iraq up on its own two feet and getting out of there.

Yet Iraq was in complete chaos, and by then Phillips knew the MPs were faced with a very long process.

At this point the 18th MP Brigade was in place in the Baghdad region, and on May 9 they conducted the first joint patrols with some of the comparatively few Iraqi police willing to return to work amidst the tangle of looters, criminals, desperate citizens, members of al-Qaeda, and squabbling sectarian tribes.[2]

Approximately 7,000 prisoners who had been captured during the official invasion were released, although the MPs still detained 2,000 more for processing and background checks. The detainees at that time reportedly included 200 foreign fighters, 178 street criminals, a number of midranking Iraqi military officers, and some members of the Fedayeen Saddam paramilitary forces.[3] There was no other choice; sections of the despicable prisons at Abu Ghraib and elsewhere would have to be pressed into use since more suitable holding facilities simply weren't available yet, at a time when thousands of detainees had to be secured.

It was at this precise moment that L. Paul "Jerry" Bremer—a civilian diplomat—suddenly replaced Lieutenant General Jay Garner as the director of the Office for Reconstruction and Humanitarian Assistance, which was subsequently renamed as the Coalition Provisional Authority (CPA).

Bremer had an impressive background, previously serving as chief of staff under Secretary of State Henry Kissinger, as counterterrorism ambassador-at-large under President Ronald Reagan, then later as chairman of the National Commission on Terrorism, and eventually, in late 2001, cochairman of the Heritage Foundation's Homeland Security Task Force. On 9/11 he had been heading the crisis management division of Marsh & McLennan when the planes hit the Twin Towers, killing 295 of their employees and 60 more of their associates.

Bremer arrived in Baghdad on May 12, 2003, under the CPA banner as President Bush's personal envoy to Iraq under orders to report directly to Secretary of Defense Donald Rumsfeld and the president himself. Although he had no official authority to issue commands directly to coalition troops, he would later demonstrate that he had de facto control over not just the military but over the civil affairs affecting millions of Iraqi citizens.

The MPs assigned to protect Bremer and help carry out many of his controversial decisions would have more than their share of run-ins and disputes with the man. From the beginning there was also a lot of resentment since it appeared General Garner—who had been forced to work with only a fraction of the number of troops that were needed during the invasion—had unfairly been left holding the bag for the chaos that Iraq had become. In many ways Garner had become a major target of the international outrage directed at the situation as a whole, only to be replaced by a civilian diplomat that the world media dubbed to be the new "Governor General of Iraq."

On May 13 Bremer flexed his new muscles with a startling announcement: U.S. military forces, including the MPs patrolling the streets, were being authorized to shoot looters on sight.[4] There was no question that the ongoing rampage had to be stopped, and that hardened criminals were having a field day pillaging the city. Yet many soldiers also recognized that a great number of looters were simply desperate Iraqi citizens struggling to survive the collapse of their already feeble economy and overcome years of suppression and abuse under the thumb of a maniacal dictator. After months of unabated destruction, was the best solution to have U.S. troops suddenly open fire?

Another equally stunning decision: A new policy of "debaathification" designed to exclude all officials from Saddam's ruling Ba'ath Party from "positions of authority and responsibility in Iraqi society"—a move that would displace up to thirty thousand senior members of the Ba'ath ruling class.[5] While it was understood that some of Saddam's worst vipers were among their ranks, where would all these people go? And what about the low-level Ba'ath Party members who joined only because they could not be hired as teachers, doctors, or policemen otherwise?

Thankfully, at least the president's personal envoy recognized that the MP ranks were sorely lacking in troop strength, and by May 16 Bremer publicly promised to double their numbers in Baghdad from two thousand to four thousand. Countrywide, the population of U.S. military police would be increased from seven thousand to thirteen thousand.[6] With a direct line to Rumsfeld and the president, Bremer had been able to communicate a high-priority requirement in a manner that cut bureaucratic red tape, a process denied to Garner. Nonetheless, Rumsfeld was still stuck on keeping troop levels at a minimum whenever possible. It would be many months before Bremer's public promise would be fulfilled.

Appearances and promises were one thing, while realities often proved to be quite another. This would be demonstrated in a small but significant way to the MPs when, a few days later on May 21, in one of his first public appearances, Bremer pulled what a number of soldiers would see as a cheesy public relations stunt.

With great fanfare Bremer appeared alongside MPs from the 18th Brigade and a number of Iraqi police officers for a ribbon-cutting ceremony to reopen a small jail in downtown Baghdad. It had taken just ten days to paint over the blood on the walls and hire local Iraqi electricians, plumbers, and other laborers to transform the battered facility into a suitable holding unit.[7]

The problem was that this new Al Kardt Jail could hold only one hundred detainees, whereas the MPs were scrambling to investigate, house, feed, and care for thousands more. The grand opening of a comparatively "pretty" but entirely too tiny renovated jail seemed to some to be a very pathetic attempt by Bremer to divert public attention away from the harsh realities of Abu Ghraib and other detention facilities.

The same day world headlines screamed the news that, as part of the continuing debaathification process, Bremer was disbanding the entire Iraqi Army and other security bodies.[8]

Back at Fort Hood, David Phillips realized in a flash that a difficult but salvageable situation had been converted into a looming disaster. Nearly half a million Iraqi soldiers—armed, trained, and with weapons intact—had been told to return home with no prospects of employment, no back pay, and little chance to find a job or feed their families. Phillips knew that not only had all sense of honor been stripped from them but even basic pride—their ability to care for their families—had been arbitrarily torn away. In a pen stroke all semblance of civil control had been removed.

By then it was painfully obvious that many of the tens of thousands of murderers, rapists, kidnappers, robbers, drug dealers, and street thugs that Saddam had freed in October had now reorganized into gangs and were terrorizing a helpless populace.[9]

Joining them now would be pools of new recruits—many of them former Iraqi soldiers and police—who were desperate to survive.

Other officers agreed. "It was absolutely the wrong decision," a former aide to Garner, Colonel Paul Hughes, later told *The New York Times*. "We changed from being a liberator to an occupier with that single decision," he said. "By abolishing the army, we destroyed in the

Iraqi mind the last symbol of sovereignty they could recognize and as a result created a significant part of the resistance."[10]

Adding to the many problems, paperwork—ranging from personnel records to secret Iraqi documents—had been systematically destroyed. Captain John Petkovich, who had been among the MPs stuck in Kuwait while waiting for the 4th Infantry Division to cross the berm some months earlier, ended up in the Al Rashid district of Baghdad, working to rebuild Iraqi police units.

"Once the Iraqi Police were disbanded by the Coalition Provisional Authority," Petkovich recalled, "they shredded or burned all the records. So when we were later ordered to reconstitute the IP force, suddenly we had all of these guys who claimed to be former police officers showing up looking for work, and we didn't have any way of vetting them. All the records were gone."

In June 2003 Phillips's own unit, the 89th MP Brigade, was alerted to deploy to Baghdad. *Now they want us—after I already sent some of my best into Iraq with 720th MP Battalion!* Phillips thought, reading the orders. With his brigade staff stripped of some of its key players, Phillips scrambled to prepare for deployment. It was obvious that they were now paying the penalty for trying to do the war "on the cheap."

The frantic call for augmentation by the 89th MP Brigade originated from Major Carl Packer, an MP on Third Army staff, an in-theater organization. Packer and his superiors recognized that they still did not have enough MPs in the field and that they needed more right away. Perhaps bolstered by Bremer's promise for more military police professionals, the request was approved by General Tommy Franks's Central Command, and landed as an official request for forces on the Joint Chiefs of Staff. The approved formal request was quickly run through the Pentagon chain of command to Secretary Rumsfeld's desk.

To the astonishment of all concerned, Rumsfeld initially refused the request.

By this time the relatively few MPs on the ground in Iraq were fully engaged and had their hands full, and not just full of looters or detainees.

As anyone would expect, Saddam's supporters—almost exclusively Sunni Muslims like him, were not at all happy that their country had been overthrown. The Sunnis were concentrated in the Sunni Triangle of Iraq: a roughly triangular region bordered by the cities of Tikrit in the north, most of metropolitan Baghdad on the south, Ramadi on the west, and Baqubah on the east. Within this area lie the cities of Samarra and Fallujah. Predictably, opposition and attacks against coalition forces were particularly fierce in these Sunni strongholds.

In recent weeks the situation inside Fallujah in particular had escalated, with several U.S. soldiers killed, two in firefights and one when his convoy was ambushed. U.S. forces in the city, there to secure and patrol the area, were regularly attacked. The situation was worsening.

So, on June 4, some 1,500 soldiers from the 3rd Infantry Division accompanied by MPs from the 18th MP Brigade moved into Fallujah in an attempt to stabilize the area and flush out al-Qaeda fighters there.

Just after midnight one soldier was killed and five others wounded when they were hit by a rocket-propelled grenade at a checkpoint set up outside a local police station. "There was blood everywhere," one local resident remembered. The MPs spent the next day blocking off the streets, searching houses in the area, gathering intelligence that might help lead them to those responsible, and broadcasting prerecorded messages in Arabic from loudspeakers mounted on their Humvees, warning local residents to either evacuate or risk bodily injury.[11]

They weren't even sure exactly who was attacking them, yet there was no question they were facing one or more organized forces that were coordinating their attacks. A few days later an MP riding in a convoy through Fallujah noticed a red flare overhead, followed by a grenade that exploded directly behind them while unknown assailants opened fire from the rooftops above them. While a crude method of communication, the red flare he had seen had clearly been used to mark their position and commence the attack.[12]

On June 7 in another Sunni city, Saddam's home of Tikrit, Private Jesse M. Halling with the 401st MP Company died when he was shot in the face while performing community outreach operations; five other soldiers were wounded. They had been going door to door collecting complaints about stolen vehicles, looting, and missing persons while answering questions asked by the locals. At the same time gunmen on the rooftops opened fire on other soldiers who were working at the neighborhood civilian assistance office. The building was then hit by six to eight rocket-propelled grenades. The simultaneous ambush demonstrated the attacks were carried out by a coordinated force, although again, nobody was sure exactly who they were.[13]

Were they being attacked by the Sunnis; displaced members of the recently disbanded old Iraqi Army; members of al-Qaeda already known to join in the fighting in Iraq; or by some faction of foreign fighters who were pouring over the border from Syria? Or some noxious combination of some or all of these groups? The limited number of MPs in theater were doing their best, yet they were stretched so thin that it was literally impossible to stop in their tracks to carefully and systematically investigate the answers to these questions.

The situation was explosive and getting worse.

In the blistering hot afternoon of August 19 in Baghdad, Staff Sergeant Andre Valentine from the 812th MP Company, soaked in sweat, encumbered by the bulk and weight of combat gear, wiggled through a nightmarish labyrinth of jagged concrete chunks and twisted steel retaining rods amid intense heat inside the massive wreckage of what was left of the United Nations Headquarters at the Canal Hotel.

Half of the building had virtually disintegrated when an old Soviet-made flatbed truck carrying about a thousand pounds of weapons-grade explosives detonated at the concrete wall directly under the third-floor office of Sergio Vieira de Mello, the UN coordinator for Iraq. The explosion wiped the façade off the building, sheared through walls, and blasted a six-foot-deep crater into the ground outside. Huge sections of the second and third floors completely collapsed. The roof crushed down onto the rubble. Horribly mangled bodies of UN employees had been carried to a grassy patch outside the blast zone. For the moment the dead lay alongside the injured who had been lucky enough to be dragged out.

MP Valentine, worried about the likelihood of secondary explosions, was a professional paramedic. He saw his duty as not to wait for rescue crews but to help those he could. He crawled down from a narrow opening on the third floor through the shifting debris below. He was trying to reach First Sergeant William Von Zehle from the 411th Civil Affairs Battalion, who was desperately working to free two men pinned from their waists down. The first man, Gil Loescher, was in extremely bad shape. He had obvious signs of slipping into a state of life-threatening shock. His battered body completely blocked access to the second man, who lay in agony just a few feet away, and who calmly, yet very simply, identified himself by his first name only, "Sergio."

Valentine and Von Zehle—also an EMT and the former fire chief of Wilton, Connecticut—struggled in the cramped hole for several hours before successfully amputating Loescher's legs so that he could finally be lifted to safety. Loescher survived, yet tragically, Sergio Vieira de Mello succumbed to his injuries before the exhausted sergeants could reach him.

Nearly two dozen United Nations employees and associates had been killed and over a hundred more wounded in what was the most violent direct attack on the UN ever.

During their initial investigation the FBI found body parts near what remained of the truck that had delivered the explosives, thus indicating a suicide bomber was responsible. This was a significant find, as al-Qaeda and other jihadists were best known for carrying out such attacks, making them more likely suspects than angry Sunnis or Shi'a. It was further found that munitions-grade explosives had been used—including a five hundred-pound Soviet-made bomb from the 1970s or 1980s, and Soviet-made mortar rockets and artillery shells. Material like this had almost certainly been looted from one of Saddam's abandoned bunkers.[14] Perhaps it was from one of the hundreds, if not thousands, of arsenals that had been left unsecured as the MPs from the 18th MP Brigade were waiting around in Kuwait for clearance to enter Iraq months previously.

In the wake of the devastating bombing it then became clear that the UN had deliberately rejected offers of protection from the U.S. military. Except for a new concrete wall, UN officials at the headquarters refused the sort of heavy security that the U.S. military has put up around some sensitive civilian sites—because the UN "did not want a large American presence outside," said Salim Lone, a key UN spokesman.[15] UN Secretary General Kofi Annan reluctantly admitted that the UN may have turned down military protection, saying, "If they did, it was not correct, and they should not have been allowed to turn it down."[16]

An Armenian-Iraqi clerk who worked in the UN communications department, herself a longtime resident of Baghdad, lay battered in the hospital with her head wrapped in bandages, suffering from assorted puncture wounds, coughing up blood caused by internal injuries. She didn't know where her younger sister, who had also been wounded in the horrific attack and was last seen being evacuated on a stretcher by a U.S. military ambulance, was being treated. She told *Newsweek* magazine, "The whole country is destroyed, looted. Look at what the Americans have brought us."[17]

It apparently never occurred to her that the suicide bomber and mysterious networks that carried out the attack were to blame, not the military that had been denied permission to provide protection inside the UN compound in Baghdad.

Most astounding, the UN had recklessly continued to employ security guards originally provided by Saddam Hussein's government before the war. "Of course it's an enormous security risk—people who were members of Saddam Hussein's intelligence corps acting in any security capacity," Representative Adam Schiff, a Democrat from California, noted. Yet UN distaste for the military ran very deep: One UN official said that even after the attack they would still not increase the number of U.S. soldiers standing guard outside UN facilities. "We will always remain a soft target . . . we are conscious of that, but that is the way we operate. We are an open organization," explained their Iraq coordinator for UN humanitarian programs.[18]

A latent and undefined insurgency was growing into a full-blown war. Phillips and the 89th were told to stand ready but wait on orders. Among leaders in the Military Police Corps as well as other senior leadership, the sense of frustration and helplessness mounted. *The faster we can get into this thing,* they thought, *the better chance we have to control it. Wait too long and this is going to turn a quick victory into a long-term disaster.*

The witch's brew of insurgents was composed of breakaway political groups driven by sectarian ideology who were eager to take over the emerging government. Sunnis feared loss of primacy in the social structure and anticipated revenge by Shi'a elements long oppressed by Saddam. Shi'a were organizing and eager to collect a blood debt from the now disenfranchised Sunnis.

Al-Qaeda operatives, ever eager to engage "Crusader" fighters, swarmed across porous borders from Syria and joined the fight, primarily insinuating themselves into the northwest Sunni areas. Iranian elements, essentially Qods Force special operators from within Iran's Army of the Guardians of the Islamic Revolution (Revolutionary Guard), moved into the Shi'a communities and began organizing a revolt.

All groups took full advantage of the convenient pool of available fighters and the burgeoning presence of organized criminal gangs, recruiting heavily from them. In return they offered protected territory and ideological top cover. The smoldering fuse burned to its end and the situation exploded.

Bremer's order to disband all security organizations—army, police, and national police—triggered an avalanche of unintended consequences. At the time, many observers were urging that the Iraqi Army units be kept intact. Take away their weapons, it was said, and use the former troops to assist in rebuilding infrastructure crippled from war and decades of Saddam's neglect. Here were organized units, with plenty of idle hands, eager for useful work. They could quickly have been paid back wages for the six months Saddam had stiffed them (in the long run considerably less expensive than fighting them later) and immediately put to work. Purging of committed Ba'ath Party members, in accordance with the wishes of Bremer and others, could have been initiated simultaneously and proceed over time. Altogether it was a less intrusive, more cooperative and understanding manner than outright dismissal. It was a humane—human—solution for an otherwise no-win situation.

Instead, many of these men defaulted to what they knew. They simply took up arms—again abundantly available in the postwar environment—and began to fight the U.S. and coalition forces and each other. With police forces disbanded and Saddam's last-minute opening of prisons, criminal gangs were energized and found all the recruits they needed to launch large robberies of banks, public buildings, and other sources of wealth.

Concomitantly, the emergence of sectarian groups like the Shi'a militia and al-Qaeda in Iraq gave the criminals sufficient top cover so that they were cloaked in righteousness rather than illegality. Murder for hire, kidnapping for ransom, protection rackets, extortion, and armed robbery became a daily nightmare for ordinary Iraqi citizens who had hoped for a better future in a liberated Iraq.

It was a classic instance of opportunity lost.

"We could never get that time back," David Phillips later recollected. "Where things went to hell after the initial fighting died down were strictly MP missions: route security, law and order, civilian control, reestablishment of police forces, gathering intelligence from the population, and—most important from a public perception—stopping the rampant looting." An opportunity missed, Phillips knew, was an opportunity gone forever.

Saddam Hussein's vast arsenal dumps—scattered about the country and in some cases composed of thousands of bunkers over vast multiple-square-mile installations—were completely stripped.[19]

Even more disturbing to Phillips and his colleagues was the thought that whatever weapons of mass destruction material Saddam may have had in place had been destroyed or removed and hidden. Like many in senior positions in the military, Phillips believes that it was highly probable that such material existed. In the rush to win the fight quickly, such installations were bypassed, with inspection units arriving only after the facilities had been stripped of incriminating evidence. Again, the specter of a lost opportunity haunted Phillips.

"Maybe we couldn't have stopped it all," he noted. "But we could have protected some of the key sites."

As summer turned to fall at Fort Hood, the 89th MP Brigade was notified by higher headquarters to begin active planning for a Christmas deployment. *This looks like the real deal at last,* Phillips thought.

As part of his responsibilities as a leader, Phillips scheduled a predeployment site survey—a firsthand look at the situation on the ground into which he would be leading his soldiers—for October. After landing in Baghdad, Phillips received briefings and situational overviews from the higher headquarters and from senior leaders in the 18th MP Brigade, the unit he would be replacing.

He needed to see the turf and hear from the lower-level officers and soldiers just what challenges they would be facing. Accordingly he arranged to spend a few days on roving patrols, and joined members of the 709th MP Battalion (out of Hanau, Germany) in their area of operations in western Baghdad.

In those days, MPs ran a lot of night patrols. Phillips was riding with Lieutenant Colonel John Garrity, the battalion commander, through the Abu Ghraib district. They were hit repeatedly by small-arms fire as they rolled through the narrow streets. Once Phillips held his breath as a rocket-propelled grenade arched over the vehicle, exploding on the far side.

"What the hell is going on, John?" he asked.

"Just business as usual, Colonel," Garrity replied. "This is about what we encounter on average every night."

Later they sat on the roof of the battalion headquarters building across from the Baghdad Zoo in what would shortly be termed the

"Green Zone." Multicolored tracers raced across the sky, crisscrossing the city. Phillips was stunned. "I thought the time of major combat operations were over. We were getting into a far more dangerous situation than anyone back at Hood had realized."

Phillips gave the grim information he learned on his trip to subordinate commanders and staff. Deployment was racing fast down on them and time was short. As he ramped up the brigade for combat, he and his command sergeant major adjusted personnel and equipment levels across the brigade, an exercise known as cross-leveling. In an unusual move, he ordered members of the special reaction team (a kind of MP SWAT team) at Hood to join the deployment. Plans were for the unit to be augmented once in country to bring it up to a full platoon.

Led by First Lieutenant Roman Reese, the platoon, excited about the chance to go to war, all had their arms tattooed with a large unit design subtitled with the words NO FEAR. Of the original fourteen members in the platoon, two would later be killed in action, six wounded, one would receive a severe noncombat injury, and three would suffer traumatic brain injuries or treatment-unresponsive post-traumatic stress disorder. Reflecting on the outcome of the decision he made that fall of 2003, Phillips noted sadly that the ultimate losses "cause me to lose the most sleep and haunt me to present day."

7

THE YEAR FROM HELL BEGINS

By mid-January 2004, Phillips was relieved on the one hand and troubled on the other. The 89th MP Brigade already had a major in-country presence. That was good. Just about every soldier he wanted to bring to the fight had arrived. The bad aspect was that it wasn't enough. Because of pressing requirements in late 2003, Phillips was experiencing the shortcomings of a staff that had been stripped of senior talent prior to deployment to reinforce the battalion that deployed early. He saw the stress of running a tactical operations center in a combat zone take effect on some of his less experienced officers.

The tactical operations center (TOC) is the heart and brain of a combat unit. In Iraq, because of the deteriorating political situation, a highly convoluted coalition forces chain of command, a growing insurgency, and the need to hit the ground running, officers and noncoms in the TOC were under unrelenting 24/7 pressure. By January that pressure was intensifying. Experienced operators learn quickly how to establish and impose an "ops tempo" in their TOC, to manage the flow of incoming and outgoing message traffic, set schedules, mitigate pressure on personnel, and deal with daily events in the same manner that a distance runner handles a marathon: One controlled step at a time over a long haul.

Inexperienced operators, on the other hand, try to sprint. They are quickly overwhelmed by the confusion, noise, contradiction, and myriad of necessary details to mount out operations. Mistakes, even little ones, can mean soldiers' lives lost. But it never slows. There are no do-overs. The treadmill rapidly increases in speed and eventually they can't keep up: The heart pounds to bursting and the brain flat-lines. This was happening in the 89th MP Brigade's operations center.

And things were about to turn farther south again.

That January, Phillips received a call from the Criminal Investigation Division (CID) people who were located on the southern side of Baghdad International Airport. There was a case under investigation, Phillips was told, that most likely would have a very significant effect on the military police and their mission. *What is this all about?* Phillips wondered as he made his way to CID headquarters.

A similar call went to Colonel David Quantock, whose 16th MP Brigade had only recently deployed into Iraq. Quantock, son of an Army officer, and a Norwich graduate, had been friends with Phillips since both were captains in the career course together. The 16th Brigade was a proud paratrooper unit out of Fort Bragg, North Carolina, where it had been part of the XVIII Airborne Corps. Originally sited at Camp Bucca in the south, the 16th's area of responsibility had spread, now reaching up to western Bagdad districts, including Abu Ghraib and the Triangle. On receiving the call, Quantock was concerned. "Something is happening in your AO [area of operations] that you need to know, right now," he had been told.

They were met by Colonel Gerald Mocello, CID commander. Phillips, Quantock, and Mocello were longtime colleagues. Coincidentally, all three had been on the same brigade command selection list published in 2001. Now they had assumed those command positions, in a place and time none could have predicted. "Take a look at these," Mocello said, laying out a series of photos. "This is going to land right in the lap of the MPs. You need to be aware of what's happening."

The photos looked amateurish but the subject was grotesque. A cold chill ran up Phillips's spine. "Where were these taken?" Phillips asked, but in his gut he knew. "Abu Ghraib prison," answered Mocello. "These are guards from the 800th MP Brigade."

Mocello turned to Quantock. "Dave, this is probably going to be your tar baby. It's right in your area of operations."

"Is General Karpinski aware of this?" Phillips asked. Janis Karpinski, a Reserve force MP officer, commanded the 800th MP Brigade.

"It's an ongoing investigation," Mocello replied. "We're looking at everybody connected with the prison and the unit. This investigation is on General Sanchez's desk as we speak. We're the most senior MPs in theater and you have people running the roads every day. You need to know this is going to blow back on your soldiers."

"Keep me posted as much as you can on developments," Phillips said. He walked from the meeting with his stomach in a knot. Outside the office Phillips and Quantock conferred briefly. Both commanders knew immediately that they faced an incident with international strategic implications, all of them bad, for the United States and the coalition, not to mention Iraqis and Muslims across the globe, too. "This is going to be our My Lai," Phillips muttered on the way back to his unit. Three months later the grungy photos exploded on global media outlets. The reaction would be worse than either Quantock or Phillips anticipated.

On January 14 Quantock was told to go to Abu Ghraib to notify Karpinski that she was suspended from command and that he would be taking over two weeks later. As Quantock waited outside, he learned that CID personnel were with Karpinski. Later he heard that they showed her photos of the atrocious behavior of her 800th MP Brigade soldiers in the depths of the prison. Quantock said in an aside to Command Sergeant Major Jeff Butler, "If this hits the press it's going to be a disaster."

Throughout her command, Quantock found out, Karpinski had very rarely visited the prison area. Once the lower enlisted realized that they were without senior leadership supervision, they ran the place like a frat house on steroids—with compliance of senior enlisted and junior officers. Opinions may differ as to whether their actions constituted torture, but everyone agrees that it seriously violated MP standards of "safe and humane care and treatment."

Quantock immediately put a new commander, Lieutenant Colonel

Lenny Upshaw, his adjutant general, into the slot and told him to clean the place up. "It's all about standards and discipline," he said. When he had first visited the prison in November 2003, Quantock had observed that all of these, including morale, were "incredibly poor." Determined to right the wrong, he spent one or two nights weekly at the prison. "We see you more than we ever saw General Karpinski," he was told up and down all levels.

The provost marshall general, Don Ryder, came temporarily to train soldiers up on 31E skills. After six weeks he wanted to go home, but Quantock insisted on what he laughingly calls the "Quantock Hostage Program."

"You go back, General," he said, "but I need you to leave a sergeant first class at Abu Ghraib and at Camp Bucca to continue training." Quantock got his noncommissioned officer on a permanent basis and the clean-up began in earnest. It would all come to a head in just six more weeks when the investigation released its findings.

A month later, in the middle of February, the lack of experience the absence of the tough-mindedness necessary for a battle staff to function in the midst of high-input, maximum-stress conditions—caused Phillips's tactical operations center to spin out of control. It started over a simple misunderstanding.

Phillips and his unit chaplain were having a meal at the Bob Hope Dining Facility over on the airport side of the base. Like many of the larger facilities in Iraq and Afghanistan, this one was peppered with large-screen televisions, usually tuned to sports on ESPN or a cable news channel like Fox News or CNN.

Phillips watched Secretary of Defense Donald Rumsfeld telling reporters at a news conference at the Pentagon that "there was no insurgency in Iraq, just a few bad people and criminals" carrying out violent incidents.

At that precise moment "all hell broke loose." Four rockets—launched in all probability from Sadr City by Mahdi Army fighters—exploded with enormous force near the mess hall. Several soldiers were wounded outside; the ground actually shook from the repeated impacts of the munitions.

Phillips and the chaplain—both completely unaware of the extent of the damage—had simply picked up their plates, ducked under the table, and continued to eat. Phillips made a sarcastic remark that since there were no insurgents the "bad people and criminals" had just fired on them.

In what would later be described as an unfortunate "play on words," the noncommissioned officer in charge of Phillips's security team, Sergeant Stacey Howell, radioed the operations center and reported that they had "lost" Phillips. Howell really meant to report that in the aftermath of the attack, with the dust, confusion, concern for the wounded, and normal chaos, that he and the squad had lost track of where Phillips was physically located.

It turned out, somewhat predictably in hindsight, that people at the operations center interpreted Howell's report to mean that Phillips had been killed in action by the rockets. A key staff player, who was an MP officer, was mentally unprepared for such news. He began to behave frantically, shouting, yelling, and issuing disjointed, contradictory instructions. He lost his composure so badly that the brigade deputy commander, Lieutenant Colonel Bob Raye, had to interject himself and calm him down.

Finally, a second report, clarifying Phillips's actual condition, came over the radio and order was restored. But the initial damage was done—the officer lost much respect from his colleagues. He was prescribed antidepressant medication, but for all intents and purposes had become operationally ineffective. He was kept in place for the moment, with the hope that he would recover.

Almost immediately thereafter another incident stunned the operations center and broke the same [S-3]'s spirit. On February 5 the [S-3] had coordinated independently with what are euphemistically referred to as "other government agency" personnel—sometimes these are CIA, DEA, FBI, or in this case National Security Agency (NSA) agents—to support a signal intercept operation within Bagdad. The idea was that MPs would provide force protection for the NSA team while they set up their equipment to capture cell phone and other wireless traffic from possible insurgents.

Once on site the NSA team leader directed the MP sergeant who had been assigned to him by the officer to have his MP squad set up a traffic checkpoint, which the sergeant did. Unfortunately none of this had been coordinated or approved by the battlespace owner, the 1st Infantry Division.

In the complex hierarchies that make up modern warfighting, such coordination is considered essential to avoid fratricide incidents; battlespace owners also need to be prepared to coordinate fire support or medical evacuations if the need arises. Still, had nothing untoward occurred, the operation might have drawn, at most, a stern counseling session directed at the officer to improve his staff procedures.

But on February 10 everything—to use a common military expression—"went to shit." During the course of the operation, an Iraqi driver either didn't understand that he was supposed to stop or decided to run past the checkpoint. The MPs opened fire on the vehicle, in accordance with approved rules of engagement at the time, and both a father and son were mortally wounded. The 1st Infantry Division now had a serious incident report situation involving MPs who they didn't even know were in their area.

When the reports began to come to the operations center via radio, the burden of his error proved more than the officer could handle. He collapsed on the floor in a fetal position, moaning and incoherent. The following day, February 11, the officer was sent home for psychological treatment at the Army hospital at Fort Hood, Texas.

No one ever knows when their time of testing will occur or how they will react. Some soldiers rise to the challenge, others are unable to cope. Even those who have proven quite capable in a peacetime military environment may disintegrate mentally when deployed into combat. While many were sympathetic to the officer's plight, the exigencies of the situation were best served—not to mention the individual's needs—by rapid removal from combat, followed by ultimately awarding him a medical discharge from further service for severe post-traumatic stress disorder.

•　　•　　•

By March 2004 the 16th MP Brigade (Airborne) was well established, including supervision of the detention center at Camp Bucca. The camp, originally set up by the British, was renamed by U.S. forces after Ronald Bucca, a soldier from the 800th MP Company (National Guard) who was also a firefighter killed in the 9/11 attack at the World Trade Center.

Along with Camp Cropper in the north, Bucca was a major collection point. At the time it was taken over, more than six thousand Iraqi detainees were being held there. After the insurgency grew it would expand to hold up to almost thirty thousand.

The 16th Brigade MPs had more on their plates than the Bucca facility. The main supply route for the entire country ran right through their operational area. They picked up convoys from the moment they crossed the Kuwaiti border headed north until they transferred to the 89th MP Brigade's area about midway up-country. By this time the Iraqi port of Umm Qasr had been cleared of sabotage and war damage so it too was now functioning as an entrepôt for incoming cargo.

It was still challenging for convoys to make the long trek north, but at this stage of the war things were settling down and IEDs and ambushes were less frequent. All that was about to change for the worse.

Quantock and his staff knew where the hotbeds of insurgency festered long before they deployed, and had therefore spent significant time developing tactics to deal with them. Because so much of the coalition forces' ability to function depended on reliable logistics support, the insurgents focused on convoys running the routes up from Persian Gulf ports as especially vulnerable targets. Typically soldiers or civilian contractors riding in these convoys had limited response capability and were less able to defend themselves and their trucks. Quantock knew he had to develop new tactics to counter the ambushes.

The 16th MP Brigade directed units to take a "shadowing" approach: MP units routinely ran Humvees tight against the rear of supply convoys, ready at a moment's notice to engage any attackers. While this tactic proved effective, it came with a cost.

One of David Quantock's favorite soldiers was Staff Sergeant Wentz Shannenberger. Nicknamed "Baron" by his fellows, Shannenberger was a staff NCO—essentially a desk jockey—who continually pestered Quantock to assign him to a platoon. He felt frustrated and not a little guilty that he was safe on base while raw soldiers were taking risks that Shannenberger thought he could mitigate through his experience and maturity. Reluctantly, Quantock agreed, and assigned him as the new platoon sergeant to the 21st MP Company (First From Above), one of only three airborne-qualified MP companies in the U.S. Army. Shannenberger exemplified the paratrooper spirit: *Send me!*

On March 24, 2004, one of Shannenberger's squads was tasked to escort a convoy from Baghdad International Airport[1] up to Taji, north of Baghdad. Normally the platoon sergeant did not have to accompany each squad, but Shannenberger elected to ride with them that day. As the convoy neared Taji base they spotted a vehicle with suspicious-looking individuals inside. "Pull alongside," Shannenberger told his squad leader, Sergeant Sholah Yi. "Let's check it out."

As the two soldiers approached the car, insurgents piled out, firing AK-47s at them. Hit several times, Shannenberger fell, mortally wounded. Yi, wounded in the wrist and thigh, was armed only with his pistol. He returned fire and ran back to the Humvee to get his M-4 rifle.

A wild firefight erupted. Suddenly they were taking fire from nearby buildings, where insurgents had previously centered their ambush. Only Shannenberger's suspicions and initiative had thwarted their intent to catch the soldiers in the middle of the intended kill zone. A grenade exploded as Yi reached the truck, knocking out his gunner, Specialist Jourdan Frain.[2] Yi was wounded again in the chest and arm, incapacitating his left arm. After snatching his rifle from the Humvee, Yi killed one approaching insurgent and then turned to empty his magazine into the car. As the MP squad took the fight to the enemy a Marine response force pulled up and together they destroyed the insurgents.

Wentz Shannenberger was later awarded a posthumous Silver Star and promoted to Sergeant First Class. Sergeant Yi and Specialist Frain were each given the Bronze Star with Valor device along with a Purple Heart.

But the loss of such a popular unit soldier hit everyone hard. Shannenberger was the first killed in action that the 16th MP Brigade faced since its January deployment. Quantock felt pangs of guilt for having agreed to move Shannenberger to a dangerous leadership position. But as bad as things were for the deployed soldiers, back home the rear detachment headquarters was not prepared for the situation.

Melissa Quantock, Quantock's wife and the informal mother to the unit's wives, was among the first to hear the news of Shannenberger's death. She and two other wives rushed to headquarters. Due to their unit's lack of previous experience in handling such a tragedy, Melissa worried that there was a lot of room for potentially devastating errors in breaking the horrible news to Shannenberger's wife. Officers specifically instructed Melissa to stay away. But she had heard about how these things had been mishandled in previous wars. "We're going to follow them," she told her friends.

Unfortunately the unit notification team had gone to Shannenberger's home without first checking to see that his wife was there. Shannenberger's wife, Corey, an Australian citizen, was at work when she got a call from the unit to come home immediately. Naturally, she was in an emotional panic as she picked up her kids and raced home. When she pulled into the driveway and spotted the notification team she fell to pieces. Her four young children were momentarily forgotten, still belted into their car seats.

When Melissa saw Corey Shannenberger's state of complete hysteria she knew that they had to step in. First they took the children out of the car and played with them under a tree in the front yard. Later they tried to calm Corey, but she was inconsolable. After this bitter first experience, Melissa noted that the unit began to learn how to better deal with casualties. They recognized that these were all young wives whose husbands had not been in combat before. Indeed, this was the first time other than the brief Grenada incursion that her husband had been deployed in harm's way. They knew it was a dangerous profession—and all their husbands were paratroopers—but facing the harsh facts of casualties for the first time, the unit responded poorly. She set out to fix that as best she could.

No one told her what she needed to do, but as the commander's wife she took it on as a personal responsibility. She formed "care teams" and tried to get the wives involved in volunteer and unit activities. It got increasingly serious as the deployment wore on for fifteen months. Casualties continued, both killed and wounded in action. Panic, depression, and boredom took their toll at home. She watched some spouses gain strength through the care teams—"they got out of their heads and became much less self-focused"—while others were unable to stand the strain.

In some ways Melissa thinks that the lines of instant communications that soldiers have today with easy access to Internet and telephones exacerbates the situation. "When you talk to them constantly over Skype or the phone, or e-mail all the time, you begin to think that things are normal; that he's just right over the hill. Then something bad happens and you're not prepared for it."

She is convinced that the Army is doing it better now, but acknowledges that it is a painfully difficult situation that is almost unsolvable. Melissa worries about the National Guard spouses who lack even the basic leadership and mutual support networks that the active Army employs. She thinks back to that first poignant conversation with a distraught Corey Shannenberger. On her refrigerator one of Corey's children had affixed a yellow ribbon with the words scrawled on it, "Keep Daddy safe."

"What do I do with that now?" Corey asked, eyes filled with tears. Neither Melissa Quantock, nor any of us, can answer that question.

8

FUELING THE FLAME

As is the case with all turbulent events, the elements of a major disturbance in Iraq had been gathering ominously for some time. The Coalition Provisional Authority (CPA) under Paul Bremer provided the catalyst. Everything in Iraq seemed to revolve around Bremer's volatile personality and the influence it had on his judgment, although in his defense it ought to be noted that guidance from Washington was frequently contradictory and confused. However, he was known for an explosive temper and an egocentric overconfidence in his own infallibility that led to stubbornness and intransigence. At his staff meetings, opposing viewpoints were not welcome and anyone with the temerity to challenge his decisions generally found themselves out of a job. As a consequence he found himself surrounded by sycophants and neophytes, often both.

Because of his status, Bremer was given a special security detail that included a platoon of military policemen. First Lieutenant Jonathan Tessmann's platoon of MPs who previously served as General Garner's personal security detachment (PSD) were now working to protect Bremer.

The MPs under Tessmann's command functioned as the first, outermost ring of security. When the Big Boss headed out to visit a particular location, it was Tessmann's people who cleared the route, managed traffic to allow the convoy to speed through intersections, and checked out the destination before the main group arrived.

As would become trademark with Bremer, he expanded his body-guard detachment with civilian Blackwater contractors who clustered around him like drones around the queen bee. "Individually they were good," Tessmann remembered. "Unfortunately this kind of duty required more group training than they had. They were making some bad mistakes that could result in holes in security." After watching the charade for a while, Tessmann finally put his foot down and compelled better training for inner perimeter security.

Tessmann was staggered by the scarcity of operational information. Maps, for example, were nonexistent or hopelessly outdated. "The best maps we had, on many occasions," he recollected, "were actually place-mats used to promote a restaurant." On several missions elements of the platoon got misoriented on convoluted city streets and had to find their way out by trial and error. Feeling your way across Baghdad traffic alone is a scary proposition. Under threat of ambush or IED it becomes a high-risk, no-win activity.

"Our lack of proper maps and guides was of no consequence to Bremer," Tessmann remembered. "He wasn't interested in those kinds of things. 'Just get it done,' we'd be told." At one point Tessmann was directed to drive up and back to Tikrit, 125-plus miles each way, with no maps. "I had to take my unit up and down with nothing more than cell phone communications and no guides. We were damn lucky we all got back safely."

Tessmann conceded that Bremer had a hard job to do, but he was frequently put off by displays of the CPA leader's temper. "He was volcanic. Without warning he might go off on tantrums for no apparent reason." Those around him, even somewhat distant like his security people, learned to walk on eggshells when they heard Bremer might be in the area. Moreover, Bremer appeared to be extremely thin-skinned when it came to criticism. As early as June 2003 a BBC report recounted stories of biting local media satire directed at him.[1] Several of the newspapers and outlets that proliferated after Saddam's removal published cartoons lampooning Bremer, in some instances quite nastily. Word from coalition headquarters was that the man had seen them and was not amused.

This was, of course, not the only source of criticism against Bremer. American media outlets, especially those with an agenda opposing either the war or the reconstruction, were merciless in their hostility, finding fault even with the successes. If a project worked, then stories carried dark hints of U.S. contractor overbidding and kickbacks. Reporters focused heavily on unsolved problems—water, electrical power, infrastructure repair and improvement—to the point that anything the Coalition Authority did was subject to endless nitpicking and complaining. A favorite trick of reporters was to find an Iraqi who would proclaim that "things were better under Saddam," thereby reinforcing their preconceived hypothesis that the war itself was a mistake.

The endless criticism, compounded by Bremer's acerbic, eccentric personality, only led him to greater errors in judgment, including selection of staff. It was, Phillips recalled, "the Original Amateur Hour over there." Ultimately, in early April 2004, Bremer's prickliness impacted David Phillips in a very personal way.

Like many officers Phillips had come to the fight with the intent of making Iraq a better place. After thirty-five years of brutal oppression, he reckoned, the door was finally opening to a freedom and democracy that Iraqis had never previously enjoyed.

Based on American values, it was clear that a key part of the new freedom centered on the existence of a free press. Prior to liberation only Ba'ath Party–approved newspapers and broadcast outlets had been permitted to stay in business. After liberation, scores of newspapers, radio and TV stations, Internet sites, and other communications outlets had sprung up across the country, each with an agenda and a voice. Phillips and others saw this as an expression of newly discovered freedom. The fact that even hostile outlets were permitted—even encouraged—to exist he saw as a tangible manifestation of beliefs put into action.

The message was clear: In a free society we can withstand criticism and complaint—even if unjustified—because that is what ultimately makes the society strong.

Phillips was aware that many of the newspapers that popped up across the country were highly critical of the coalition, and many personally attacked Bremer. After all, as head of the CPA he was an automatic target for all that Iraqis saw was wrong—looting, lack of control, failure to bring electrification and water quickly enough, economic turmoil—justifiably or not, such criticism was laid at Bremer's door.

One small paper, *Al-Hawza* in Baghdad, particularly delighted in publishing cartoons attacking Bremer. The newspaper was the official organ of the Mahdi Party, headed by the violent cleric Moqtada al-Sadr. Bremer insisted on seeing these cartoons, each time growing more infuriated. In late March 2004 Bremer, according to Philips, had a tantrum over the latest in the series, exploded, ordering his military subordinates to close down *Al-Hawza*. Bremer indicated in his memoirs that he made the decision to close the newspaper to quell violence. If so, it backfired. In any event, it fell to the 89th MP Brigade to enforce the order.

Phillips was stunned to receive an order that directed him to shut down the newspaper. He gasped in dismay and sought to rectify what he was certain must be an error. Anxious to get clarification before incalculable damage was done, Phillips called his boss, begging him to reconsider the order. Phillips felt emotions taking over. "Isn't a free, independent press what we have come to promote?" he asked. "This flies in the face of everything we stand for."

"Dave," he was told, "this is an incredibly stupid, intellectually dishonest move. I'll talk to the CPA myself." Feeling better, Phillips went back to the daily grind.

Shortly thereafter Phillips's phone rang again. It was his boss. "Dave," he said, "I'm sorry, but we're going to have to shut it down. Orders from Bremer personally."

Torn by mental anguish, Phillips reluctantly called Lieutenant Colonel Byron Freeman, commander of the 759th MP Battalion, to issue the order. Freeman, a combat vet from Desert Storm, argued with Phillips with the same logic that the latter had argued against the order. "Our hands are tied," Phillips said, trying to hide his bitterness. "Carry out the order." Phillips slowly hung up the phone, deeply troubled by an impending sense of dread, knowing that what they were doing was incredibly stupid and self-destructive to the coalition effort.

Shortly after receiving the order, Freeman selected his 984th MP Company from Fort Carson, Colorado, to carry out the operation. Following a personal reconnaissance, the company commander briefed Freeman and offered recommendations. They decided that the most effective way to accomplish the order was to close *Al-Hawza* at night to avoid a direct confrontation with Moqtada al-Sadr's newspaper staff.

On March 28, 2004, Freeman's company moved out to the Karada Peninsula, just outside the Green Zone—a mixed neighborhood on a land mass that jutted into the muddy Tigris River like a large, swollen tongue. MPs hung thick chains across the entrance with a large wooden sign that stated in Arabic: *By order and direction of the Coalition Provisional Authority, this newspaper facility is closed.* Meeting no physical resistance, the MPs were able to carry out the closure order. That was the easy part.

The next morning, *Al-Hawza* workers arrived to find their newspaper closed. They pulled out cell phones and speed-dialed local militia leaders. Adverse popular reaction was immediate. Understandably, the general Iraqi press erupted with anger and outrage. Even media normally sympathetic to the coalition expressed bitter criticism. Accusations of hypocrisy (justified in many Western minds as well) flew wildly, fanning the propaganda fires that had already been started by anti-government, anti-coalition elements.

The closure of *Al-Hawza* had played right into their hands.

Both Phillips and Freeman had anticipated an explosion of hostility. "I knew that once we completed this mission, tensions would certainly increase," Freeman reported, then added with classic military understatement, "I alerted my senior leaders to be prepared for a significant change in our operating environment." In other words, *They're going to come at us, guns blazing.*

The MPs didn't have long to wait.

Freeman's units began to be attacked more frequently than they had been over the previous three months. Targeted assassination attempts against Iraqi governmental officials and facilities spiked. Where they were strong, especially in districts like Sadr City, the Mahdi Army began to attack Iraqi Police stations in an attempt to take them over.

Bad news proliferates. Crashing on the heels of the press closing, a crushing new embarrassment emerged. Days later the Abu Ghraib photos broke across the world media. Phillips found himself in the midst of an incredible mess, agonizing that so much of it had been of the coalition's own making and could have been so easily avoided.

West of Baghdad, in Anbar Province, Sunni disenchantment with what they perceived to be a Shi'a-dominated new Iraqi government became coupled with nefarious influence from hundreds of foreign al-Qaeda organizers who had infiltrated through Syria to produce a violent uprising. The region exploded.

On March 31 four Blackwater contractors were passing through Fallujah on their way to deliver food to an American military outpost. They were ambushed on the main route north that transects Fallujah. Not only were the contractors brutally murdered—reports say they were forced to stay inside the vehicle while the crowd set fire to their SUV and burned them alive—but they were hung in pieces from the nearby bridge. The depravity of the act sent the message from the insurgents that there would be no quarter or humanity in the upcoming fight. The coalition, appalled by the brutality, accepted the challenge and rose to confront it.

While the coalition prepared a response, the situation deteriorated across Anbar. Between Fallujah and Baghdad lies Diyala. At 1030 hours on April 3, 2004, just days after the massacre in Fallujah, a sergeant from Keeseville, New York, with the Wild West name of Jesse James Shambo was a turret gunner in a Humvee with 3rd Platoon of the 984th MP Company based nearby at Camp Muleskinner. Shambo, who stands five foot seven and weighs in at 186 pounds, is an accomplished body builder.

He was a recent high school graduate and spent his spare time working on his father's logging business and boxing. Before joining the Army he had boxed in New York state competitions. Asked to define an outstanding physical characteristic, Shambo noted two facial scars from logging. His fellow soldiers volunteered that he ran around with a "pissed-off look" on his face.

So far the Army had been a whirlwind. Two months after raising his hand to take the oath of enlistment in July 2003 he had completed training as a 31B military policeman. By November he was in Iraq, rolling as a Humvee turret gunner through the dangerous territory surrounding Baghdad. Now his unit was headed toward what they were certain would be a firefight in Diyala.

Having learned that insurgent forces had taken control of the city, their mission was to get to the Iraqi Police station as quickly as possible and reestablish a coalition foothold. As they left the gates they called in a status report: "Start patrol time, now. Rolling with twenty-nine MPs and seven vehicles."

There are only two major roads into the city, which lies about thirty minutes away from Muleskinner. The road they entered on splits into two bridges just before getting into the city proper. Halting at the bridge, Shambo's platoon sergeant called to him to assess the situation. You see a lot more while perched high in the turret that was Shambo's fighting position than in the low-riding Humvee cab. Shambo noticed about fifty-plus people milling about on the far side of the bridge. He ducked into the turret to relay the report. When he stuck his head back out again the people had eerily disappeared. The platoon sergeant called again for confirmation.

"Shambo, where are they and how many?" Shambo's answer was not what he wanted to hear. "I don't know. There were around fifty or so. But they're gone. I can't see anybody anymore."

The mood was ominous. Cautiously, the platoon sergeant gave the order. "Push across the bridge. Everyone watch your sectors!" Moving slowly, as the bridge accommodated only one vehicle at a time, they assembled on the far side. Still no one in the city showed his face. Previously the platoon had taken the right-hand fork when it visited the police station. Today, with a heightened sense of impending trouble, the platoon sergeant intentionally broke the pattern. "Take the left fork to the station," he ordered.

As the convoy rolled toward the main road they were met with a massive explosion. A shock wave rocked the trucks. Greasy black smoke blossomed in the street and obscured vision. It was estimated that two 155 mm artillery rounds had been emplaced as an IED. Insurgents, waiting for the detonation, initiated their ambush before the debris settled. Suddenly the MPs were in the middle of a killing zone.

Insurgents fired a rocket-propelled grenade aimed directly for Shambo's truck. "It looked like a flaming softball coming right at me." Shambo yelled, "RPG!" and ducked instinctively as the round flew over his vehicle. He immediately opened up on the gunman with the light machine gun—a 5.56 mm M-249 squad automatic weapon—mounted on his truck. At that time the platoon did not have heavier, more effective .50 caliber machine guns on all the Humvees, but Sambo was able to swiftly take out the enemy gunner before swiveling his weapon to engage more targets.

Insurgents seemed to be everywhere. In seconds the MPs were deep into an intense firefight. RPGs flew at them from windows and alleys. The distinctive rattle of AK-47 and machine-gun fire deafened soldiers. In the background they heard scores of bullets bouncing off the trucks.

For the quarter-mile run to the station they were under constant attack. Every truck was heavily engaged. The noise and smoke were everywhere, and the explosions were deafening. When they turned left into the road to the station, the enemy was waiting in force and hit them with everything they had. "We had to drive right into that fatal funnel," Shambo later recalled.

Struggling to make it to the police station, each truck maddeningly had to negotiate a too-tight passage. Drivers were forced to stop outside the station and maneuver in order to clear it. This meant that others waited, under constant attack, slowly pushing forward under continuous heavy fire, while one after another of the trucks slowly surrounded the station.

Once in place, the platoon sergeant ordered a team to dismount and prepare to force open the gate. Sergeant Shambo was the lead man in the stack of MPs ready to act. The order was given and they pushed back the gate, weapons ready, unsure of what lay behind that barrier. The team was faced with six armed Iraqis—not in uniform, not police. Since the Iraqis did not raise their weapons as a threat the team did not engage them. Without an interpreter they were unable to find out who the men were, other than listening to them mutter "friend, friend."

Brushing the men aside for the moment, the team cleared the station in minutes then set up defensive positions. They released the six suspicious Iraqis, who then crossed the street, entered the mosque, and began to broadcast over a loudspeaker. "We had no idea what they were saying, but it sounded hostile," Shambo remembered.

Shambo took up a fighting position on the roof once a rudimentary defensive perimeter was established. He faced the main road and double bridges. Enemy mortar fire began to impact all about them, crunching explosions threw shards of red-hot shrapnel and pieces of rock and concrete all about. Machine guns, RPGs, and small-arms fire whined overhead and smacked into the walls of the station. "We were in a three-hour fight without a second of silence," he remembered. The platoon was using prodigious amounts of ammunition. "We were burning through two hundred rounds an hour per person." Worried that they would shortly go "black" (empty) on ammo, the platoon leader, a lieutenant, hastily called for emergency resupply.

Unpleasant word came back over the radio: Because of higher priorities for an ongoing fight in Sadr City, the platoon in Diyala would have to wait. *How much longer can we hold out?* they thought. They counted precious magazines and prepared for the worst.

As far as the insurgents were concerned, the battle had just begun. More than a quarter of the village was burning furiously because of the number of rounds being fired, many of them tracers. Suddenly the armored support vehicle gunner—who was manning a large dual .50 caliber machine gun and a MK-19 grenade launcher—got eyes on the enemy mortar team he had been looking for. He immediately lit them up with intense fire from both weapons. The powder charges for the mortar rounds ignited and the mortar pit burst into flames. *One weapon and crew out of the fight!* The gunner tracked, picking out new targets.

Fighting continued unabated into long nighttime hours. Ammunition levels were reaching the critical point. The platoon leader called again for assistance. This time they were told that a support squad would be at their location in an hour.

Just before daylight a convoy of Iraqi Civil Defense Corps (ICDC) soldiers pulled up. They had to fight their way through enemy fire to reach the MPs at the station. A special group founded only months before in September 2003, the ICDC fighters were largely an unknown force. This was the first occasion when most of these MPs would fight side by side with Iraqis.

By then the combat intensity had calmed down a bit. Shambo had a moment to survey the area. "Looking around and seeing all of the smoke, debris, and dead bodies made me think of a World War Two movie," he recalled. MPs, taking the initiative, dispatched a recon squad from the now-secured police station to see what was happening outside the gates. They picked up weapons, counted the dead, and looked for surviving enemy fighters.

To their pleasant surprise they watched individual policemen from the overrun station return to the job, picking their way through debris. Together they searched the dead, stacked bodies, and collected weapons and ammunition. By mid-morning, with the help of the Iraqi Police, they counted thirty-two enemy dead and had moved a stack of weapons back into the station.

As twilight began to fall on Diyala the next night, April 4, tension inside the station grew. They sensed that the coming night was going to be just as bad as the first had been. Already large groups of people gathered in front of the station, appearing to check out what was happening inside.

Despite the growing crowd, Shambo and his platoon members still felt more confident than could be expected under the dire circumstances. During the afternoon a platoon from the 1st Armor Division had roared into Diyala to assist them. Now, in addition to an ammo resupply, the MPs had two M-1A1 Abrams battle tanks, a Bradley fighting vehicle, and thirty-two additional infantrymen standing shoulder-to-shoulder beside them. *We might get overrun,* they thought, *but it would cost a lot of enemy dead to break our lines.*

Despite the reinforcements, the pace of the battle was beginning to tell on soldiers. Other than quick catnaps during the afternoon, most of the MPs had already gone more than a day without sleep or even rest. They were living on MREs and whatever snack food they had stuffed into cargo pockets before leaving Muleskinner. Water wasn't an issue, for the moment, but leaders were keeping an eye on it. Combat anywhere—particularly in hot desert climates—is physically draining. Just staying on your feet demands a lot of hydration.

Word filtered up from the Iraqi Police that the city had been locked down for the night. No citizens were allowed to roam about. For the defenders this greatly simplified the rules of engagement: If anyone was outside, they were bad guys. Shortly after dark the enemy started firing mortars at the station. They had the range. Rounds fell among the soldiers and armored vehicles. So far no one was seriously hurt. But that could change in the flash of an exploding round.

A tanker spotted a group of twenty or more men carrying weapons and moving stealthily toward the beleaguered police station. He yelled down at the crew: "Enemy in the open, advancing!" Without warning one of the Abrams tanks fired the 120 mm main gun, which the crew had lowered till it was practically parallel to the ground. The explosive force of the huge 120 mm round blew the insurgents out of the picture.

Darkness comes quickly in the desert. Already taut nerves tensed with dread. *They'll be coming again*, the soldiers thought, checking and rechecking ammo supplies and fields of fire. The sun dropped and the muzzle flashes began to appear and spread. The next four hours were a repeat of the previous night's firefight. Mortars, RPGs, machine guns, and AK fire hammered at the police station and its defenders.

But on this night there was a big difference: The night-vision equipment on the tanks—thermal and infrared sights that strip away the enemy's cloak of darkness—allowed tankers to identify targets. Inside the tanks the deadly chant began: "Target! Troops in the open. Load a high-explosive round. Gunner: fire!" For the insurgents the price of jihad had gone up. Steadily, systematically the tank main guns swept through the night with deadly intent, eliminating the enemy. For several hours they literally blew away insurgent strongpoints with their big main guns.

Near midnight, having had enough, the insurgents withdrew to their hiding places. Things quieted down considerably.

On April 5, entering the third day of the fight, U.S. and Iraqi soldiers were starting to think that they had the battle won. Both the daylight and nighttime hours passed without serious exchanges of gunfire. Soldiers began to come down from the high adrenaline levels that marked the past two days. They were exhausted and hungry.

Early on the morning of April 6 the first sergeant from the tank unit brought a relief convoy to the police station. Even more welcome for the MPs was the delivery of their first hot food in days. While they eagerly chowed down, armored vehicles patrolled the city. "We won't be attacked during daylight," one soldier told Shambo. Everybody began to relax. Big mistake. The armor unit relieving them was in the process of trading places with those already there. Soldiers milled about, vehicles were clustered in groups. In their overconfidence they let their guard down. "We had set ourselves up for an ambush," he recalled.

The Sunni insurgents, patiently waiting for an opportune moment, brought it to them with devastating effect.

Near the main gate the outgoing armor commander was briefing his replacement when, seemingly from nowhere, a smoking RPG round flew toward an Abrams tank. A flash. An explosion against the tank hull. Suddenly a soldier lay on the ground wounded. In a rush like a breaking wave, small-arms fire hit all around the station. The enemy had crept up close and surrounded them. Incoming bullets appeared to come from every direction. For the first time in combat Shambo heard the terrible, chilling cry, "Medic!"

Running back to take up his fighting position, Shambo noticed flashes coming from a clump of bushes alongside the river. *That's where the RPGs are being fired from!* he thought. It was a long shot away but in range of his squad automatic weapon. Training kicked in. He scrunched into a steady firing position and took his time. *Got to get a good sight picture on the target,* he thought. He squeezed the trigger. Shambo poured controlled eight-to-nine-round bursts into the bushes. *Fire. Get the sight picture back. Fire. Repeat.* After minutes of pounding the enemy position RPGs ceased.

Rather than retreating as the soldiers first thought, the insurgents had spent the quiet day reinforcing their positions and bringing in more fighters and ammunition. In some cases they piled lumber, furniture, sandbags, and concrete blocks against walls and windows, converting them into instant bunkers. Reinforcements like this made a weapon like Shambo's automatic weapon that fired a light 5.56 mm round ineffective. He was taking fire from a nearby house and unable to suppress it because of the protective layer the insurgents built. Soldiers needed something heavier to knock out that fighting position. The tank couldn't maneuver to engage the house because the wounded soldier lay in the way. In frustration, Shambo fired an AT-4 shoulder-fired antitank rocket at the house but couldn't see much damage. Finally, during a lull in the shooting a team was able to retrieve the wounded soldier.

Now the tank could maneuver against the enemy. Swinging around into firing position the Abrams gunner slammed a heavy round into the house. The force of the explosion was dramatic. "The house almost imploded before it disintegrated," Shambo recalled. With U.S. casualties slowing, the soldiers fought back with everything they had. Tanks unloaded on the enemy in every direction. Still, enemy fire poured into the station.

Finally more reinforcements showed up, and this time the gloves were off. U.S. combat units surrounded the city from the outside with twelve more Abrams tanks and fourteen Bradley fighting vehicles. The 1st Armor commander decided that if the bad guys wanted a fight to the death, then he would give them one. He began to commit more assets to the fight, determined that they would not lose Diyala. An entire company of infantry soldiers were added to the defensive strength, and Apache attack helicopters buzzed low over the enemy positions adding awesome, pinpoint firepower to the fight. Shambo watched the display of raw power with awe: "They destroyed anyone who tried to stop them."

Having been taken by surprise once, the MPs inside the city were not going to be fooled again. Shambo and the other defenders "improved their foxholes," a military slang term for continuing to work on strengthening individual fighting positions during lulls in the battle. Sandbags were added for protection, ammo accumulated and stacked in arm's reach. CamelBaks (small backpacks filled with water) were topped off, and a package or two of MREs stowed in the corner. They worried that with the coming of night the enemy would renew his attack.

Thankfully, as the night unfolded and stayed relatively calm, MPs began to realize that the worst seemed over. Shambo, who had been up for three straight days, fell into the deep sleep of the exhausted. By morning a new MP convoy arrived to relieve Shambo and the rest of the 3rd Platoon. "We were glad to see them," Shambo commended with understatement.

The immediate fight for Diyala was over. More than fifty-two enemy dead littered the streets. No one knew how many wounded and other bodies had been dragged away and hidden. Captured weapons continued to be stacked inside the police station.

One American soldier with the 1st Armor Division had been killed and three wounded in the fighting.

Shambo rolled out of Diyala that morning tired like his battle buddies, but with the sense of satisfaction that comes from having been tested and then having prevailed. Yet somewhere in the back of his mind he knew that this fight was a long way from finished.

9

GROWING PAINS

In a constant combat environment, working around the clock every day of the week, a phenomenon known as "groundhog day" emerges. Ask any soldier who has been deployed and they will chuckle. "What's the date," and "what day is this" are common conversational questions. Quantock, deciding to try to break the grinding routine in his headquarters, started what he called the Loose Grip Award. It was to be given—ostentatiously and with elaborate fanfare—to any commander or staffer who screwed something up. The award itself is modest: a small green Army notebook (Government Printing Office number 7530-00-222-3521) with "Loose Grip Award" scrawled across the cover in black Sharpie, attached to a ripcord from a reserve parachute. For the paratroop brigade the implication was that the miscreant was unable to successfully "pull his reserve" thereby "crashing and burning."

Along with facing the public humiliation associated with being identified as a recipient, the "winner" was required to write a detailed report in the notebook about his or her misdeeds. The staff members quickly caught on and began to outdo each other exercising creative writing skills explaining their transgressions. Such entries as "There I was working diligently at my computer when vicious space aliens sent messages that altered my brainwaves . . ." became typical, as individuals invented explanations for why they overlooked or neglected a task. Soon members of the 16th MP Brigade began to treat the Loose Grip Award as a point of pride, and exercised great pains to contrive the most outlandish tales of why they had—usually in their opinions, inappropriately—been designated an awardee.

It was one of the few tension relievers and a great source of humor as days wore into weeks and into a long, seemingly endless fifteen-month tour in the Iraqi sandbox.

Sergeant Mike Williams had been in Iraq a few months already, leading his squad up and down the Baghdad portion of Route Tampa, the main supply route (MSR) stretching from Kuwait almost to the Syrian border. Like a lot of MP units at the time they were sent out as bait, driving openly, showing a coalition presence, and daring the hardcore Saddam supporters and other malcontents to come out and fight. They mixed it up occasionally, but for the most part up until April 2004 Williams and most coalition forces thought the situation to be under control.

Williams, of medium height and a solid build, is a self-described "Army brat" born near Hanau, Germany, and a career soldier. When they arrived in Iraq just a month earlier, many of the MPs figured that conditions would be similar to Kosovo two years prior—lots of patrolling, lots of interaction with local security forces, but overall fairly quiet.

But that April the weather began to heat up. So did the fighting. There were at first disturbing indicators that the mood had changed for the worse. Williams and the MPs began finding IEDs sewn into the bellies of dead dogs. The road was suddenly littered with them. They knew the situation had gotten more dangerous.

On April 8, a Thursday morning, Williams's truck—he was rolling in the first version of the up-armored Humvee—sideswiped a previously damaged guardrail on Route Tampa and slashed the rear tire. He called the situation in to his platoon leader, then pulled the squad back to their base at Baghdad International Airport for repairs.

As they slowly rolled back to the camp the MPs saw something they'd never seen before. It made the hair rise on the back of Williams's neck. Trucks, busses, even industrial-type dump trucks clogged the roadway into the city. Each was loaded with black-clad men with green flags sewn to their sleeves, all heavily armed.

When they spotted the Americans they made throat-cutting gestures and angrily pointed and shouted. *What the hell is going on?* Williams wondered. He would later learn that was the day that the renegade Shi'a cleric Moqtada al-Sadr had declared revolt against the coalition and Sunnis. Within hours the eastern Baghdad district named after Sadr's father was flooded with thousands of fanatic Shi'a fighters who called themselves the Mahdi Army or the Jaish al Mahdi (JAM).

Meanwhile, the revolt had begun in earnest. A squad from 4th Platoon, 230th MP Company (Hellraisers), led by Sergeant Edwin Rossman, had been caught by Mahdi Army insurgents inside Sadr City. They had been entering Sadr City area along Route Sword when an ambush broke out on both sides of the road. Everywhere they looked pockets of fifty or more black-clad insurgents were clustered, weapons at their shoulders, shooting at them with everything from RPGs and machine guns to AK-47s. The volume of fire was deafening. Bullets ricocheted off the sides of the Humvees and rocket trails arched overhead. The squad leader knew the road. *Keep pushing*, he thought, *and we can break out at the far end.*

Fighting desperately to break free of the complex ambush, the squad endured four kilometers of fierce fighting. Abruptly they saw insurgents had anticipated this move. Their only way out had been hastily blocked by concertina wire and junked cars spread across the road. If they stopped they would be destroyed piecemeal. Rossman had no choice: "Turn the trucks around quick," he ordered. "We'll have to fight our way back out!"

Once they turned back the Mahdi fighters were waiting for them. They faced a run back through a four-kilometer-long killing zone. The MPs knew they were in a deathtrap. In their open turrets, gunners burned through boxes of ammo. Expended brass rattled and jingled down in a torrent. Focusing on his job, Rossman continued to work the radios, trying urgently to get some supporting fire or reinforcements to assist. The thought flashed through his head: *We may not be able to make it out of this one.* Pushing it aside he continued to lead his soldiers in the fight.

Back at the airfield Williams and his people heard tense, urgent voices over the radio. Everyone knew their MP buddies were engaged in a desperate firefight. Williams's trucks were not ready to roll—the flat tires were not yet replaced—but time was of the essence. He had to get help to them *now*! Fingering switches on his radio, Williams called higher headquarters. "We need to move out there and support Fourth Platoon!" In seconds he got the green light to assist the outnumbered Hellraiser squad: "You're cleared for the mission," a voice from the operations center called.

"Let's roll out of here," he told his squad. Four vehicles roared out of the gate and turned up Route Tampa, tearing into the fight. Their tires were flat, but their weapons were locked and loaded. Williams's driver, a female MP, was apprehensive. From the radio traffic it sounded like they were rolling into an inferno. Over the internal intercom set Williams quietly reassured her. "Pay attention to your job, pay attention to what you're doing. It'll be all right." As they drew closer to the fight she settled down and focused on driving.

Heading north on Route Tampa they were burning up tires when they spotted the beleaguered squad emerging from the narrow Route Sword. Two JAM pickup trucks were in hot pursuit. Enemy gunners standing in the beds peppered the retreating squad with machine-gun fire and RPGs. As they watched, a fleeing U.S. vehicle took a hit from an RPG, seriously wounding the gunner, Specialist Jonathan Kephart, in the head. Shrapnel entered the front of his head and emerged from the back.

Kephart dropped momentarily in the turret, then popped back up and continued to man his gun till he collapsed. Up to that moment, Kephart had been instrumental in keeping the enemy at bay, first firing his .50 caliber machine gun until it had been disabled by an RPG exploding almost in the turret, then switching to an M-249 squad automatic weapon until it jammed, and finally firing his M-4 rifle at the insurgents with deadly effectiveness.

As he led his rescue convoy into the fight, Williams shot past Rossman's four 4th Platoon trucks rushing out of the ambush. The audacity of the move hit him suddenly: *We're in the enemy's kill zone.* "Turn the truck sideways. Block this road!" he ordered. Now his truck became the primary target for the pursuing insurgents. In a bold move, Williams had blocked the road to the attackers, allowing Rossman's squad to slip away.

Williams and his squad were raked by a massive amount of small-arms and RPG fire. Abruptly Williams noticed that his truck was not returning fire! His gunner was frozen at his post. Desperate, Williams yelled at the gunner but got no response. Twisting around, Williams punched him repeatedly in the legs, trying to break the lock of fear that gripped the soldier, who was in his first serious firefight.

Fearing that they would be knocked out of the fight, Williams crawled over the seat, dragged the gunner out of the turret, tossed him into the back, and manned the MK-19 automatic grenade launcher himself. First he focused fire on the direst threat. He walked his rounds into the two JAM pickup trucks, bringing down a rain of 40 mm grenades upon them. In short order the explosive rounds shattered glass and metal, broke both Toyota trucks to pieces, set them on fire, and blew away the crews.

Got 'em! Williams thought. The main threat was suppressed. He turned the gun, seeking targets. MPs were still being hit with constant fire from surrounding buildings. Madhi insurgents in nearby buildings were raining fire at them from windows and openings. Williams went to work with the MK-19. Systematically he walked the explosive grenades from window to window, blowing away fighters. Within minutes he had cleaned out the windows and suppressed the attack. The bold violence of his squad's counterattack on the ambush force pushed the insurgents back into Sadr City.

Williams's analysis was simple: "It was them or us."

They turned around and moved back to the Tampa-Sword intersection where Rossman, joined by other reinforcing units, had set up a hasty perimeter. They called for casualty evacuation but incoming helicopters were twice diverted for "higher priority" wounded. While the squad medic worked frantically to keep Kephart stable and alive, the minutes ticked like hours. After almost thirty minutes, they were finally able to get a medevac chopper on the ground for the two wounded soldiers. Tragically, Kep died of his severe wounds the following day.

Kephart was a personable young man with a consuming sense of responsibility. He had been extremely popular with other soldiers and leaders. Kep proved himself that day to be an exceptionally brave and competent soldier also. "We were surrounded by five hundred insurgents and fought through eight kilometers of pure hell," Sergeant Rossman described the fight. "Kep was shot twice yet continued to pour fire into the enemy till he was mortally wounded." His actions, his fellow soldiers agree, "Ensured his brothers and sisters made it safely out of the ambush." For exceptional bravery Kephart was awarded the Silver Star.

Williams was also cited for exceptional bravery because of his courage and leadership that day, and was recommended by his immediate superiors to be awarded the Bronze Star with V device for valor.

In a sad commentary on awards for soldiers, repeated too often, a higher officer in a staff position then decided that Williams was "only doing his job" and downgraded the award to an Army Commendation Medal with V device.

If he is bitter about the award, Sergeant Williams hides it. "The most important thing about that day is that we were able to get in there quickly and defeat the enemy before they were able to hurt our soldiers more."

The following day, April 9, Sergeant First Class Jackson Varner, also a platoon sergeant of the 230th MP Company (Warmasters), was rolling on Route Tampa south of Baghdad. He was in the same company as 3rd Platoon, which had just lost Kephart the previous day.

His Humvee hit an IED. The world exploded around him. "That was the first time I was blown up." Varner, a native of Cleveland, Ohio, had been an MP since joining the army in November 1990. He had served for years prior in Germany, deploying twice to Bosnia and Kosovo. This was his first combat tour. It would not be his last.

The vehicle interior was a dark, smoke-choked chaos of lifting, turning, then falling violently back on the road from the explosion. A heavy metal .50 caliber ammunition can flew down from the turret and smashed against the back of Varner's neck, cutting his neck and crushing two vertebrae. Smaller pieces of debris were thrown around the inside, lacerating his face. "I was selfish at first. I just thought about me—the pain, the shock, the fear. Then training kicked in. I ordered us out of the kill zone, organized supporting fires, and medevacs."

Fortunately no one in the truck was killed. "The experience was so frightening that my gunner quit, then my team leader, a buck sergeant quit, too. It was more than they could handle. I was eligible for the Purple Heart for my wounds but turned it down. It was just a day after Kep died and I didn't think I'd earned it."

The Abu Ghraib story finally broke publicly in late April. It would have long-term catastrophic effects on America's global image and would unfairly tarnish the reputation of all military police. Though the media had the story for several weeks, at first there was minimal reporting on it. This is a visual age. Only when the photos taken from inside the Abu Ghraib prison were released did the world recoil in shock and horror.

Lieutenant General Ricardo Sanchez had already launched a formal investigation on January 14 and brought in Major General Antonio Taguba as an outside party to conduct the inquiry. Taguba had met with Phillips and Quantock in early April to get their input.

In the interim, the 800th MP Brigade assets were removed from Abu Ghraib. Its commander, Brigadier General Janis Karpinski, had been suspended pending results of the investigation. The 800th MP

Brigade, an Army Reserve unit, drew members primarily from Pennsylvania and New York, and had been in-country since spring of 2003 when it was activated to open detainee camps at Bucca, Cropper, and other sites. Originally scheduled to rotate quickly, in May 2003, the brigade was extended for prison guard duty, including responsibility for Abu Ghraib. Some blame what happened on low unit morale due to the extension, others place the fault squarely on the shoulders of officers and noncommissioned officers who failed abysmally in their leadership responsibilities.

Career military policemen like Sergeant Gary Watford were incensed. "The whole thing was a slap in the face for MPs. We were supposed to set the standard for the Army: of troops, for troops." He considered the behavior of the 800th MP Brigade "disgusting" and "offensive." Not to mention incredibly stupid. "Those shitbags actually captured their gross behavior on camera. They behaved like thugs on the street. They disgraced us all."

Most bothersome to Watford and most of his fellow MPs is that the actions at Abu Ghraib remained in the American public mind as the image of a "typical" military policeman. "They don't think about MPs in Kosovo, Bosnia, Croatia, Afghanistan, or anywhere else in Iraq. Instead we hear them talk about these assholes."

He is appalled that they were so undisciplined and poorly supervised. "We get values drummed into our head from day one in training and throughout our lives. These guys represented the complete opposite."

Dave Quantock was told to get into Abu Ghraib immediately with 16th MP Brigade assets. Karpinski was finally officially relieved of command. On his preliminary inspection, Quantock was disgusted. "The place was nasty. I was wading through raw sewage. There were still human bones from the Saddam days scattered about." His orders were direct and simple: "Fix that place up!"

Quantock moved with alacrity. He instituted several immediate corrective steps. MPs were not to be involved with interrogation issues. No more "softening up" detainees prior to interrogation. The MP's full attention was to be on safe and humane care for those confined. Strict standard operational procedures were put in place regarding oversight, care and treatment, and full accountability from the top down.

Quantock created a separate facility called Camp Redemption. He called in engineers and contractors to move forward on the job of cleaning up the physical plant, still a disgrace from Saddam's day when body parts and meat hooks were the norm. Soldiers of all ranks realized the damage that had been done and worked diligently to rectify an unfortunate situation. "We had a good mix of Reserves and National Guard augmentees. They brought a lot of great civilian skills and we were able to build a decent infrastructure."

Within a short time new facilities were under construction at Abu Ghraib so that detainees could be moved to upgraded facilities. Discipline and standards imposed and enforced by leadership at all levels transformed a place of horrors into a model prison.

But to the world at large Abu Ghraib remains an indelible stain, and it may take years—if it is even possible—for the MP Corps to erase it from its otherwise proud history.

The Abu Ghraib incident gave further motivation to insurgents to target coalition and especially MP vehicles. "From then onward," Phillips noted, "the words 'Military Police' stenciled on the sides of our trucks may as well have been a neon sign saying 'shoot me.' We became rolling targets for disgruntled, vengeful Iraqis."

Meanwhile, Major General Geoff Miller reported to Baghdad on April 30 to assume command of all detainee operations in Iraq. Miller, in the eyes of Pentagon officials, had straightened up the confusing mess at Guantánamo when he took over there in late 2002 and would be the ideal person to fix whatever was broken in the Iraq detention system.

When he arrived at Baghdad, Geoff Miller had an attitude, and it wasn't pleasant. He immediately crossed swords with Dave Phillips over the conditions of Saddam Hussein's internment. Confined since capture at Camp Cropper, specifically in the specially constructed Griffin Rock facility, Saddam was known among coalition members as "HVT #1" or high value target number one. Responsibility for Saddam fell under Phillips's 89th MP Brigade. Phillips, as part of his commander's duties, frequently dropped in at Griffin Rock and visited with Saddam and the other seven former Ba'ath officials confined there.

Phillips found these visits useful. He occasionally conversed with the former dictator while checking on his health and well-being. Like most career MPs, Phillips was singularly aware of the need for both safe and humane care—an MP imperative—and also maintenance of certain standards of common decency. Though this man had arguably been one of the worst human rights violators on earth, that did not mean that he was to be treated as an object of derision or contempt. "You can feel about him as you will," Phillips commented. "He was a brute, no question. But treating him badly would have reflected poorly on us, not him."

Phillips was upset with Miller's attitude toward Saddam. "He wanted to make Saddam and the others part of a petting zoo. He'd invite in visitors, lord it over everyone, ham it up, all for his personal aggrandizement." Phillips relied heavily on his deputy, Lieutenant Colonel Rob Raye, to keep Miller and his touring groups out of the Griffin Rock facility. Raye was good at it. As a consequence Miller was not pleased with Phillips's reluctance to support his behavior. The two officers began to cross swords on this and other issues. "We fought every day," Phillips recalled. Their relationship had begun on a sour note and continued to deteriorate.

At Camp Ashraf, north and a bit east of Baghdad, Phillips had Lieutenant Colonel Terri O'Brien in charge of operations. On one visit, Miller noticed that there were three MP dogs on the site—special search dogs, trained to sniff out explosives. Chuckling, Miller suggested that they move the dogs to his theater internment facility and use them to intimidate detainees. "They scared the hell out of the detainees at GTMO and were very effective," Phillips remembered Miller bragging.

O'Brien was adamant: The dogs were under his control and they would not be relocated or used in that manner. Phillips stood behind him. But Miller would not let the issue go, continuing over time to insist that the dogs be turned over to his intelligence officer for use at the facility. Finally Phillips had had enough. He ordered the dogs transferred down to Lieutenant Colonel Byron Freeman's 759th MP Battalion in Baghdad, away from Miller's sight and grasp.

Phillips was convinced, as he recalled, that at that point his relationship with Miller had truly "gone to the dogs."

Dave Quantock, on the other hand, found that Miller gave him "top cover" when other units were trying to take assets from his unit. "He was very demanding, but overall was my savior in a couple of situations." By that point Quantock's unit was responsible for almost 90 percent of detainee issues. From his perspective, having someone with Miller's experience working the higher command levels on his behalf was a gift.

By May, fighting was nonstop. Sergeant Jackson Varner remembered, "We were pulling route security out toward Fallujah where the big operation was under way, trying to keep Route Tampa open." By that time Tampa was a graveyard for civilian and military vehicles. Each destroyed vehicle marked a victory for the insurgents and a place for future IEDs. "Sadr had declared war," Varner recalled. "On any and all U.S. forces—civilians, contractors, or military, didn't matter. We were all targets." Colonel Quantock loosened the rules of engagement. "If he's got black clothes and a green headband or flag on," the 16th MP Brigade commander ordered, "engage him. He's the enemy and we've got to suppress them."

Varner felt a knot in his stomach whenever they rolled, the results of his first IED strike in April. He experienced bouts of irrational anger alternating with frustration and fear. Finally he went to the aid station for diagnosis. He still had severe pain from the wounding weeks prior.

"Sergeant," he was told, "you're suffering from a concussion and fractured vertebrae. You're on the next evac out of here." He was shipped first to Landstuhl hospital in Germany, then back to his home base at Fort Lewis, Washington, where disks C-4 and C-5 were fused. "It was my wife's birthday," he recalled, "May 24."

Then Varner went back to the fight in Iraq. "I wanted to go back. This was what I'd trained for [for] more than ten years. And I didn't want to leave my platoon down there without me."

"We were ducks in a shooting gallery." That's how Williams described the period in Iraq when everything appeared to unravel. Across the country, others agreed with his sentiments. "We got hit every time we left the wire," Varner recalled. Or as Watford succinctly summarized the situation: "It sucked. Big time."

The flash point was Baghdad, and the timeless desert once again was soaked with the blood of fighters and innocents alike.

The military police—in-country for the first time in force—were told to establish a law-and-order environment amidst the chaos. But at this stage, rebuilding the Iraqi Army had priority, and the Ministry of Interior—boss agency for police—was itself in turmoil because of political infighting.

Shi'a cities in the south were in full-scale riot. MPs like Platoon Sergeant Henry Stearns acknowledged that the place lived up to its name: the Triangle of Death. In Anbar Province al-Qaeda in Iraq, with Sunni tribal leaders' acquiescence, controlled cities like Tal Afar, Ramadi, and most of all, Fallujah. Criminals released by Saddam flooded the cities, where they joined in loose alliance with former Baathists who had disbanded and gone into hiding. Add infiltrating foreign al-Qaeda fighters to the mix and it became a witch's brew for violence.

MPs were angry over the coalition's ineffective response to the contractor killings in Fallujah. "We knew at the time that it was a half-assed effort," Watford recalled. "Worse, we knew we were going to have to go back one day and finish the job. On the one hand we wanted to get it on and over with. On the other we knew that we'd be going into a shitstorm." Watford, from Florence, South Carolina, had been an MP for six years and, like many of his compatriots from the 230th MP Company, was on his first combat tour. "It was exhilarating, I have to admit. We were pulling route security, had lots of freedom of movement, were allowed to shoot back, and we were looking for a fight."

Watford's platoon was told that they needed to boresight their weapons on the armored support vehicles (ASVs) they had just been issued. Until the weapons were boresighted and tested, they were basically ineffective and were not to be fired. They were told that the only available location—oddly, in a country that was essentially a shooting gallery—was at Taji base, more than a two-and-a-half-hour drive north. "Get up there and get it done," they were ordered. "Be prepared to stay about a week or so."

They hit the road, with six ASVs running north on Tampa without maps or directions. "Where are our maps?" Watford had asked. "How in the hell do we get there?"

"Just head north and you'll run right into it," was the answer. The officer added smugly, "You can't miss it." *Right,* thought Watford. Making matters worse, the MPs were not told that they would be leaving one maneuver unit's battlespace and transiting into another. "They didn't give us frequencies, call signs, points of contact. Nothing."

Resigned to make do with what he had, Watford got his unit on the road, driving north. By the time the sun was setting over the western desert horizon they hit a little town. "It was quiet, way too quiet. And we got worried. Here we were all by ourselves with weapons that weren't ready to fire."

Suddenly they saw Mahdi Army fighters pour out of buildings and alleyways. Black clothing with green flags sewn on their shoulders, weapons at the ready, shooting. The small convoy tried to push forward but found the route blocked with razor-sharp coils of concertina wire strewn across the road. Unable to go forward, Watford and his soldiers began to back up slowly—"maybe three miles an hour, tops"—through the roaring ambush. First one RPG then another flew over the truck. So far the insurgents were shooting high. Watford knew that in minutes they would find the range and began to strike the ASVs with devastating consequences.

Mahdi insurgents were shooting, shouting, and storming out of buildings. Rounds sparked off the slanted sides of the ASVs—the first up-armored version in-country—and ricocheted into the streets and buildings. The stench of cordite, explosives, and burning buildings filled the air.

In the middle of the fight an RPG shooter got a direct hit on one ASV, but it failed to damage the vehicle seriously. *This up-armored stuff really works!* Watford thought.

Working the radios frantically the American convoy called for air support through the battlespace owner of the area they had left, not aware that they were now in another unit's area of operations and that they were breaking all kinds of rules because they had inadvertantly not informed the new landowner of their presence. (Even if they had known at the time, though, breaking the rules was less important than staying alive.) Responding to the calls for assistance, a small, two-seat OH-58D Kiowa Warrior helicopter gunship buzzed in at rooftop level. Carrying both a .50 caliber machine gun and 2.76-inch rockets, the Kiowa is a frighteningly deadly air-ground weapon. Instantly assessing the critical situation, the pilot engaged his guns and rockets. Raging fire tore into a group of Mahdi fighters trying to plant an IED on the convoy's exit route. Working up and down the street, the helicopter suppressed fire long enough for the MPs to work their way out of the town—backing up and shooting small arms the entire time—until they got to a main road that allowed them to bypass the town. Watford was relieved they were able to break out of the ambush largely unscathed. But it wasn't over.

"I got into a flaming argument with a captain from the cavalry unit after we arrived safely at Taji," Watford recalled. "He was seriously pissed off that we hadn't coordinated with him, didn't tell him we were entering his battlespace, and that we might need fire support. After what we had been through—hours on the road, a serious damn firefight, and confusion that wasn't of our doing—I lost my temper and gave it back to him." It especially upset Watford that he was a pawn in the affair.

The entire convoy movement ought to have been coordinated by and through the 16th MP Brigade, his higher headquarters. Not informing the respective units that they would be exiting one landowner's space and going to another was an especially egregious oversight. These are the kinds of procedures that have to be reflexive in a smoothly running operations center. Such processes are not about commanders' egos but directly affect soldiers' lives. Watford and his MPs were extremely lucky to have gotten air support; medevac, if needed, or quick-reaction forces would have been almost impossible to coordinate once the fight started.

After the mutual outburst the captain realized that the sergeant was right and graciously apologized. Watford continued the mission, determined not to get caught in a screwup like that again.

Incidents marked by gross failure to communicate with higher and adjacent headquarters were alarmingly high in Iraq during this especially violent period. The number and repetition became a disturbing pattern. During a long discussion about this breakdown with Lieutenant Colonel Tom Lombardo, one of the most cerebral and deep-thinking of the generation of battalion commanders emerging from these wars, some basic but overlooked factors emerged.

Principal among his (and our) conclusions is that most of the senior officer and NCO leadership at the time—the colonels, generals, and sergeant majors—while having decades of experience in the Army, were in fact at their first real war. Prior combat experience, if they had it, was based primarily on short, decisive actions such as Grenada, Panama, and Desert Storm, conflicts that lasted only for days or weeks in a highly limited environment. In Iraq they were forced to deal with prolonged conflict in a highly complex environment for the first time in their careers.

While most leaders focused on preparing rookie soldiers for their first combat tour, almost all missed the fact that for them it was also their first rodeo, as it was for their senior staffers. Leadership was quite properly concentrated on two essential tasks: accomplish the mission and take care of the soldiers. Lost in the shuffle, however, were the bothersome but necessary coordination procedures that experience demonstrates are vital to success of both basic tasks.

Lack of experience alone was not entirely responsible for the confusion. As units rotated through areas of operations (AOs)—some added, some removed entirely—basic guidelines such as delineation of boundaries and degrees of responsibility seemed constantly to shift and change. Much of the blame for the confusion can be laid at the doorstep of a system of military instruction that continued to emphasize linear warfare—a highly structured layout similar to European fronts in the Second World War—in an environment that was totally different from the clean, clear map overlays presented at Leavenworth and branch schoolhouses.

Commanders, by temperament and training, are told to take charge and get the mission accomplished. The system demands aggressive, bold commanders in order to defeat a determined enemy. This is a formula proven by history and essential in warfare. As a consequence, when leaders in Iraq were told, "This is your area of operations," they took such guidance seriously. Problems arose in the complexity of the theater itself, many self-inflicted by higher command and staff.

A combat arms brigade commander was told that a certain area belonged to his complete responsibility, for example. Complicating the matter, a support commander—someone commanding an MP brigade like Phillips and Quantock—would be told that their AO extended from this city or province to that one. Lost in translation was the confusing result that AOs overlapped and were assigned to multiple commanders. What is astounding is not that there was conflict and confusion among staffs and commanders but that there was not more of it.

Initially each unit commander proceeded from the basis that he "owned" the territory assigned to him, and maneuvered his units within that area at his discretion. Thus it becomes easier to comprehend why an MP unit, whose AO included both Baghdad and Taji, would casually dispatch Watford or another subordinate command up the road without comprehending the necessity of coordinating with tactical brigades whose commanders thought that they in fact were the real "landowners."

"We often sat there and watched our commanders or S-3s order companies and battalions to run the roads with no thought about linking with the tactical brigades," Lombardo recalled. "When we'd suggest that we contact those brigades we'd be brushed aside. 'To hell with it,' they'd say. 'That's our AO and we can go anywhere we want to in it.' It led to a lot of senior leader conflict and needless danger to our soldiers."

Unfortunately the situation required several serious incidents and concomitant loss of life before adequate procedures were finally worked out to resolve these seemingly trivial but absolutely essential "ownership" disputes. Standard operating procedures now require that tactical brigades for the most part "own" terrain, and combat support units like MPs, engineers, and others, routinely call in to their TOCs (tactical operations centers) every time a unit clears the wire. As a result, unfortunate incidents such as those that occurred in the most tumultuous days of Iraq fighting are now largely a thing of the past.

In June, Jackson Varner had his platoon on clearance missions on Route Detroit, south and west of Baghdad. His platoon spotted an IED and halted. They were on a narrow part of the street with houses close to the road. Perhaps in panic, the insurgents triggered the IED near the right side of the lead truck. Immediately the ambush was sprung. RPGs and machine-gun fire poured in, pounding the sides of the trucks. Alerted by the premature IED, the platoon was ready and in position and returned devastating suppressing fire on the gunmen. The entire engagement lasted for about three minutes till the insurgents who were still alive fled the battle.

"None of our guys got hurt," Varner remembered, "and we were able to give back more than we got for a change."

10

COALITION UNDER SIEGE

There was a minor panic in the late morning on June 30, 2004, at Dave Phillips's 89th MP Brigade headquarters. For six months the MP brigade had oversight of the confinement facility in which Saddam Hussein and seven of his henchmen were held. After endless wrangling and delay, intrusive interference from international agencies and nongovernmental organizations, and constant media carping, the trial format and dates were fixed.

The dictator and his coterie were scheduled to appear the very next day for their first hearing before the newly constituted Iraqi judicial system. Abruptly the phone rang. Colonel Marc Warren was on the line. Warren was staff judge advocate for the coalition commander, Lieutenant General Sanchez. "What are the high-value prisoners going to wear at court tomorrow?" Warren asked.

For a moment Phillips was nonplussed. It was not something that anyone had given much thought to. "I planned on having him wear his orange jumpsuit," Phillips answered. Later in the day the phone rang again, this time from Sanchez's office. When the general came on the line he issued crisp orders: "I want them in suits. Dress them up. Oh, and make sure Saddam gets a fresh haircut too."

Phillips was stunned. This was the eleventh hour. Where in the hell where they going to get the kind of clothing the general demanded? The best the PX (post exchange) had to offer was cargo slacks or blue jeans and a wide assortment of T-shirts. Saddam standing before the world audience in a bright red T-shirt with OPERATION IRAQI FREEDOM on it probably wasn't quite the image Sanchez was fishing for. Searching for ideas, Phillips queried his deputy, Lieutenant Colonel Bob Raye, and Major Pete Lydon, head of a special police assistance team. Among them they decided that the commander's order gave them sufficient latitude to be creative.

Maybe, it was suggested, we could take the money we need from the operations fund? Phillips administered a fund of approximately half a million dollars to be used for rebuilding the Iraqi Police. This was the beginning of what would eventually become a multimillion-dollar concentrated program to rebuild the entire Iraqi Police structure, but in those days was indicative of the lower priority of police operations. Phillips ran the idea through his brigade judge advocate officer, the in-house unit lawyer, who "begrudgingly concurred" with the plan to purchase suits, sports jackets, dress shirts, ties, shoes, and socks on the local economy. Now, who was going to make the purchase? It was not smart or safe for any of the American officers to go on a shopping spree in downtown Baghdad.

Lydon nominated his "terp," an interpreter called Khalid to disguise his true identity, as the man to make the purchases. "He knows Baghdad, he's from here. If he's willing, he's the guy." When Khalid was consulted, he was given a list of requirements including sizes and quantities. Hearing the detailed request, Khalid raised an inquisitive eyebrow. Being pretty savvy, Khalid figured out who the clothing was for, but kept his mouth shut about it.

"I can get this stuff," Khalid said. "But I'll need cash. And a lot of it."

"Go for it," Phillips directed, shoving ten thousand dollar in cash into his hand. "Take one of the civilian cars parked outside. And your phone. Call if you get in trouble."

For several hours they worried. Phillips had alerted some MPs to be ready to respond if Khalid was attacked but knew realistically that they could never get to him in time if it was serious. That evening the terp returned with a trunk bulging with brand-new clothing. Phillips was thrilled.

"Did he bring back any change?" the judge advocate officer asked hopefully.

"I'm not even going to ask!" Phillips replied, parceling out bundles of clothes for each prisoner. Luckily the new stuff fit well enough to meet Sanchez's requirements. But the problem wasn't completely solved. "The boss wanted him to have a haircut. Where are we going to get that done at this time of night?"

While Raye and others were mulling it over, one of the young female MPs in the operations center said softly, "Sir, I can cut hair."

Phillips turned a suspicious glance on the soldier.

"Yes, sir, she can. Look," a male soldier offered, proudly pointing at his head. "She cut mine!"

Phillips squinted. The soldier had been shorn almost bald. He remained unconvinced. "Sir," the female offered again. "I took cosmetology classes in high school."

Unconvinced, but resigned—"What else could I do that late?"— Phillips gave the go ahead. Saddam got a haircut in his cell.

The next day all of the cable networks carried the Saddam appearance, and the talking heads breathlessly described his fancy, expensive clothing in detail. Other commentators had lots to say about his stylish haircut.

"We watched all that from our operations center," Phillips recalled. "If only they knew the behind-the-scenes machinations that went on to get that done! What creativity and ingenuity from young soldiers! It gave us our laugh for the day."

The female soldier in question is reticent to this day about having her identity released. She is now a civilian again, and remains concerned about possible retribution.

Not more than a few days after Saddam's court appearances began at Camp Victory, Phillips received a call from General Miller, then commander of Task Force 134, in charge of all detainee operations in Iraq. During the hearing Saddam had waved a pen about during his frequent rants. Miller didn't ask, but demanded: "I want the pen he used in the hearing!" In some ways, Phillips could be sympathetic. Everybody wants a piece of history or a special souvenir from an important occasion. But Miller's "arrogance and self-aggrandizement" had been grating on Phillips for several months already and the tone didn't sit well.

Regardless of personal feelings—even if Phillips had *wanted* to give Miller the pen—it simply wasn't proper, or, for that matter, legal. Nor was this the first time Miller pestered Phillips for personal items from the detainees. During his confinement Saddam had written three books of poetry using small green notebooks provided by the Army. It was commonly known to the MPs who guarded him that he passed much of his time this way. Miller learned of this and repeatedly demanded to have the books. Phillips politely but adamantly refused to comply.

"To accept things from the detainee—or worse, confiscate them for some officer's personal aggrandizement—was in violation of several international agreements and the Uniform Code of Military Justice." Over time the conversations grew increasingly heated as Miller insisted on having the poetry books. Now he was adamant about the pen. The demands were way out of line, in Phillips's opinion. "General," he told Miller when the issue came to a head, "I'll need to have that request in writing." That never happened.

From time to time, Saddam had offered small gifts to his guards, but the MPs, obeying orders, had refused. To waive this directive to please a general officer was not something Phillips was comfortable doing. It would, he thought, make him a hypocrite.

Still, the pressure from Miller was growing. Finally, Phillips got an idea. "Bring me two boxes of those Skilcraft pens like the ones we gave HVT number 1," he directed his headquarters company supply sergeant. Later he laughed. "Miller got his pen, and so did more than a dozen people who were screaming for Saddam souvenirs. My executive officer and I never did say 'this is the actual pen,' we just said, 'we're sending a pen over' and let them make their own assumption." In recounting this story Phillips added impishly, "I still have a few. Do you want one?"

• • •

Like many who wear silver wings, First Lieutenant Alvin Shell loved being a paratrooper, describing himself as "airborne all the way, going one hundred miles an hour." Deployed to Iraq with Quantock's 16th MP Brigade, Shell was an aggressive platoon leader in the 21st MP Company (Airborne). He always pushed to get outside the wire of the Camp Victory headquarters.

Shell was there to do his job as best he could, whether that meant engaging a hostile enemy or befriending impoverished Iraqi civilians. He regularly brought extra food and supplies to a homeless Iraqi family scratching out their existence at a nearby dump, and sought to help other villagers whenever he could. At the same time Shell also lived by the fundamental Army dictum of "accomplish your mission; take care of your men."

For the past four months he had participated in operations in western Baghdad, out to the Fallujah area where the fighting had been intense. Now back at Victory, he was supposed to be standing down on the night of August 31, 2004, but a fellow platoon leader had made a scheduling error. Shell volunteered to lead her patrol out into the highly volatile area near the airport, on Route Tampa. Locked and loaded, the MPs rolled out of the gate headed to patrol the main supply route.

The radio crackled with a report that a supply convoy had been hit. Shell ordered his platoon to speed to the ambush. Approaching the mess, Shell saw that a large tractor-trailer loaded with fuel had hit an IED and sat disabled in the road, clogging traffic. Shrapnel from the blast had ripped the main tank open, spewing a river of diesel fuel onto the road. Ordering soldiers to set up security, Shell dismounted and trotted over to assess the situation. They were able to pull the driver out of the burning semi, and then, sloshing through the fuel, began trying to hook up a winch so the truck could be cleared out of the traffic lane. The convoy had to be able to exit the kill zone before more vehicles were hit.

Without warning an RPG flew over Shell's shoulder. It was so close that he felt the heat from the round as it narrowly missed. He was knocked temporarily unconscious into a fetid ditch beside the road. Shaking off the blow, Shell stumbled out of the ditch to see that the same grenade that had almost killed him had ignited the river of diesel fuel on the road. It erupted into an inferno of hell.

Shell saw people racing around on fire. His platoon sergeant, Sergeant Wesley Spaid, was screaming for help while engulfed in the middle of the blaze. Without hesitation Shell ran through the flames and grabbed his diesel-soaked sergeant, frantically doing everything he could to extinguish the fire. Shell rolled him on the ground, hugged him close, and threw dirt on Spaid. Convinced he was going to die, Spaid asked Shell to shoot him. Shell yelled back that if he'd wanted to shoot him he could have done it outside the inferno from a more comfortable place. Finally, after Shell completely covered him with dirt, the flames went out and Spaid was able to run to safety.

But Shell was burning, and now found himself trapped in a circle of raging fire. There seemed to be no way out. Soaked through with diesel, Shell clutched his M-4 rifle, protected his face with his left arm, and plunged through the flames to try to get to safety. Instantly he was engulfed in fire. "I lit up like a Christmas tree," he recalled. He stumbled from vehicle to vehicle seeking vainly for a fire extinguisher but realized that they had been used up. Desperately he stripped off his body armor and shirt, seeing in horror that his skin was on fire, while he ran back to the ditch, plunging himself into the contaminated water.

Finally the flames were out. "I remember when I got out of the ditch, I still thought I had my weapon in my hand," he recalled. "I looked down, but my weapon wasn't there. It got so hot that it had melted the skin in my hand and my weapon fell on the ground."

Shell, ever the leader, ordered a report on personnel and weapons status. Satisfied, he decided that the fastest way to get his wounded soldiers evacuated was to drive the two miles back to Camp Victory rather than wait for helicopters. When he arrived at base he exited his vehicle and collapsed into the arms of his soldiers.

As the company commander loaded him onto the evacuation helicopter, he told Shell that he was a hero for saving Sergeant Spaid. "I'm not a hero. A hero is a sandwich," Shell replied. "I'm a paratrooper!"

With burns over more than a third of his body, Shell was placed in an induced coma. When he was brought around at Brooke Army

Medical Center in San Antonio—which specializes in treating severe burn cases—he first saw his wife, Danielle, and his father beside his bed. Shell was furious, thinking he'd only been out for a few hours. Why had the Army brought his wife and father to Iraq? For the next several days he kept asking for his rifle. "We'll find it," his father, a retired Army noncom, replied calmly.

After more than eighteen months and thirty surgeries, Shell had recovered to the point that he could walk before his youngest son, Jochim, took his first steps. That had been the challenge the family gave him, and he met it. Promoted to captain, Alvin Shell was awarded the Bronze Star with V device and Purple Heart for his actions that night. It gave him much satisfaction that the presentation was delayed until he could receive the awards standing with his brigade back at Fort Bragg.

Now medically retired and working as a physical security specialist with the Department of Homeland Security, Shell is partially blind in his right eye, still hurting, and will bear permanent damage from his wounds, particularly on the right side of his body where his leg and arm were burned to the bone. But he has no regrets, nor does he want the dreams that continue to haunt his sleep to ever go away.

"It would be an injustice to those who were involved, those who didn't make it. It's who I am. I don't want to get over it."[1]

From the time of commissioning forward, an officer is taught that two basic principles must be held sacred: accomplish your mission and take care of your soldiers. In that order. Third, and definitely last, is to take care of yourself. One of David Phillips's most visible characteristics is his unswerving adherence to those principles. He made his position crystal clear to subordinate commanders: "I will not stand idly by and witness soldiers' lives being wasted."

Such focus on duty often comes with a personal price. In August 2004 his command sergeant major, senior NCO in the brigade, was clearly troubled. Part of the creed of the noncommissioned officer states that he will carry out management details so that his officers can focus on their responsibilities. This time the issue was too big for him to handle alone. Reluctantly the sergeant major had to involve his colonel. Fortunately, he and Phillips had a special relationship. The commander's door was always open and so were his ears and his mind.

The sergeant major brought in a sordid report. One of his battalion commanders was having an illicit affair with an enlisted female soldier in his unit. Not only was this a violation of General Order Number 1—the military's "thou shalt not . . ." list of prohibitions, but it violated ethics, leadership principles, and basic common sense.

Phillips was concerned. Such blatant behavior was deleterious to unit morale and welfare. He decided to give his commander an excuse to break off the affair. *Remove the temptation,* he thought, *and solve the problem.* "Let's get her out of there," Phillips directed. "Reassign her to a COP or FOB far away from the battalion headquarters. If she's out of sight, maybe she'll be out of mind."

Agreeing, the sergeant major left the meeting and phoned his counterpart at battalion. "What's the most distant outpost you have?" Hearing the reply, his directive was clear. "Get her ass up there. Immediately!"

For a while it seemed to work. Then the situation blew up—almost literally—in their faces.

"Colonel, we've got a problem," the grim-faced sergeant major said. "The battalion commander sent a four-vehicle convoy up the road to pick her up and bring her back to headquarters so that they could go on R and R together in Qatar."

Phillips was livid. The round trip was a minimum eight-hour drive along IED-mined roads in a very dangerous AO. How could one of his commanders be so reckless to endanger soldiers' lives over a sexual liaison? He was stunned by the brazen behavior and disregard for soldiers' safety. For a long minute he was dumbstruck by the sheer idiocy of the action.

"Sergeant Major," Phillips directed, voice tight with anger, "I can put up with most anything, but when it comes to playing fast and loose with soldiers' lives I draw a hard line. We are going to inspect that battalion as soon as the two of them return. Make the arrangements, but keep it quiet."

True to his word, Phillips and the sergeant major dropped in on the battalion unannounced. Phillips patiently allowed the commander and his staff to give him a situation briefing then asked the commander to step aside privately. "Let's go talk somewhere," Philips said. "In fact, let's go to your room."

The battalion commander, a lieutenant colonel, went ashen-faced. He stammered through a litany of excuses as to why it would be better to talk here. "My room is too small," he said, "it's trashed, it wouldn't be good . . ." Stone-faced, Phillips was adamant: "Let's go to your room. Now."

Visibly shaking, the battalion commander led the way. When he opened the door to his room, two cots—placed side by side—occupied most of the space. Nothing more needed be said.

Phillips turned to him, dark eyes flashing anger and disgust. "You're suspended from your command," he said, watching the officer melt inside. The following day Phillips explained the situation to Lieutenant General Thomas Metz, commander of the Multi-National Corps–Iraq.

"What do you recommend?" Metz asked.

"I want him relieved of command," Phillips said.

"Do it!" Metz replied.

Twenty years of work went down the drain for that lieutenant colonel because of his gross error in judgment.

On the return trip to his headquarters Phillips was pensive. Something was troubling him. He turned to his sergeant major, his most trusted advisor and right arm.

"That officer and I had been together in the same MP company when I was a captain and he was a lieutenant," Phillips said, his voice filled with deep sorrow. "That was years ago. We had stayed in touch ever since. He was my best friend in the Army."

Many officers feel that being killed in combat is preferable to being relieved of command in wartime. It is a humiliating, career-ending action. There were several ways that Phillips could have resolved that situation under the table. Few would have been privy to details. He could have transferred the female soldier to an entirely different unit, or, for that matter, expedited her reassignment back to the States. That would have been the easy way, the line of least resistance, and many would have understood that the bond of long-term friendship trumped punitive action.

But Phillips would have known. And he would have found it difficult to live with the lie. "That officer recklessly put U.S. soldiers' lives in danger—acute danger, I might add—for purely personal pleasure. I don't care how deep a friendship is, there is no way that I can forgive him for doing that." Even though he was troubled emotionally—you don't simply destroy your best friend's life without it taking a toll, regardless of what your intellect tells you—Phillips chose the path of moral fortitude and leadership rather than give in to emotion.

Later, long after the incident, Phillips commented on the consequences. "There wasn't any more of that crap going on for the rest of the deployment," he growled.

Since the ugly series of events in April, the tension in Sadr City grew increasingly vicious. Adding to the mix, the 1st Cavalry Division, also out of Fort Hood, Texas, had replaced the previous landowner, the 1st Infantry Division. Under the latter, working relations with the 89th MP Brigade had been collegial. When the cav came to town, as Phillips recalled, they came with big talk about "saving the day" from "jacked-up" MPs who had done a lousy job of police training.

They entered Baghdad with the attitude and perception, observed Lieutenant Colonel Freeman, commander of the 759th MP Battalion, that "they were 'going to win the war.'" Shortly after taking over the battlespace, the commander decided to make a "show of force" run through Sadr City. Freeman and others had tried to pass on what they had learned the previous few months to cav leadership but were dismissed.

"They just refused to listen," Freeman said. Instead they sent a patrol into Sadr City looking for a fight, and found one. "They came in too heavy-handed and stirred up a hornet's nest." In that fight alone, the cav lost nine soldiers, and several more were wounded. Prior to their arrival the sector had settled down somewhat, but as the 1st Cavalry Division's history reports it, the division found itself "sucked into gritty combat in

Sadr City [and] the division has withstood more than 150 attacks this month, and saw too many of its fresh soldiers killed and wounded."

Prior to deployment some Cav Division staffers had spent a day with the Austin, Texas, Police Department and considered themselves experts on urban law enforcement. They thought that they could do a better job than the MPs. Unfortunately, in the near term, according to Phillips, their "arrogance" merely "inflamed the fight." They were "rank amateurs." Phillips dismissively spoke of the cav experience in Austin: "One day with a police department including a catered lunch with the deputy chief doesn't make one an expert in police operations."

In early June 2004 Phillips's 89th MP Brigade received adamant orders from the battlespace owner—then Major General Peter Chiarelli, commander of the 1st Cavalry Division, to occupy every Iraqi Police station on a continuous basis, including those in ultra-dangerous Sadr City. Till that time MP squads of nine to twelve soldiers had visited stations during daylight hours—often fighting their way in and out—then securing back at their base at night. Chiarelli reassured Phillips: His subordinate brigade combat teams (BCTs) would give necessary support to the MPs in the stations in time of need.

Phillips interpreted these orders as placing his soldiers in extraordinary danger for relatively little gain. "In most instances the Iraqi Police went home at night and the stations were all but deserted. There was no training going on. Our people were just magnets for the insurgents." But the matter was beyond discussion. However, he thought he detected a cynical reason for the order. Justifiably or not, Phillips believed it was done with the expectation that, if the policy failed, the BCTs could seek to remove the MP battalion."

Why would the cavalry units possibly want to get rid of the MPs? The reasons are complex. A strong motivation to dump the MPs came from the old bugaboo, command jealousy. At the time, Phillips actually had *three* direct bosses. The command structure was needlessly convoluted and ridiculously inefficient. Chiarelli, of course, was one boss. The others were Miller at Task Force 134, and British Brigadier General Andrew Mackay, head of the Combined Police Advisory Assistance Team.

Working for any one of them would be a challenge: It is axiomatic that there are always more missions than resources. All three were at odds over just who the 89th MP Brigade would give the most support to. Basically, like kindergarten kids in the yard, all of them wanted everything. None of the three, in Phillips's opinion, "recognized the requirements of the others. This placed the 89th MP Brigade into an untenable position of balancing support among them all." In other words, no matter how Phillips allocated support to any one of the three, all of the respective commanders considered themselves shortchanged. It was a no-win situation of enormous proportion and consequence.

As Phillips dryly summarized his quandary: "You can see why my relationship especially with MG Chiarelli and MG Miller deteriorated; neither was concerned about the other's mission." Increasing bickering between the two broke into open hostility between the cavalry commander and the task force commander. It came to a head, fittingly and predictably, in the nightmarish environs of Sadr City where, in accordance to Chiarelli's orders, Freeman had sent elements to work full time at the al Karama Iraqi Police station.

Freeman was not completely opposed to the move. He thought that having MP presence at the stations would prevent the frustrating, intimidating cycle of abandoning the stations to Mahdi insurgents at night and having to fight them off the following day. Freeman ordered squads to spend three days at a station and then rotate out as another squad replaced them. His support for the decision was predicated on one vital contingency: that 1st Brigade, 1st Cavalry had a quick reaction force to respond immediately if needed. "If you get in trouble," he told his soldiers, "the cav will come to your assistance." Very shortly that commitment would be tested.

Freeman's battle rhythm included daily visits to the stations to check on his soldiers and senior Iraqi Police officials in east Baghdad. At about 1500 on June 3, 2004, Freeman pulled his security detachment into the al Karama station in Sadr City for a visit. He was uneasy. As his Humvees approached the station he noticed shop owners closing their stores and pulling down the rolling metal overhead doors that protected the front of the shops.

As he walked the grounds of the station he noticed Mahdi insurgents on top of nearby buildings and leaning out of windows. They weren't trying to hide but flaunted their black and green uniforms with impunity. Alarm bells rang in Freeman's brain. He quickly spread the word: "Get ready for an attack!" He ordered his security detachment along with other MPs into fighting positions. Inside the station he found some of the Iraqi Police hiding in an inside room. Angrily, he ordered them to arm themselves and get out to defend their station. Taking no chances, he placed them with U.S. MPs. "If they are shoulder to shoulder with an MP they'll fight."

Within minutes Mahdi Army insurgents launched a large-scale attack on the al Karama Iraqi Police station. RPGs and small-arms fire smacked the walls of the station and cracked overhead. Freeman immediately radioed the cav landowner, but told them that he could manage for the moment. "We've got the situation under control." Next, unable to reach Phillips on radio because of distance, he contacted him via cell phone. "Byron," Phillips directed, "they're testing us. You've got to hold that station. Let me know if you need assistance."

Throughout the afternoon fighting intensified. The volume of fire increased markedly. The noise level made it difficult to hear and the acrid stench of cordite spread across the station grounds. Freeman sensed that more insurgents had joined the fight. He began to feel that he was inside a tightening noose. He contacted the cav brigade for news. Did they know anything from an intelligence standpoint? Negative, he was told. The Iraqi Police, now totally engaged in the fight, had received their own intel from cell phone conversations with officers in the area. "The Mahdi Army is sending busloads of fighters to surround us," he was told. Freeman was alarmed by the information and radioed back to the cav brigade.

"We've still got control of the situation here," he reported. "But they are bringing people in. Maybe you can interdict some of these reinforcements. And we're going to need a quick reaction force out here to give us some help." Evening turned into night and the attack only seemed to intensify. Finally after midnight a squad of Bradley fighting vehicles arrived from the cav. "They stayed for a couple of hours, killed some Mahdi Army guys, then left," Freeman reported. After the cav departed, the fighting continued into the early dawn hours. "We killed and wounded a lot of Mahdi Army insurgents, but had only had four wounded ourselves."

The al Karama station is a short map distance from everywhere in Baghdad, but a long slog on the ground for a relief force to negotiate through garbage and tire barricades, IEDs, and wild-eyed shooters. Freeman, a tall, strong officer who resembles the actor Dennis Haysbert, personally led convoys bearing food and ammunition through the fiery gauntlet of insurgents to the al Karama station. Each time they made the run the intensity of fire grew stronger despite the fact that the 759th soldiers were giving back more than they received.

During the second night the MPs were able to get limited air support from some coalition assets, but all calls to the cavalry brigade went unanswered or ignored. At one point Phillips frantically telephoned the brigade begging for help for his soldiers, who were taking a beating. "All units are down for scheduled maintenance and we can't assist," was the reply.

"I was stunned," Phillips later recalled. "American troops in a hot firefight and another American unit ignores them."

Throughout the fight the MPs were able to use the MK-19 203 mm grenade launcher. Through a stream of explosive grenades the MPs were able time and again to suppress enemy fire and beat them back.

For the next forty-eight hours, as Freeman fought continuously to break the siege, four soldiers were killed in action and twenty-eight wounded, some seriously. Even more Iraqi Police were casualties. Several MPs were later cited for valor. For three long days Sadr City lived up to its vicious reputation as a deathtrap for coalition and Iraqi Security Force soldiers. Phillips would describe it as "some of the toughest fighting that MPs had seen since the 1968 Tet Offensive in Saigon."

By the second day, Phillips himself joined the fight, leading his personal security detachment through the debris-choked, blockaded Sadr City streets. After they fought their way into al Karama what they found "reminded me of the Alamo." The station was pockmarked with thousands of bullet strikes and chunks of wall blown away by mortar fragments and RPG strikes.

"We held the al Karama police station," Freeman reported. "However, it was not much to see with its numerous RPG and small-arms holes in the structure. The station was in shambles." Bodies of Mahdi fighters littered the streets and alleys. Simply to walk on the ground was an exercise in slipping on strewn-about shell casings and rubble.

Keen to the presence of additional Americans in the station, insurgents began to drag debris, vehicles, and any kind of obstacle they could place in the exit roads. "It was an attempt to keep us 'hostage' in the center of the city," Phillips recalled. He made a decision. They would fight their way out of the blockade, engaging the enemy the entire time, and abandon the station. The price to hold it was, in his opinion, far too high for any perceived value. Under constant fire until they cleared the district, this is exactly what they did. Then, days after they abandoned the station, the Mahdi Army destroyed it.

Phillips was bitter, not about the fight itself, this was war; but about the events surrounding it. He thought his soldiers had been hung out to dry, used as pawns by rival commanders. "We were supposed to be supported by the BCTs [brigade combat teams], but one place in particular that I will vehemently stand by my belief was that the elements of the 759th MP Battalion were left to fend for themselves in Sadr City."

Amidst the shooting-gallery atmosphere of Baghdad in that ultraviolent period, Phillips was summoned to Chiarelli's headquarters. The cavalry division commander was angry, Phillips was indignant and, as he understated the encounter, "The conversation was less than pleasant." Still, though scarred from the encounter, Phillips came away somewhat pleased. His unit was officially removed from Chiarelli's supervision and placed under the corps commander, a shift that took these unit commander personality conflicts, "turf battles and battlespace ownership" off the table. Still, five MP companies stayed under cavalry division and that continued to worry Phillips. Would they be supported or abandoned if placed in great danger?

This was an issue that continued past Phillips and the 89th Brigade's rotation, and the following year would once again rear its ugly head in the distant Shi'a city of Karbala.

11

THE COST OF WAR

"The most dangerous road in the world." That was how war correspondent Michael Yon described Route Irish, the main divided highway that linked Baghdad International Airport (BIAP) to the city and the Green Zone. Littered with wreckage of blown-up military and civilian trucks, cars, and piles of garbage, rubble, and litter, there was no such thing as a routine run to BIAP. But coalition forces made the run so frequently that the gauntlet of IEDs, RPGs, and small-arms fire had been surrealistically transformed into a normal experience.

Nevertheless, Sergeant Kiet Christensen would have been the first to note that no matter how often convoys traverse a particular road, the danger of IEDs and VBEDs (vehicle-borne explosive devices, or suicide bombers) remains high. That it was a greater danger on Irish than some other routes just meant that as a good noncommissioned officer he had to have more situational awareness when his soldiers made the airport run. On July 13, 2004, Christensen was a team leader in the personal security detachment for coalition forces commander General George Casey. Early that day his squad leader passed the word down: "The boss has to go to BIAP this afternoon. Get your trucks and people ready to roll."

That day Christensen and his squad dropped General Casey off without incident. For Christensen it was business as usual. He had run the route on scores of occasions. As was normal for the season it was three-digit-Fahrenheit brutally hot. Soldiers just had to "embrace the suck" and live with the heat. While at the airport Christensen noted that the gunner in his truck was light-headed, a bit disoriented, and weak. *She's starting to show signs of heat stress*, Christensen thought. *I'd better get her down from there.*

Christensen didn't think twice: "Take care of your soldiers" is all but tattooed onto the eyelids of NCOs. Christensen brought the soldier out of the turret, made her drink water and Gatorade, and changed places. "You sit in the truck commander's seat up front. I'll gun for the run back to the Green Zone." Even though the air-conditioning units in Humvees are notoriously weak compared to those in a civilian automobile—designed mainly to keep sensitive computer equipment cool—the right front seat still provides a cooler ride than up in the open exposed to the fierce sun.

After departing BIAP, the convoy—weapons locked and loaded—picked up speed as they roared eastward on Route Irish. By Christensen's estimate they were hitting sixty to sixty-five miles an hour running down the two left-most lanes. He manned the .50 caliber gun in the open turret, scanning his sector of the roadway for possible threats. Suddenly he alerted. As the convoy approached a point where an entry ramp funneled vehicles onto Route Irish, Christensen spotted a nondescript civilian sedan speeding up the ramp and onto the highway at a rate of speed that would overtake the convoy. He must have been pushing seventy-five or eighty miles an hour. And he was headed straight for them.

In a heartbeat Christensen faced a horrible decision, the quandary that haunts every American soldier in his position. His mind raced through options.

Was this a suicide bomber in a car loaded with explosives? Or maybe just a reckless Iraqi driver, maybe drunk, driving irresponsibly? It happened. Though Muslims, many Iraqis notoriously drank like fish. Standing atop the turret with the wooden grips of the solid .50 caliber machine gun tight in his fists and thumbs pressed against the trigger mechanism, Christensen knew without a doubt that he could "light up" the car. Literally blow it to smithereens right there on the highway and stop it dead in its tracks.

But that "dead" part was the rub. A nagging little voice in his mind made him hesitate. He knew the rules of engagement. By heart, because they rehearsed and repeated them every time during mission brief before they rolled out of the gate. *If I kill this guy and it turns out he's nothing but a drunk in a hurry, I could be in a hell of a lot of trouble!* He risked court-martial and disciplinary action if someone in an office back in the rear with all the time in the world to evaluate the episode, and with the benefit of hindsight, judged his actions as too precipitate. *My Army career could be over.* With his head spinning with possibilities—none good—the sergeant waited one beat too long.

It took only that split second of hesitation for Christensen's world to explode in his face. The sedan—loaded with explosives—was driven by a suicide bomber who detonated his bomb immediately in front of the Humvee. Christensen remembered a flash, then blackness.

The car rammed into Christensen's Humvee and exploded with such force that the two-ton Humvee was flipped on its back. The sedan itself flew upward, landing on top of the burning Humvee. Sergeant Kiet Christensen was alive, barely, pinned beneath the smoldering wreckage.

Initially knocked unconscious, Christensen came to in a nightmare. Scalding hot oil and hydraulic fluid poured down over his face and body. His skull was fractured. Smoke choked his lungs. He was barely able to lift his head high enough to see his crushed body. What he saw appalled him and almost sent him tumbling down a slippery slope into shock. Shock, the fastest way for a casualty to die. His chest was crushed. Only by straining could he barely bring air into his shattered body. His legs were mashed under thousands of pounds of twisted metal, bone jutted out from flesh, legs and feet twisted into impossible positions. Waves of indescribable pain washed across his body. He couldn't move. He was completely pinned.

Agonizing pain interfered with his ability to think properly. Having suffered severe traumatic injuries, bleeding profusely, and with limited ability to breathe, Christensen had a single thought screaming in his consciousness: *Chances are I'm not going to make it!*

Still he struggled. No longer was he fighting to take care of his men. Now it was intensely personal. He just fought to stay alive.

Soldiers dragged the others in the truck to freedom. They began to treat wounds and tried futilely to free Christensen. "We've gotta get a wrecker out here quick!" someone yelled. The squad leader worked the radio. Time was against them. The other wounded could be evacuated quickly but how to remove tons of steel off a soldier's shattered body quickly enough to save him? And would any shifting of the wreckage kill him on the spot? Impatiently the squad called for help and set up a hasty defensive position. Sometimes suicide bombers came in pairs.

For more than two desperate hours Christensen lay beneath the wreckage, bleeding, struggling to get air in his broken chest, and enduring spasms of pain that took him to the edge of consciousness. He was tempted to sink back into the darkness just for relief from the overload of pain signals that his broken body sent to his brain. But Christensen was tough, wiry, and a fighter. Instead of giving in he hung on, listening to the words of encouragement from fellow soldiers who vowed to rescue him. Inside the slight frame of this Vietnamese-born, American-adopted soldier, his warrior's heart continued to struggle for life.

When the wrecker truck finally reached the scene of the attack soldiers had to work carefully to remove the destroyed vehicles— beginning with the suicide vehicle itself—from Christensen. Everyone knew that his life hung in the balance. One slip could send the truck falling back down upon his damaged body. It wouldn't take more than that to push him over the fragile edge. Soldiers struggled mightily to work as quickly as possible—everyone knew that saving him from shock, blood loss, and major trauma was a race against the clock— while using exceeding care in the removal process. Meanwhile brave medics crawled into the wreckage to start an IV and treat him as best they could. It was an excruciating process in patience, skill, and frustration. All the more so for the helpless soldier trapped beneath.

When the wreck was finally removed after two and a half brutal hours, Christensen was immediately air-evacuated to the Baghdad hospital. Doctors were horrified by the sight of his body. Teams worked frantically to get him stabilized as quickly as possible. As skillful as they are, surgeons knew that the damage he suffered far exceeded their capabilities. It was critical to get him up the medical chain with all speed, but equally important that he be in condition to fly.

Once stabilized, Christensen was flown by air ambulance to the Landstuhl military hospital in Germany. While at Landstuhl he was worked on again and again. Ultimately the decision was made: Place him in an induced coma and move him on to Walter Reed Army Medical Center in Washington, D.C. It is a normal technique for terribly injured soldiers. Putting them into the coma allows the body to relax and begin the slow healing process while not stressing the patient more than necessary. Sergeant Kiet Christensen would remain in that state for two weeks.

Back at Walter Reed, Christensen was brought out of his coma, having already undergone multiple restorative surgeries. Thankfully, the process was at the point that the question no longer was "Will he live?"—skillful medical attention had gotten him through the immediate crisis—now it was "How well will he be able to function?"

When Christensen came back to consciousness his first memory was of his father standing at the foot of his hospital bed. He was amazed. "Dad," he asked groggily. "What are you doing in Iraq?"

"You're in Walter Reed, son," Andrew Christensen, a retired aerospace engineer, replied gently. He and his wife had taken Kiet into their hearts as a baby years before when he had been abandoned. Once again they stood by him in his time of need. "You're safe back home."

Christensen has fought through more than twenty-three major surgeries to repair the wounds he suffered on that "routine run" out to BIAP that day. It would be eighteen months before he was released from Walter Reed. He was offered the option of medical retirement—indeed, almost forced to take it—but resisted with all the inner toughness that brought him back from near death that terrible day. He has spent years in agonizing rehabilitative physical therapy, fighting through pain both mental and physical, to achieve his goal of returning as a fully functioning noncommissioned officer.

Fortunately—for him, for the Army, for the Military Police Regiment, and for his country—Christensen had a strong voice intervening on his behalf. MP Regimental Command Sergeant Major James Barrett visited every wounded MP transiting through Walter Reed. After speaking to his soldiers and making certain that they were aware of the gravity of their situation no matter what it was, he always asked them what were their desires. Many, like Christensen, had been so badly wounded that the Army would offer them medical retirement in grade. By taking this option a soldier could doff his uniform, receive a lifetime pension (albeit a small one), and continue to receive treatment if needed, usually at VA facilities. Some decided on this course.

Others, again like Christensen, were adamant: They had fought hard to survive a terrible wounding and would fight with equal determination to remain on active duty. They were true Warrior Police and wanted only to be given a chance to return to the MP Regiment and the lives to which they had dedicated themselves. Moreover, soldiers of this level of commitment are consumed by a loyalty and devotion to other soldiers. They recognize that the war continues and that if they do not participate then others have to take up the slack created by their departure.

Christensen looked the command sergeant major in the eye steady and strong. He affirmed his desire to remain in the Army. "I will not leave voluntarily," he said. "I am a soldier and belong here with my buddies." Grasping his hand, the sergeant major pledged to help make that happen.

He did. By the time of our interviews with him, Sergeant Christensen had undergone more than twenty-four surgeries and remains on active duty. He was an instructor at the Fort Leonard Wood Schoolhouse, and attended the advanced leaders course. Christensen plans to submit an application for admission to the criminal investigation division of the MPs.

While Christensen's story is compelling, it is not unique. Other soldiers have bucked the system and remain on active duty today whereas in the past they would have been separated without a moment's thought. Army officials realize that the experience these wounded warriors bring to their fellow soldiers considerably outweighs any physical limitations.

Many, like Staff Sergeant Michael Murphy, a two-tour Iraq veteran, lament the damage suffered by soldiers like Christensen who try too hard to follow rules of engagement knowing that their actions will be harshly judged: "Sometimes you just have to jump the ROE. You do what you have to do and only hope that your commanders will back you up."

"It was total civil chaos," Master Sergeant Jim Eakin remembered when he first deployed to Iraq. His unit, the 630th MP Company (Team Maverick) based in Bamberg, Germany, arrived on April 20, 2004, just when the terrible days of spring were reaching a crescendo. The unit was assigned to the 793rd MP Battalion. Eakin remembered that while they had completed predeployment training it was inadequate for what abruptly faced them in-country.

Thinking that things would be fairly quiet and that missions would involve mostly law enforcement, route security, and Iraqi Police training, they had focused on what Eakin considers "normal MP missions." "We had very little preparation for what would be our ultimate mission. Things were going to hell. All of a sudden from 'take your time and get ready' it shifted to 'get on the plane and get over there!'"

In those early days as the insurgence exploded across Iraq, al-Qaeda fighters were drawn like flies to a corpse. Previously peaceful urban areas were transformed into battlefields that became the terrain of choice for the bad guys. Enclaves of Sunni occupation were particularly vulnerable for exploitation by AQI (al-Qaeda in Iraq) leadership. Disgruntled Sunnis were ripe for recruiting. Many rallied to the false flag of al-Qaeda, particularly in Anbar Province and south of Baghdad in Salman Pak.

The city sits astride the ancient Tigris River on the eastern, convex side of a sweeping curve. A long thin island splits the river adjacent to the city. There migratory birds winter prior to taking the long flight back to Europe, and fishermen and gatherers plumb the muddy, polluted waters, seeking something to sell at market or take home to eat.

A main road from Baghdad bisects the city north-south, eventually linking the greener north to the desert cities of Najaf, Nasiriyah, and ultimately Basra. Salman Pak reveals its farming roots in the stalls of lively food markets that dominate the main drag. Inside the city, the road splits around a broad median park lined with tall, spreading trees and some actual green space with benches for women to rest from shopping while their children play and old men sit and contemplate the world changing around them.

Around the park and along the main and side streets, buildings are low, rarely exceeding three stories, with flat roofs to allow families to sleep atop them on the hot summer nights. Residences and official buildings are protected from the public by high walls, occasionally topped by branches extending from internal gardens. The relentless westerly desert wind deposits dust on all surfaces, eventually turning every fence, wall, and rooftop a uniform sandy brown.

Openly defiant Sunni militiamen ran the place. Iraqi Police leaders and supporters of the new government were assassinated, policemen were gunned down on the streets or in their checkpoints, stations were attacked by open formations of AQI, and families were kidnapped and held hostage.

Team Maverick—elements of the 630th MP Company—was ordered to make a run into Salman Pak in midsummer to see what could be done to restore order.

Master Sergeant Eakin was riding in the left rear seat of a Humvee on July 20, 2004, when the Mavericks rolled into the tough city. They were about twenty miles southeast of their usual beat in Baghdad. His unit had endured a lot of IED attacks in different locales till then. "Normal stuff," he said, "mostly hit-and-run. They'd pop an IED, maybe with a cell phone command, then boogie." That day the insurgents set a deliberate ambush. "We were hit first with IEDs. My vehicle was immediately disabled."

The next IED blast came from over Eakin's left shoulder. It blew out the window and part of the door, then ripped into him, wounding him badly in the upper body and head, continuing on to wound the driver, Specialist Miles Parker. Almost immediately, a second IED blew beneath the vehicle. The explosion ripped upward, wounding Eakin again on his right side. A small piece of shrapnel slammed into the head of the turret gunner, Specialist Danny Daniels, killing him instantly.

"The first one got my head, face, and left shoulder. On the second my lung was punctured, and I almost lost my right leg," Eakin recounted.

With multiple potentially fatal wounds, fighting for his life, Eakin was trapped in the Humvee, bleeding badly and slipping in and out of consciousness. Other soldiers rushed to assist but were engaged by hidden enemy fighters. The noise was almost numbingly loud as the Americans fought off the deadly attack.

This attack was a calculated complex ambush. By destroying a vehicle, the enemy halted the convoy just where it wanted—where all their weapons would be concentrated to inflict maximum damage on American soldiers caught in the kill zone.

The battle got increasingly hot. Almost immediately after the IEDs blew, three RPGs struck the rear of Eakin's Humvee. The insurgents knew their trade: A close-range direct strike with a rocket-propelled grenade might be enough to destroy what was left of the Humvee, at the least set it on fire. Amazingly, all three RPGs were duds. They smacked the truck and fell inert to the ground. The enemy increased the volume of small-arms fire. With classic ambush tactics they emerged from cover and began to assault through their killing zone. "The killing zone: That was us," Eakin remembered.

Eakin lay bleeding and helpless in his Humvee as enemy fighters tried to gain fire superiority over the MPs. They charged from concealed positions, attempting to overwhelm the defenders. But the insurgents, smart as they were, failed to count on one thing: the firepower MPs bring into a fight. Bodies and pieces flew across the road as high-velocity rounds tore them apart. Fanatical insurgents were stopped dead in their tracks by sheer volume of fire. Throughout the fight Team Maverick never wavered. The resolute commitment of soldiers who refused to be overrun on that street, that day, won the battle. Bodies of enemy fighters littered the roadway around the convoy. Still the firefight escalated.

Other elements of Team Maverick had gone ahead and were out of the fight when the ambush was sprung. Hearing what their battle buddies were catching, they swung around and returned to help. When more MP trucks showed up, guns rattling death on the ambushers, the assault was finally stopped. Eakin was relieved. "Their quick response saved us."

Sometime in the chaos of combat, Eakin lost consciousness. Later he was told that between ten and fourteen enemy fighters were killed. He was never certain of the nature of the fighters, but given that the ambush occurred in Salman Pak, odds are that the attackers were Sunni insurgents, al-Qaeda, or a combination. In any event, they paid for their attack with their lives. On the American side several soldiers were wounded and Daniels was killed in action.

Eakin's combat wounds are painfully displayed: His face is heavily scarred and his left eye is slightly off-focus. Some of the bone structure of his head is permanently depressed. He had a lot of damage to his entire left side, suffered paralysis for a while, and almost lost his left eye. He was evacuated first to Baghdad then to Landstuhl Army Medical Center. "They put me in an induced coma," Eakin tried to recollect. "I think in Baghdad, maybe in Germany. I was doped up on painkillers. It's all pretty fuzzy at that point in time." He was airlifted to Walter Reed Army Hospital and brought to consciousness having gone through the first few of what would be several surgeries.

"I didn't know that Danny had been killed till they told me at Walter Reed," Eakin said, his face tight and solemn. "That soldier was like a son to me. I had mentored him back in Germany. It really hurt when they finally gave me the word."

After twenty-two operations, Master Sergeant Eakin decided he had had more hospital time than he wanted. "I have some permanent vision impairment in the left eye—that isn't going to get any better—and as far as the disfigurement of the face is concerned it wasn't worth more time under the knife. They offered but I said screw it, enough is enough.

"I know what I look like," Eakin said with the lopsided grin that is now his trademark. "But my wife still stayed with me so I figure what the hell. I can live with it." Like many of his badly wounded compatriots, Eakin had to plead to stay on active duty, because the Army medical staff was determined to medically retire him.

"It was thanks to the regimental sergeant major that many of us were allowed to fight the system and stay active," Eakin affirmed. "CSM Jim Barrett visited us all at Walter Reed and made a point of asking 'What do you want to do?' After we told him we wanted to stay, then he vowed to make that happen. And he did."

Before they deployed, as Christmas 2003 approached, it had been a bittersweet time for David Phillips and the 89th MP Brigade. Word had just come down that the brigade would deploy forward elements to Iraq during the holiday season. About then, Staff Sergeant Darren Cunningham worked his way up the chain of command for an office call with the brigade commander.

Phillips received him warmly. He and Cunningham had served together in MP units around the world for the past twenty-plus years. Phillips was aware that Cunningham had already submitted papers for retirement and had been offered a position with the police department in Killeen, Texas. Phillips was happy with the way things had worked out for a loyal soldier.

Cunningham, however, was unhappy. The 89th MPs—his unit—was preparing to go into combat on the other side of the world and that meant that soldiers he had trained, mentored, and developed for months would face the ultimate test without their sergeant being there to watch over them. "I want you to pull my retirement papers, Colonel," Cunningham announced.

Phillips resisted. "You've served your time honorably. You have a job and a family. You don't need to do this."

Cunningham persisted. He spoke of his soldiers and his obligation to be with them in combat. He spoke of duty. Finally, he said that knowing where the unit was headed, he could not live with himself if denied the opportunity to accompany them.

Phillips begrudgingly relented. "In his position I would have done the same thing, made the same argument." He told Cunningham, "Okay. I'll take care of the paperwork. You can come along."

As September 2004 approached Phillips had a moment to think over some predeployment decisions. He was convinced that allowing himself to be persuaded by Cunningham to delay retirement and join the deployment had been the right decision for them both, and for the brigade's mission. Cunningham had exceeded expectations, proving to be a highly critical player as the mission to rebuild the Iraqi Police developed. Phillips had assigned him to the brigade's special police team under the very capable Major Pete Lydon. The police team was considered to be essential in the building process and Cunningham had shown himself to be especially adept at working with Iraqis, analyzing and setting up training, and contributing on all levels to success.

Things had gone well over the past several months despite the fighting and the losses. By late September 2004 the 89th MP Brigade was already thinking about redeploying back to Fort Hood. One evening Phillips and Command Sergeant Major Charlie Guyette were having evening chow at their dining facility and were joined by Cunningham, who had just come from a day's work in Baghdad. The three were relaxed, joking, and chatting about going home.

With great flourish Cunningham presented Phillips with a new set of retirement papers that would be effective in early January 2005 right after they got back, together with the announcement that the Killeen PD had held the job open for him. Phillips joked about not signing it, everyone laughed—"just good-natured horseplay"—and ended the evening on a high note.

The enemy likes to fire rockets at night. Darkness disguises their movement and makes counterbattery fire less effective. On September 30, 2004, Victory Base, home of the 89th MP Brigade, took incoming rocket fire at about 0400. One hit a trailer with men sleeping inside, turning it in a gory instant into razor-sharp shrapnel and a blazing inferno. One of the inhabitants, Sergeant First Class Albert Mersch, was critically wounded but survived his injuries. Seven other soldiers in the brigade were wounded.

Mersch's roommate, Darren Cunningham, was killed instantly in the attack.

The loss continues to haunt David Phillips. "I visited Staff Sergeant Cunningham last month in Arlington," he wrote in May 2010. "I visit him every time I go to Washington."

12

DEEP IN THE TRIANGLE OF DEATH

One day in early October 2004 the brigade chaplain asked to ride on route clearance with an MP patrol. Sergeant Gary Watford was reluctant but couldn't come up with a convincing reason fast enough to deflect the request. He put the chaplain in his own truck where he could keep an eye on him and they headed north on Route Sword. Not long into the ride the chaplain had to urinate badly. It happens. More experienced soldiers learn to go easy on coffee before mount-out and make the latrine the final stop before donning gear and strapping in.

The chaplain asked Watford to stop, but the sergeant was concerned about security. "Use an empty water bottle," Watford urged. Modesty, or the prospect of trying to keep a stream of urine locked onto a narrow bottle opening while jostling in the back of a Humvee and avoiding annoying splashes, may have increased his reluctance to give it a go. The chaplain persisted, whining about the urgency of his need. Finally, with a sigh of resignation, Watford agreed to stop.

"We pulled over and found ourselves at the intersection of Sword and Tampa, where there had been that big fight back in April. We were stopped under an overpass. While the chaplain got out to piss I glanced at fresh graffiti on the concrete. It said 'We Kill USA.' I remember thinking 'This is not a good place.'"

Watford urged him to hurry. Back in the trucks and rolling, the patrol barely got fifty meters down the road when an IED went off in the space behind Watford's truck and just in front of the next one in line. Fortunately, though rattled, nobody was hurt. At that point Watford decided, "That was the last time anybody got a piss break on my truck."

By late October 2004 Fallujah was ready to explode again. Essentially the festering resentment of residents, fueled by enormous al-Qaeda infiltration, was unresolved since the previous spring when the Blackwater contractors were murdered and the Marines had moved in to clear it. The Marines had been stymied in their first attempt because of political restraints imposed by a media-adverse Washington. The U.S. presidential election was scheduled for early November. As soon as the results were known, the Bush administration greenlighted coalition leadership to go back in and clean it up. Easier said than done.

In the intervening six months al-Qaeda and Sunni insurgents had turned Fallujah into a fortified city. Ammunition, food, medical supplies, and communications networks were established and in place. Explosive charges were planted on all entrances and choke points. Houses and apartments were turned into bunkers. Mosques, hospitals, and schools became ammunition storage dumps and command centers. The local populace had been terrorized to the breaking point. Anyone who refused to accept the strict Wahhabist doctrine of the al-Qaeda fighters was killed, tortured, or locked into ad hoc basement prisons. Rape, assault, drug use, theft, and general abuse were casual and routine. Those who could do so fled at the behest of the coalition that opened pathways for them in the growing ring of military might that surrounded the city. Those who refused to leave hunkered down. The fight was on.

Military police from the 16th MP Brigade were tasked to support maneuver units. "We pulled route security, convoy protection, set up traffic-control points, and established areas for captured enemy fighters," Sergeant First Class Jackson Varner remembered.

As the fighting intensified and the noose tightened around Fallujah, work for the MPs increased. Refugee issues grew, and captured insurgents had to be processed and transported, primarily over to nearby Abu Ghraib. In Baghdad, Sergeant Gary Watford watched the fight and went to his superiors with a request. "I want to help out. Get into the action over there." They agreed and released him to the tactical operations center that was being set up in an unused part of the Abu Ghraib prison.

"It was awful conditions," Watford recalled. "We were in this strange-looking stone room, with a single high window and an odd bench-like ledge that ran the length of the far wall, for sixteen or more hours daily. There was a repulsive smell that never left the room. Just the air made people queasy. I was nauseous most of the time."

The fighting got tougher and the battle rhythm of the operations center grew even more intense. "It seemed like I was constantly sick," Watford remembered. "Just something low-grade but it kept me feeling weak and tired."

Finally, in a rare idle moment Watford turned to the senior non-com present. "Any idea what that writing on the wall means?" He gestured to brown graffiti that had been scrawled on the wall for who knew how long.

"Something about Saddam—good or bad, not sure. This was their latrine. The detainees wrote it in shit with their hands."

Horrified, Watford looked closer. Suddenly the odd configuration of the room was clear: the "ledge" was simply a long bench that had once had holes cut in it. The graffiti was fecal matter smeared on the walls. And the nauseating smell was decades of accumulated human waste lingering beneath the bench. *Godalmighty,* Watford thought, *no wonder we're all sick!* For a long time Watford wondered if the MPs had been given this space by the landowner as some sort of weird revenge or if it was pure accident.

For those who fought there, Fallujah became the epitome of grim urban warfare in Iraq. Soldiers wisely loathe fighting in cities. Maneuver space is limited, there are too many civilians around, density of buildings offers innumerable cover and concealment options for a wily enemy, and combat is almost always eyeball-to-eyeball. While the primary fighters were Marines and infantry, it wasn't long before MPs were called to assist.

"We'd go in on a variety of missions," Watford said. (He had managed to get out of the toxic air of the ops center.) "Casualty evacuation, bringing up supplies, escorting out captured fighters, and often just to give the infantry a bit of help."

Sergeant Willie Bowman was in the fight. His platoon was clearing houses in a fought-over bloody section of Fallujah, kicking doors, sending in "stacks" to clear rooms and blow up buildings. The insurgents were dug in, had constructed holes in walls and floors so that they could pass quickly from room to room or even to adjacent houses. Frequently soldiers would clear a house and follow-on personnel would be ambushed inside by terrorists returning through hidden passages. As American soldiers and Marines entered buildings their desert boots crunched scores of hypodermic needles and vials of drugs beneath the soles. "They were all drugged to the gills on amphetamines, cocaine, and adrenalin," Bowman recalled. "Several times we shot guys who were really dead but continued to fire because they were so jacked up they didn't even know it."

They had entered the ground floor of a house and were stacking again to clear rooms. Bowman remembered, for reasons he still does not comprehend, that he pushed his lieutenant aside and dashed first into a room. "Something just told me to do it. I crashed in, scanned left, and in my peripheral vision caught sight of a guy on the floor on the other side of the door with an AK pointed right at me. I must have jerked my head as I was turning to get him." The insurgent bullet struck Bowman on the right side of the neck and ran along his jawline. Bowman killed that enemy and kept moving. "I was so pumped up I didn't even realize I had been shot until about half an hour later when somebody noticed all the blood pouring from my face."

Bowman spent a few days in the hospital, then, as quickly as he could get away, returned to duty. "They needed me. I couldn't sit there while my soldiers were in danger."

One of the most enduring memories of Fallujah for Watford was the filth. "We were lucky and usually only spent three days in the city before rotating out. The grunts were stuck there for a week or more at a time. The Iraqis were supposed to clean up the bodies and haul them away but most of the time they were afraid to come up to the front. Sometimes it would be more than a week and they wouldn't come up out of fear. The stench was revolting. You'd have to sit in all that and eat MREs. It was disgusting but there was nothing we could do."

All who participated in that bitter battle came away with the same conclusion that Watford expressed. "We should have done it right back in spring but we all knew in the fall that this was the last round. No do-overs on this run. We loaded up, fought our way in, and took the place. It was a major victory."

Over the months that HVT #1—Saddam Hussein—had been under his custodial supervision at Griffin Rock on Camp Cropper, Dave Phillips had developed a habit of dropping in to the facility fairly regularly to check on conditions. The entire MP Corps had been wire-brushed by Abu Ghraib. From top down command emphasis was adamant: There will be no more infractions. It was partially from this motivation, but also largely natural compassion for detainees in his custody—regardless of how despicable their acts had been—that drove Phillips to make frequent inspection visits.

With his interpreter along, Phillips would sit in the cell with some of these high-profile men and chat. "Saddam never lost his composure," Phillips remembered. As did others who were exposed to the dictator, he noted that Saddam's eyes drew attention. "You hear the expression 'commanding eyes' but this was the first time I ever experienced it personally. His ego was enormous, his confidence almost overwhelming. Here he sat, awaiting almost certain execution, and calmly discussed what he intended to do to Iraq after we put him back in power. The man never missed a beat."

Late in November Phillips was chatting with Saddam in his cell when several rockets detonated nearby. Cocking his head, Saddam listened then gave a dismissive wave of his hand. "This is not the real Iraq," he told Phillips. "I will show you the real Iraq. Come back here later with your family and I will escort you around."

Bemused, Phillips would later recount the story to his family. His son Daniel, something of a character, quickly noted, "Oh, cool. Now we get to go to Iraq, too!"

In November 2004, the 504th MP Battalion deployed into Iraq from its home base of Fort Lewis, Washington. Sergeant Henry "Hank" Stearns was back in Iraq. He had deployed for a few months in the early stages of the war, and now brought his unit back for what they expected to be a full-year tour. The Dragonfighters are the most highly decorated military police unit on active duty. They were stationed at Iskandariyah, about twenty-five miles south of Baghdad along Route Tampa, at a base known as Forward Operating Base Kalsu. They had heard the stories; seen the reports. They knew they were going into the maelstrom.

"The Second Battle of Fallujah was ongoing," Stearns recalled. "My soldiers were going to have to run those roads, take the hits from the IEDs. We read intel reports that special snipers from Egypt had come in with the al-Qaeda guys. They were picking off gunners right in the turret. We knew it was going to be bad." In the next few months Stearns and his soldiers would find out just how bad their area had become.

Very shortly, as the area became a focal point for sectarian violence, it was known as the start of the "Sunni Triangle," a hotbed of Sunni tribes linked with al-Qaeda in Iraq. "Later," Stearns recalled, "we started calling it the 'Triangle of Death.' "

●   ●   ●

In December 2004, after months of steady, intense fighting and losses, Phillips looked back on what was a very difficult year. On the bright side, many of his and other units' soldiers performed exemplary service. The fighting had been intense at times and on every occasion his MP soldiers rose to the challenge and prevailed. The brigade put a much bigger hurt on the enemy than they received. He was also pleased with the new police training-team programs. They had accomplished a lot with the program of rebuilding the Iraqi Police, and though much remained to be done and the preponderance of resources went to the Iraqi Army, he could see progress.

On the other side of the ledger he was bitter over the fact that many of the disasters were preventable. Too many of the bad decisions that led to chaos had the fingerprints of the Coalition Provisional Authority in the person of Paul Bremer on them: disbanding the Iraqi military and police, closing the newspaper, and general mishandling of Sunni and Shi'a alike. In his mind it was a long list and contributed directly to the loss of many good soldiers.

That month, with great fanfare at the White House, Paul "Jerry" Bremer was given the Medal of Freedom by President George W. Bush. Phillips could only shake his head over the irony.

13

NATIONAL GUARD WEEKEND

For months Sunni insurgents and al-Qaeda back in Iraq had been targeting a key supply route running north through the Salman Pak region into Baghdad. Coalition convoys used the road extensively and were thus tempting soft targets. National Guard men and women out of Kentucky in the 617th MP Company had been shadowing convoys—driving behind them while being prepared to respond to emergencies. This was one of David Quantock's tactical innovations and it was proving successful. Some of the MPs employing this tactic were about to be tested once again on Palm Sunday, March 20, 2005.

A patrol of three Humvees, call sign Raven 42 with the 617th MPs, had been patrolling Iraq Route 6—aka Alternate Supply Route Detroit—just north of Salman Pak.

Staff Sergeant Timothy Nein, a thirty-nine-year-old printer with International Paper Co. and the father of two young sons, led their security unit of nine MPs and a medic from the first Humvee. Nein's gunner, manning a .50 cal in the turret above him, was twenty-year-old Specialist Casey Cooper, with Sergeant Dustin Morris driving.

They were a tight team that strove to be prepared for anything. As squad leader, Nein had insisted that his soldiers always perform thorough vehicle and weapons maintenance checks and services after every mission, no exceptions, and that weapons, ammunition, and other equipment were always kept in exactly the same place within each vehicle. Since their arrival into Iraq four months earlier he constantly pushed his squad in relentless drills to help ensure that every individual would be able to react instantly, and with precision, when attacked. Nein also strove hard for his unit to "be better organized, attack as soon as you can, dismount when you need to dismount, stay in the trucks when you need to stay in the trucks, and not have everybody do their own thing."

Following directly behind them in the second Humvee rode Sergeant Leigh Ann Hester, a petite twenty-three-year-old shoe store manager from Nashville, Tennessee. Specialist Ashley Pullen drove while Specialist Jesse Ordunez was prepared to use his M-240B machine gun, an MK-19 grenade launcher, and a squad automatic weapon as needed in the turret above them.

Trailing at the rear in their third Humvee was the squad's medic, Specialist Jason Mike, a former Florida high school football star who'd earned All-District, All-State, and All-American honors but gave up his dream of going pro to join the Army just after the 9/11 attacks. Specialist Bryan Mack was driving while specialist William Haynes manned their .50 cal, and Sergeant Joseph Rivera served as the vehicle commander riding in the front passenger's seat.

Their small security force, driving north on Detroit, encountered a half-mile-long convoy of thirty coalition tractor-trailers headed south. Within the convoy three Humvees from the 1st Battalion, 623rd Field Artillery (call sign Stallion 33) escorted the mix of Army and civilian vehicles. "Turn around," Nein directed.

"We're going to shadow these guys till they leave the area," Nein called over his radio, alerting the squad.

Meanwhile, a northbound convoy of approximately thirty trucks, escorted by three armed trucks from 518th Guntruck Company (call sign Regulator) were approaching a convergence point that none realized was a complex ambush by approximately fifty insurgents.

About ten minutes later the convoy halted. Up ahead Nein saw that some vehicles were trying to pull off the road. "They're being hit! Go! Go! Go!" shouted turret gunner Cooper. Nein alerted his ten-soldier squad to follow him. Morris zipped through a gap in the tractor-trailers, and at Nein's direction led the vehicles right into the kill zone between the insurgent ambushers and the convoy.

Nein realized that the supply convoy had inadvertently driven into a carefully planned complex ambush. Dozens of enemy fighters lined two irrigation trenches, forming an L-shape to the main road. Others were positioned in a nearby two-story house and an orchard. They were pouring machine-gun fire and RPGs into the convoy. Three drivers were already dead, and six more wounded.[1] Insurgents seemed to be everywhere around them. As Nein pushed his soldiers into the teeth of the ambush, several of them noticed a line of civilian vehicles—BMWs, Chevrolet Caprices, and Opel sedans—parked some distance away, doors and trunks left open.[2]

"Initially, when we made the turn to flank the anti-Iraqi forces, I counted seven cars, all with four doors open, and I did the math real quick in my head, and I was like, 'That's twenty-eight [insurgents] against ten.' That's two point 8 to one odds. That's not very good," Nein recalled. "Little did I know it was five to one odds, which is even worse."[3] These carefully positioned escape vehicles also suggested the enemy's possible intent to try to take hostages for ransom or for use in grotesque beheading videos. Later, insurgent bodies were found carrying handcuffs and they discovered that one of the dead had been filming the firefight, confirming the worst—that they intended to broadcast videos of the ambush, and possibly executions, to the world.

By then at least three U.S. soldiers from the original escort units had been wounded, their vehicles knocked out of action. To stop the insurgents from inflicting further damage on the convoy, and hoping to outflank them, Nein's squad pressed hard down a parallel road, blazing fire at the trench line with .50 caliber. heavy machine guns and automatic MK-19 grenade launchers.

While rushing some 250 meters down the access road under heavy fire Nein's Humvee had its tires flattened and a round hit the engine block, spraying hot oil across the hood and windshield.[4]

His gunner, Cooper, suddenly saw smoke and a black dot before his eyes, thinking, "Oh crap!" an instant before an RPG exploded as it hit the rear passenger door, knocking him out cold. From her vantage point of the driver's seat in the second Humvee about twenty meters behind them Specialist Pullen saw the lead vehicle had actually been picked up in the air on impact before slamming back down on the ground. Cooper collapsed forward in the turret as Nein shouted "Coop! Are you okay?" while simultaneously starting to move his body aside and man the big gun. Within seconds Cooper, wounded in the face, jolted back into consciousness and sprang up like a jack-in-a-box. "I'm good!" he shouted before seizing the .50 cal to reengage.[5]

Gunner Ordunez, in the second Humvee, fired to provide cover so that Nein and Sergeant Hester could dismount their vehicles. Both leaders exited in the face of heavy enemy fire. Morris piled out of the heavily damaged lead vehicle to follow behind them. Pullen's vehicle was still operational so she dismounted and took up a position on the left rear side, staying close just in case she might need to leap back into the driver's seat.

Nein, Hester, and Morris all raced forward into the face of the enemy, firing weapons as they advanced. Though they were outnumbered, Nein remained determined to take the fight to the insurgents. While Cooper and Ordunez used the .50s and MK-19s from their turrets to clean out one trench line, Nein crawled to the top of a dirt embankment and saw that several insurgents were holding position in the adjacent ditch. "We're going to have to go in there!" he shouted to Hester. While Nein was reconning the situation, Hester had already killed two enemy fighters in the wood line with her M-4, including one insurgent who had been preparing to launch an RPG.

The pair advanced slowly, yard by yard, throwing hand grenades and launching grenades from Hester's M-203. While Nein held their line Hester ran back under fire to the vehicles to retrieve more grenades and bandoliers of ammunition, pulling them out of a different truck. Nein's insistence on always storing ammo in exactly the same places within all their vehicles paid off, allowing Hester to grab what they needed without fumbling around or taking her eyes off the firefight for little more than an instant.

Meanwhile, the squad's third Humvee, commanded by Sergeant Rivera, was far behind them, more than one hundred meters away by the main road, fighting hard against insurgents lining a trench. Rivera had ordered his driver, Specialist Mack, to stop there so that this key trouble spot could be dealt with. Gunner Haynes began blasting away with his .50 cal from the turret as Rivera, Mack, and medic Jason Mike dismounted, positioned themselves on the left side of the vehicle, and opened fire.

In short order Mack yelled out that he'd been hit. Medic Mike put aside his weapon to drag Mack to safety while Rivera and Haynes laid out hailstorms of suppressive fire. Mack had been hit in the arm, the round ricocheting into his torso and landing between his heart and lungs. "I bandaged him up, threw him into the vehicle, and picked back up my sector of fire," Mike later recalled, knowing at that moment that his M-4 marksmanship represented better value for saving lives than his medical skills could.[6] The medic was delivering his shots with surgical precision. "I was picking out targets very, very carefully, making sure I was hitting guys left and right."

Then Sergeant Rivera yelled that he'd been hit and couldn't feel his legs, after taking a round that entered his back and exited through his stomach, barely missing his spine.

It suddenly dawned on them all that both Mack and Rivera had been using the left side of the truck as cover when they were hit— meaning that insurgents were now lining both sides of the road.

A moment later a piece of shrapnel hit gunner Haynes in the left hand. "Wrap it!" Mike told him, snatching up the Haynes' squad automatic weapon (SAW) while still clutching his own M-4. The medic then crouched over the hood of the Humvee and raised both weapons, glancing back and forth while aiming at insurgents on either side of him until Haynes was able to get back into the fight. "He would look in one direction, aim and fire, then turn in the other direction to engage on that side," Nein said.

Then Mike and Haynes yanked a pair of shoulder-fired rocket launchers—AT-4s—from the truck and engaged the enemy, who were using a nearby abandoned farmhouse as cover, quickly knocking out fire coming from that direction.

In the distance ahead of them, Nein, Hester, and their MPs had no idea that three of their comrades had been hit, for they still had their hands full. A round hit the SAW that gunner Ordunez had been firing, briefly knocking him to the floor of the second truck. Gunner Cooper in the lead Humvee was calling out to Nein to throw a grenade over the berm to stop an insurgent he could see nearby on the south side of the road. Hester turned, shot, and killed another insurgent on the north side. Nein threw a grenade over the berm, then scrambled up to peek over, finding that his intended target had escaped.

But then Pullen, still positioned just outside the second truck, heard screaming over the radio inside. She opened the door and recognized medic Mike's voice but at first couldn't understand his words over the din of the firefight all around her. Turning toward the main road she then saw Sergeant Rivera lying on the road in the distance. It was then that she heard Mike's report that Rivera, Mack, and Haynes had all been hit.

Relaying the news to squad leader Nein, Pullen fired up her Humvee and drove it back about one hundred meters to get as close as she dared before dismounting and sprinting some 90 meters more— roughly the length of a football field—to reach Rivera. She applied pressure to his wound as he screamed in agony. She talked to him calmly and comforted him. "Keep thinking of your son," she pleaded, desperately trying to keep him from sinking deeper into shock.

By this time convoy escorts who had been focused on casualty evacuation and moving the convoys out of the kill zone had heard Nein's radio calls for assistance. Responding immediately, surviving trucks from Stallion 33 and Regulator 3 raced over to help assist Raven 42's wounded.

Nein had been calling over and over again for air support but now recognized there was a real possibility that his entire squad would be overrun before such help arrived. Although most insurgents had been eliminated from the fields and buildings around them, at least four more were down in the trench on the north side of the road—and they had the capacity and intent to kill them all. *We need to go on the super offensive,* he realized. *We need to start going into the canal system; we need to charge these guys.*

He jumped into the trench with Hester hot on his heels, while Morris covered them from above and simultaneously monitored the civilian getaway vehicles to ensure that insurgents wouldn't have a chance to escape. Nein and Hester advanced down the trenchline in ten-meter rushes, firing their M-4s and throwing grenades as they went.

After Nein and Hester disappeared into the trench the gunner, Cooper, began to systematically destroy the enemy getaway vehicles, making it impossible for them to escape. He demolished all that were within his line of sight, yet knew there were more that he could not see from his current position. He suddenly realized that his damaged vehicle's engine was still running. He jumped down and moved the vehicle closer up the dangerous road until he could get a clear field of fire. When his truck died in an explosion of oil, he remounted the turret, took the remaining enemy cars and SUVs under fire and destroyed them. Now the enemy was trapped on the battlefield.

The Stallion and Regulator teams assisting medic Mike with the wounded then opened fire on the field as well as the trench line, and with Nein and Hester continuing their advance toward the main road, they pinched in and eliminated the remaining insurgents. Mike then saw Nein and Hester and yelled, "Cease fire! Cease fire!"

It was at that moment that one last insurgent appeared out of nowhere and sprayed an entire magazine at Nein and Hester. Shooting from the hip thankfully spoiled his aim and, shocked but uninjured, they promptly shot him dead.

After forty-five minutes of hell the battle was finally over. More assistance arrived on scene from the 617th Company and a Marine quick reaction force. The wounded were treated and medical evacuation helicopters were called. Air support, now superfluous, finally showed up on station.

At final count twenty-seven enemy fighters lay dead, while seven were captured alive, along with twenty-two AK-47s, six RPGs, sixteen rockets, six machine guns, forty grenades, and a video camera containing footage of the firefight that would have undoubtedly been used as a recruiting tool on jihadist websites.[7] No American soldiers were killed, although Rivera lost a kidney.[8] The others recovered over time.

For gallantry in action Nein, Hester, and Mike were awarded the Silver Star. Nein's award was later upgraded to the Distinguished Service Cross. Leigh Ann Hester became the first woman since World War II to be awarded the Silver Star and the first in history for actions in combat. Others in the squad, including Pullen, received Bronze Stars with V device, and Army Commendation Medals with V device. Several received Purple Hearts for being wounded that day.

Hester, in a later interview, acknowledged that she thinks of the incident almost every day and sometimes gets through a night without dreaming about it. But she notes that these memories come with the job.

Despite the media attention given to Hester and Pullen, their commander, Captain Todd Lindner, knew the score. MP women had been in combat for a long time. "They shouldn't be held up as showpieces for why there should be women in combat," he commented. "They should be held up as examples of why it's irrelevant."[9]

Later, remarking on the way his squad had responded to the complex ambush, Nein just grinned. "We're infantry with badges," he said.[10]

14

DEPLOYMENT CYCLES

It had been a long haul for Dave Phillips and his family, but he finally brought his 89th MP Brigade home from Iraq in December 2004. He was tagged to be the provost marshal for Central Command in Tampa, Florida, and both he and Dawn were excited about the upcoming move.

The reception at Fort Hood for the returning soldiers was bedlam. The place was packed with happy people. A DJ blared music and was flashing lights and pumping "fog" from a machine to give the place a disco air. "We could hardly see any of the families," Phillips remembers, "because the DJ couldn't make the damned fog machine stop. That part was disappointing." It was 0400 in the morning. Despite jet lag, exhaustion, and the early morning wakeup, everyone was tremendously excited: The brigade was home at last!

Dawn rushed down to meet Dave on the floor. They were grinning and hugging each other after a too-long separation. There was a lot to get caught up on. Abruptly, out of the artificial fog, the provost marshal general, Major General Don Ryder, came up behind them. He had flown down from the Pentagon for the brigade's homecoming earlier that day. Ryder welcomed Dave then said with seriousness not usual for the occasion, "I really need to see you later this morning before I fly out."

Damn, thought Phillips. *This can't be good news.* Over the noise,

Dawn, who had overheard the exchange, whispered in his ear. "Why do you need to see him this morning? You just got home." Phillips whispered back, with a touch of bitterness, "Sounds like we're not going to Florida anymore." There was little they could do, so they just stood on the crowded floor and continued to hold each other.

After too few hours at home, Phillips slipped into a fresh uniform and drove over to the MP station. He had hugged the kids, caught a nap, showered and shaved, but was still fighting the kind of bone-weariness that is endemic to military troop movements. First the emotional letdown of being out of combat and free of immediate danger, then the endless tedium and nit-picking of getting more than a thousand men and women and their tons of equipment loaded onto cramped, cold aircraft. Top that off with multiple hours of troubled half-sleep on the plane. Then repeat the process after landing to make sure everyone gets organized, all weapons and sensitive gear are accounted for, and nobody is lost in the process. He was, in a word, mentally and physically fried.

Ryder was happy to see him and very cordial, but he brought the kind of mixed news message that Phillips dreaded. Ryder wanted Dave to come up to Washington and be his deputy commanding officer for the Army's Criminal Investigation Command (CID). It is a great honor to get these kinds of by-name requests from senior officers. But the request also wiped off the books in a single stroke what the Phillips family had thought of as a welcome dream assignment. "I was so worn out and tired, I don't recall my exact words," Phillips remembered. It didn't matter. They were on the way back to Washington.

But not right away. Not until June 2005 did Army Chief of Staff Peter Schoomaker reluctantly release his replacement-designate, Colonel Mike Galloucis, to take over the brigade.

The change of command ceremony was a moment of mixed emotions for Phillips and his family. Having run the 89th for an unheard of thirty-six months—three full years including an intense combat deployment—Phillips estimates that he may have set an MP Corps record for length of service as a brigade commander. For exemplary service in Iraq during 2004–2005 the 89th MP Brigade was awarded the Meritorious Unit Citation.

Dawn Phillips carried much of the weight of these ripples from the combat pool. Even though she didn't wear the silver eagles of command, she readily accepted the unwritten responsibilities and burdens that come with being the commander's wife and senior spouse in the unit. She and Dave had walked side by side during his entire military career. Not that it started all wine and roses. Having dated from junior high school, the Cleveland, Ohio, couple attended college together. Financially Dawn was struggling. Her parents had died young and left her in a tough position to meet tuition and costs. Dave and Dawn got married on June 17, 1978, when they were both sophomores.

There are some few soldiers for whom a combat tour seriously messes up their heads. Thankfully they are few but their impact is large, and for a small family, overwhelming. Alcohol issues predominate. After months of enforced abstention, the impulse to get dead drunk on return seems irresistible. Most will binge out once or twice then get over it. For a few others, the lure is too great, the drinking becomes habitual, and alcohol is a problem.

Other issues associated with difficulty in adjusting from a combat deployment—spousal abuse, depression, wild spending sprees, and blinding, unpredictable rages of anger—are typically problems that will end up in the laps of commanders' spouses who are involved. Dawn Phillips, who had committed herself to the role of taking care of the stay-behinds, was involved to her eyeballs.

Even soldiers who don't exhibit the most extreme symptoms of combat stress are affected. Loud noises startle them. They feel defenseless—remember, they have carried a weapon close at their sides for more than a year. Now they are unarmed. Their heads are on swivels, eyes constantly watching for the IED or hidden ambush site, ears continually alert for the sound of incoming rockets or mortars. They are terribly impatient, particularly with those who don't have the sense of urgency that combat imposes on every action, however small. That impatience translates into abrupt actions with spouses and children and frays the fibers that bind families together.

When these spouses—primarily young wives with little life experience—are unable to cope with the stress brought home by their husbands, they have options. The military services provide medical and mental health professionals to assist, and for the religious, chaplains are available. But often the first port in the storm is the commander's wife. Understand, not all commander's wives perform this role. Some remain a bit aloof, others dip a toe. But Dawn Phillips was all-in with what she perceived as her immutable duty to soldiers and their wives.

The danger in such a commitment is that for the weak of spirit it can be erosive to their own psychological health. Dawn waded into the situation full-bore, dismissing her own stresses as irrelevant to the accomplishment of her goals: to take care of soldiers and their families at home just as her husband was caring for them while they were off in harm's way.

Dave Phillips recognized this exemplary trait in his wife and appreciated it greatly. Through the informal officer-NCO grapevine he listened to many stories about how this soldier or that, this wife or family, were comforted and assisted by his wife. His gratitude was deep and sincere.

So that day in June, when the flag of command would finally be passed to a worthy successor, Dave and Dawn entered the large Fort Hood gymnasium along with their three children, Noelle, Sarah, and Daniel. Everybody attended: soldiers, staff, families, and visitors. This was the culmination of what for many officers is the high point of their careers. Torn with conflicting emotions, Phillips made his outgoing comments to a group that had become in many aspects part of his extended family. And he blew it.

"I really, really screwed up," Phillips recollected. "In all the excitement and action, with all the stuff going on inside me, I forgot to thank my wife and kids for the support they gave me for those long, often dangerous three years in the saddle." He knew his omission, as understandable as it was in all the tumult of the occasion, was only human. He also knew that because of his distraction he inadvertently caused them great hurt. His sense of regret was profound. "It causes me great angst and pain to this day."

Turning the sad experience to a positive, he noted, "It was a changing point for me that helped me really focus on what was important in my life: my family."

So though the formal occasion has passed, this may be a good time for Americans to thank military wives and families, especially those like Dawn Phillips and Melissa Quantock who voluntarily accept the mantle of responsibility for those who the system generally ignores or brushes aside. Their dedication to soldiers and their families is exemplary and serves as a model for what the institution ought to do but doesn't. We all owe a deep debt of gratitude to women like Dawn and Melissa who, as the poet John Milton described, "also serve who only stand and wait."

By April 2005 Sergeant Henry Stearns and other MPs had become a bit cynical. They didn't need to watch the large cable news TV screens in the dining facility to know that their AO was heating up. "We were constantly getting attacked," Stearns remembered. "Mostly from IEDs. That was the big casualty-producer."

In fact they had become somewhat contemptuous of the Iraqi insurgents as fighting men. Long firefights were rare. Most of the time snipers took shots at exposed soldiers, particularly when dismounted or exposed in turrets. Other times a bomb would blow, the insurgents would empty a magazine on full auto without aiming—what soldiers call "spray and pray"—then flee the scene before MPs wiped them out. On the down side, the insurgents were becoming extremely inventive, imaginative, and proficient with IEDs.

The emerging generation of explosive devices was considerably more technologically savvy and sophisticated than what soldiers had previously encountered. Insurgents could detonate IEDs remotely by cell phone or buried wires, and were proficient at innovative ways to disguise mines. They tried new tricks like burying smaller antipersonnel mines around the main device to kill or wound explosive ordnance personnel who tried to defuse it, and placing secondary or tertiary devices nearby so that rescue vehicles would be blown up, too. These guys were getting good. Way too good, in Stearns's opinion, because they were killing his soldiers.

It was those terrible IEDs that were giving Stearns and soldiers from the 504th MP Battalion fits. By April 2005 they had been deployed to Iraq almost six months. The learning curve had been steep and bloody. And things were about to get worse.

On a routine route patrol on April 17, an IED blew up under a truck. One of the most popular soldiers in the battalion was critically injured. Private First Class Sam Huff, a bright, cheerful young woman from Tucson, Arizona, lay battered and bleeding beside the dirt road. As the medics worked frantically, assisted by MP soldiers trained in combat lifesaving skills, the squad leader worked the radio. "We need an air casualty evacuation," he called. The squad was stunned by the cold reply. "Negative. Your casualty is not high enough priority. Proceed to ground evac."

"Maybe it was all a big misunderstanding," Stearns remembered, as he morosely fingered the remembrance bracelet on his left wrist. The bracelet has the inscribed names of the soldiers lost in his unit. "But because it took us so much time to get her out and to a hospital it turned out to be too late." On the following day, April 18, Private First Class Sam Huff died of her wounds.

The weather on August 20 was typical brutal Iraqi summer: steaming hot with blowing dust from the western deserts. Sergeant Willard Partridge, a career soldier from Ferriday, Louisiana, was driving with his squad in Anbar Province on a rescue mission. They had picked up a frantic radio call from another squad from the 504th MP Battalion that they had been hit by an IED. Partridge and his buddies floorboarded the accelerators on their Humvees. As they closed on the halted vehicles, Partridge's truck momentarily disappeared in a blast of dirty, black smoke and debris. It had triggered a secondary IED specifically placed to blow up anyone coming to help.

The IED had detonated under the driver's side. Partridge fought to steer his Humvee to avoid running over his fellow MPs. "Hit the brakes!" the truck commander beside him yelled. "I can't," Partridge shouted back. "I've lost both my legs!" Fighting desperately to keep the vehicle under control despite intense pain, shock, and blood loss, Partridge gripped the wheel and steered his Humvee off the road safely. His concentration and focused effort kept it from overturning and averted collision with other trucks. Thanks to his dedication no other soldiers were injured.

Medics worked on him and a helicopter took him to the major military hospital in the Green Zone. When he arrived he was unconscious from massive lower body trauma and blood loss.

His platoon sergeant, Henry Stearns, raced to the hospital in the Green Zone to see him, but Partridge was deep in a coma from which he would never wake. Stearns leaned over and spoke softly to his dying soldier. Willard Partridge became one more name on the remembrance bracelet Stearns wears constantly.[1]

With great fanfare, the new Iraqi government in August announced that Saddam Hussein's trial would begin on October 19, 2005. They wanted to show off the new judicial system in a big way and ordered construction of a special venue in which the trial would be held. While not a "show trial" in the sense that it was rigged, the proceeding was designed to display to the world that the dictator was out of power and that true justice could be achieved in the new Iraq. Work on the project proceeded apace.

Meanwhile, Captain Sam Harvill had his own problems. As operations officer of Task Force 134, the unit responsible for all detainee operations in Iraq, Harvill was told to make sure the trial venue was suitable. That was fine, but by the time he got the order, the place was ready to open and the Iraqis were reluctant to let him or anyone not directly associated with the process enter, supposedly for security reasons.

"If something goes wrong, it's your ass, Harvill!" Those words from his boss were sufficient motivation. He was aware the eyes of the world would be focused on that venue and that if anyone up the long food chain above him that ran from Baghdad to the White House was upset by a deficiency real or imagined, the resultant anger, like the proverbial ball of shit, would roll downhill to "plop" on Sam Harvill's head.

"We gotta get a team in there," Harvill told his operations sergeant. So on the morning that the trial would begin Harvill pulled up to the venue with a scratch crew of fellow MPs to do what they could. Already press, lawyers, witnesses, and anyone who could cadge a seat crowded the small venue. "It hadn't even started and the place was bulging at the seams." In fact, as the team soon discovered, this was literally true.

The design included a mezzanine-balcony that overlooked the floor of the wider audience and court. People had crammed their way into the space until it was overloaded far above rated capacity. "The floor was actually bowing in front of us," Harvill remembered. Horrified, imagining what chaos would result if the structure collapsed from the weight, Harvill and his people frantically came up with a solution: "Grab some four-by-fours," someone suggested. "We'll wedge them in here to prop the balcony up."

Scrambling to make it happen, MPs scrounged lumber from a nearby pile of unused construction material and began hammering long makeshift beams into place, bracing the sagging mezzanine. "We were able to do it while everyone continued to wander around. Some of those idiots were still fighting up the stairs to get a spot even though they saw us sweating out the balcony below. It was just lunacy." But the balcony held, the trial began, and until now, the world was not wiser.

"We got a tip through an Iraqi source of the location of one of Saddam's mass graves. Your guys are gonna go out there and find it. Take the Iraqi Police colonel with you." So much for Thanksgiving dinner at the DFAC, thought Stearns. It was November 24, 2005, and his unit had less than eight weeks left in Iraq before scheduled redeployment back to Fort Lewis.

The convoy rolled out of their west Baghdad base into the Triangle of Death, headed for a spot that was adjacent to an irrigation canal. The Iraqi Police commander and the interpreter rode in one of the lead Humvees, driven by Specialist Marc Delgado and commanded by the squad leader, Staff Sergeant Steven Reynolds. The gunner was a nineteen-year-old woman, Private First Class Marissa Strock, an Upstate New York native who had joined the unit in April 2006.

As the unit pushed slowly alongside the canal looking for the burial site, a massive IED detonated under Sergeant Reynolds's truck. The force of the explosion killed Reynolds, Delgado, and the Iraqi colonel outright, sending their bodies into the air and scattering them on the other side of the canal. The interpreter was thrown from the vehicle into the canal where, barely conscious, he clung to wreckage to keep his head above the rancid water. When soldiers got to Strock they found her alive, but barely.

She had suffered serious head and body injuries. Both legs were mangled, her skull appeared to be fractured, and her breathing was shallow and labored. She had puncture wounds in her abdomen and back. Frantically, the team called for priority one emergency medevac.

Meanwhile soldiers swam out into the fetid canal to rescue the interpreter, who was in shock. "They had to punch his hand and arm to get him to release the wreckage he clung to desperately," Stearns recounted. "It was that or let him drown."

Soldiers crawled in the weeds to stay low while they searched for bodies and pieces. "Ammunition for the destroyed truck was scattered all over the place," Stearns said. "They were incredibly brave because that stuff was 'cooking off' all over the field and rounds were exploding randomly. Any of them could have been hit."

Strock was successfully medevaced to Baghdad, where her left foot was amputated. Given the serious nature of her wounds she was immediately evacuated to Landstuhl hospital in Germany, where eventually both legs were amputated and she was treated for a lacerated liver, traumatic brain injury, and bruised lungs. Deep in a coma, she was subsequently transported to Walter Reed Army Hospital for advanced care.

After months of rehabilitation Strock accepted medical retirement. She spent months learning to work with her double prosthesis.

Just more than one year later, in September 2006, the guest speaker at the Military Police Ball at Fort Lewis was Marissa Strock. To a highly emotional standing ovation she walked out on stage—unassisted for the first time on her new legs—to deliver her speech.

"If I could," Strock said, "I'd go back in a heartbeat to hunt down the terrorist bastard who killed my friends."

15

THE FORGOTTEN THEATER

When Staff Sergeant Gary Watford landed in Afghanistan in summer 2006 he was a bit surprised to find that he was appointed to lead General Karl Eikenberry's personal security detachment. A PSD assignment brings soldiers into closer contact with high-ranking persons than is usual, thereby offering chances both of grand success and spectacular failure—either of which the soldier is painfully aware will be performed under a glaring spotlight.

In March, President George W. Bush made a surprise official visit to Afghanistan's president, Hamid Karzai. As commander of the International Security Assistance Forces (ISAF), Eikenberry was expected to be a major player at the meeting, along with U.S. Ambassador Ronald Neumann.

Because Eikenberry visited the presidential palace even more than the ambassador, it made good sense that his security detail would be in charge of the planning, liaison, and execution of Bush's visit. Karzai's palace was a complex of multiple series of concentric walls, with a gate to the driveway that separated a soccer field and an open area, then a heavy inner automatic lift gate, and corresponding layers of security. While having a cooperative relationship with the inner circle of the guard force (who operated strictly by the book; Afghan nationals trained by Blackwater), Watford was frequently aggravated by their pompous, arrogant behavior, summarized by his opinion that "they acted like a bunch of assholes."

Nor was he particularly impressed by similar attitudes from White House security. Watford had painstakingly planned the entire operation—in constant liaison with Karzai's counterpart staff—and had furnished the Secret Service with detailed schematics of the two separate helicopter landing sites (the soccer field for staffers and security, and the open area for President Bush), and specific routes to be taken: driving ISAF-supplied security vehicles preparked alongside the soccer field landing site across the driveway to meet Bush's helicopter, then back to the driveway to enter the inner gate), and the need to have an *exact* count of vehicles that would enter the inner sanctum.

On the day of the visit, security party helicopters landed in a blinding cloud of dust on the soccer field as planned. The sparkling clean, shiny SUVs, standing ready with doors open, were inundated by choking dust. Then the Secret Service agents leaped onto the field, dove into the prepositioned heavily armored Ford Expeditions, and instead of swinging to the back of the building to pick up the president, headed directly for the inner security gate.

Afghan presidential guards were unimpressed. The gate remained closed.

Watford politely walked up to the vehicle and tapped on the window to point out the error. No answer. Through the bulletproof glass he could see the driver staring at the gate operator in frustration and talking to his fellow agents. But the agent wouldn't open the door for further instructions. A long minute passed. Watford repeatedly tried again, pointing at the open field at the right and shaking his head while looking toward the gate. No acknowledgement from the president's best.

Finally the driver flung open his door. "Why won't they let us through?" demanded an agent.

"Don't you think you ought to pick up the president first?" Watford asked dryly.

"Christ, isn't he in there? Where is he?" asked a now-panicked agent.

"Follow the friggin' schematic I drew for you and briefed you on and pick him up behind those buildings." Watford pointed, adding, "He's probably waitin' on you fellows."

With a roar they zipped off to collect the POTUS, then returned, except that an additional few vehicles—including General Eikenberry's in the number five spot—had been peremptorily added to the convoy.

Watford watched and counted as the agreed number of four vehicles buzzed through the gate. He was not surprised when the guard force abruptly closed the gate in front of the fifth vehicle. "If we told them four and added one at the last minute, then *bam*, down would slam the gate after the fourth vehicle. They didn't care."

Out popped Eikenberry, who waved casually to the Afghan guard, who knew him well and gestured him through the walking gate. Almost immediately after Eikenberry disappeared through the gate, a large individual dressed in American civilian outdoor wear, sporting a full black beard, and carrying a submachine gun approached Watford, who incidentally was the only soldier present.

"We've gotta get in there," the large man told Watford.

"Who are you?"

"I'm a Navy SEAL, and we think the president is going to be assassinated."

"What makes you think that?" Watford asked, stunned.

"They won't let us through the gate."

Watford tried in vain to explain the ironclad gate policy to the SEAL. Meanwhile, from the corner of his eye he watched guards from Eikenberry's and other cars quietly get out, walk off, and magically disappear. One minute they were there, the next, gone. Where in the hell did those guys go? he wondered.

"Okay," the SEAL continued to an increasingly incredulous Watford. "You're gonna kill this guy." The SEAL gestured to the Afghan guard who stood about five feet distant and had been smiling and nodding throughout the episode, devoid of an understanding of English.

"*I'm* going to kill him?" Watford asked, realizing that this had turned into a black comic opera. "Uh, what about those two guys up there with the RPK machine guns? The ones who're already pointing their weapons at us, and will stay trained on me as soon as you walk away from the gate?"

"Don't worry about them, we'll take care of them," the SEAL said. With a half smile he discreetly gestured toward the guard. "You kill him; then we'll break in."

"What about me? I'm the only soldier here. Will your guys shoot me by accident?"

"Don't think so," the SEAL reassured him. "Just kill that guy."

Watford shot a glance at the guard, who was smiling contentedly at them, oblivious to his imminent demise.

After a minute the SEAL faded away. Watford thought for a moment, then decided. Okay, guess I've gotta kill this guy. He casually brought his small submachine gun from around his back and cradled it in his arms folded across his chest, all the time flashing a big grin at the now-puzzled Afghan guard. Then he reached over and flipped the switch to "fire."

At that moment the guard, suddenly realizing something was amiss, decided to seek refuge behind the security barrier and promptly disappeared. Watford sneaked a look up at the two guards above his head on the wall, both of whom had RPK machine guns pointed directly at him.

Ah, shit, he thought. *It's gonna be one of those kinda days.*

For the next three hours he stood there alone—"I'm the only Joe in American uniform anywhere in the yard"—wondered where the disappeared SEALs were, and contemplated the fact that he might soon be dead while two presidents played Xbox games together inside, or whatever the hell they were doing in there.

Finally the presidential party roared out of the gate, the SEALs emerged from hiding places, Eikenberry walked out and motioned for him to come over. "Let's get going, Sergeant."

"Roger that, sir," Watford replied, casually slinging his submachine gun over his back.

Another day of fun and games in downtown Kabul.

●　　●　　●

For a lot of soldiers, Afghanistan only comes in two flavors: straight up or straight down. "You can't believe the terrain we rolled along in Afghanistan," Captain Cassandra Facciponti remembered, thinking about some of the missions they ran in Afghanistan. During her year-long tour she took her platoon through "unbelievable terrain." Route security topped the mission requirements on that deployment. Given that virtually every stretch of road is a potential ambush alley, and that drivers were usually civilians who did not have the capability of defending themselves, it was vitally important that MPs showed up to protect coalition supply convoys.

The passable roads are few, narrow, in horrible condition, and as familiar to Taliban as the AK-47 clutched in their fists. In Afghanistan it isn't the old joke "you can't get there from here," but rather, "you might get blown up or killed trying to get there."

The Taliban and independent "warlords" have enough historical knowledge and are sufficiently savvy about strategic terrain and modern logistics to recognize that the Khyber Pass, the K-G Pass, and other chokepoints are critical for the survival of U.S. and coalition forces. Counterinsurgency theories, winning hearts and minds, these are all valid tactics but, without the supplies necessary to carry them out, they may be impossible to implement over the long haul.

"Amateurs talk about tactics, but professionals study logistics," former Marine Corps Commandant General Robert H. Barrow said in 1980. Since World War II, route security and rear-area security missions have fallen primarily on a single branch of the Army: the Military Police Corps. In this fight, too, that fact has not changed. Want the supply routes kept open? Call the MPs.

In the Afghan back country, roads quickly become camel caravan tracks and goat trails. The Polo brothers would be familiar with the routes. "One time we were on a dirt trail in the mountains that kept getting narrower and narrower," Facciponti remembered. She got concerned. "Stop the truck," she ordered her driver, thinking she'd better make a visual check. "I opened my door. Our wheels were right on the edge of the cliff. I was looking at a thousand-foot drop just below my boots dangling out of the door. How we missed rolling off that cliff I'll never know. A skilled driver and good luck, I guess."

For much of her Afghanistan combat tour Facciponti's unit was based out of Bagram, pulling force protection duty for the large detention facility as well as local route security missions. On July 12, 2005, four terrorists made a daring escape from the Bagram Collection Point. All four were foreigner fighters, al-Qaeda hard men, from Syria, Libya, Kuwait, and Saudi Arabia. More disturbing, the Kuwaiti, Omar Al-Faruq, who was using one of his numerous aliases, "Mahmoud Ahmad Muhammed," while in prison, was in fact the planner for the notorious Bali bombing of October 12, 2002, in which more than two hundred people were killed. Bali had been the worst case of terrorism in Indonesia's history. When they were belatedly informed of his escape, Jakarta authorities were incensed. This was yet another highly embarrassing issue for MPs in the same year as the release of the investigatory report on detainee abuse from 2002 that led to several courts-martial for essentially beating two detainees to death.

Exacerbating the humiliating escape were the circumstances surrounding it. Facciponti, who was there when the escape occurred, noted with some sarcasm, "Imagine four guys in orange jumpsuits making it through the wire and then disappearing into a crowd. They'd stand out, right?

"Well, there were always lots of kids in the adjacent field playing soccer. And for some reason that day they all showed up in bright orange T-shirts. So it was easy for the bad guys to disappear into the crush of the crowd. We thought at the time it was an inside job."

In late spring, Phillips, still at Fort Belvoir working for Criminal Investigation Division, was asked by his boss General Ryder for a favor.

"Dave, would you call Colonel James Harrison and ask him to reconsider his decision to retire?" Ryder explained his unusual request. "We've got issues out in Afghanistan with the Afghani corrections program. Jim recently commanded the Disciplinary Barracks at Fort Leavenworth. He's one of our most experienced MPs and we need him badly to deploy out there and take charge of the overall program and square it away."

Harrison, tall, grizzled, with short-cropped, graying hair, was a dedicated soldier. After Phillips explained the request—"no one else is as qualified and the Regiment needs you"—Harrison voluntarily pulled his request for retirement and packed his rucksack. He was headed to Bagram.

In September 2006 Colonel Harrison flew into Guantánamo Bay to call on Admiral Harry Harris, commander of the joint task force. By now Harrison was in full command of the detainee operations in Afghanistan, based out of Bagram. He was essentially on a fact-finding trip, trying to find what the "best practices" were that worked in Guantánamo and which of them might be transferable to the considerably larger facility at Bagram.

He spent two weeks on the island, working with Colonel Wade Dennis and others at the detention group, exchanging information. "I'm headed back to see my wife for a short visit in Kansas," he noted. "Then back to Afghanistan."

Sergeant Willie Bowman was now back in Iraq, scarred neck and all. His unit had replaced the MPs guarding Griffin Rock at Camp Cropper, which housed Saddam Hussein and a coterie of seven additional top former Iraqi war criminals including Tariq Aziz and Ali Hassan al-Majid, aka Chemical Ali.

As were many who were proximate to Saddam, Bowman was stunned by the former dictator's absolute composure. "He was always in control. Absolute control. He never, ever showed fear of any kind. That man could walk into a room and control the place with just his eyes. I can see why the guy was able to take over a whole country."

Late in the year, when the trial, appeal, and judicial proceedings were completed and the outcome of execution known to all, Saddam never wavered. "Even when he walked up to the gallows, the man still intimidated everyone in the room," Bowman recalled. "It was an amazing performance. Here he was about to be hung, surrounded by enemies who wanted him dead, and still scared the hell out of everybody."

Bowman was disgusted at the behavior of the Iraqis after the gallows sprung. "They were like a much of immature jerks, shouting at him and calling him names. None of them had the balls to do it while he was alive, but seeing him hanging there gave them all kinds of fake courage."

16

BETRAYAL IN KARBALA

In the year 680 AD the Prophet Muhammad's second grandson—Imam Hussein—was brutally murdered along with seventy-two of his followers and family members in the desert just outside what is now the Holy Shi'a City of Karbala, some fifty miles south of Baghdad. The assassination was carried out by an army intent on preventing Hussein from challenging the caliphate, the foundation of Sunni rule. That massacre caused the original split between the Sunni and Shi'a tribes.

Now millions of Shi'a followers from across Iraq and Iran commemorate the fortieth day after the anniversary of Hussein's death by making a pilgrimage to Karbala, home to over nearly a half million regular residents, during the annual festivals of Ashura. Saddam Hussein's Sunni regime had banned the celebrations for several decades, yet in 2004 after his fall from power an estimated two million Shi'as resumed the pilgrimage.[1]

Shi'a followers often slash themselves with knives or swords and let their blood run freely to show their sorrow their inability to save Imam Hussein over 1,300 years ago, a practice sensationalized by the world media, eager to show photographs of parents slicing the heads of small children and even infants.

The religious significance of Ashura and truly enormous crowds of Shi'a worshipers are unfortunately very tempting targets to Sunni militants, and each January there are very deadly attacks on Shi'a around the world.

When festivities in Karbala first resumed in 2004, at least five explosions killed an estimated 112 Shi'a (hospital officials weren't entirely sure, since the bodies were so dismembered that it was difficult for them to determine the exact count) and wounded another 220.[2] Blood-stained worshipers who had already beaten and slashed themselves in remembrance of the Prophet's second grandson rushed to donate blood to the injured.[3] A year later security was tightened to the point where bombers shifted their attention to other holy cities in Iraq, although in January 2006 the deadly attacks commenced when a suicide bomber killed 60 Shi'a and injured more than 100 more outside the sacred Imam Hussein Shrine.[4]

One might conclude that what started with the murder of Imam Hussein in ancient times has remained a tradition of betrayal, murder, and massacres.

In January 2007, Sergeant First Class Michael King of the 127th MP Company, 3rd Platoon (Wolfpack) based out of Germany, was deployed to FOB Iskan in Iraq. He had no idea about Karbala's bloody history and hadn't heard that some four million pilgrims from across the Middle East were already heading for the Holy City.

In-country for just two months so far, King had other things on his mind. The thirty-one-year-old platoon sergeant held his children close to his heart in the form of a tattoo portraying three little horned monsters. It hadn't been too long ago that King himself had closely resembled the mischievous "You'll shoot your eye out!" Ralphie of *A Christmas Story* fame, although he'd finally ditched his oversized glasses after PRK surgery less than a year before. A talented artist known best for his witty sarcasm and blunt leadership style, he purposely shoved aside thoughts of home to fully focus on the Wolfpack and their police transition team assignment at the Karbala Provincial Joint Coordination Center.

Every other week King or his platoon leader would lead just over a dozen MPs on the harrowing four-hour drive to Karbala, where they worked mentoring the Iraqi Police for an average of seven-day shifts before returning to FOB Iskan.

The soldiers of Wolfpack always dreaded the trip. There were only two ways to get there from FOB Iskan. The main route took them past an old Republican Guard Ammunition Supply Point, which had been informally converted into a jihadist flea market for explosives and other IED supplies. The alternate route, through the canal system, meant driving with water deep enough to engulf a Humvee on one side and steep six- to eight-foot drop-offs on the other with not enough room to turn around. If something blew up in front, the only retreat option available was to have the whole convoy back up for long distances.

Yet what bothered King and many members of the Wolfpack most was the Karbala Provincial Joint Coordination Center (KPJCC) itself and the main Provincial Police Headquarters (PPHQ) building within it. The compound was roughly two city blocks in size, smack dab in the middle of a busy neighborhood, and guarded primarily by Iraqi Police, along with only nineteen or twenty MPs, plus another dozen or so soldiers from the 377th Parachute Field Artillery Regiment (PFAR) typically rotated in and out during weeklong shifts there—too few to properly secure the compound. The compound that they only half-jokingly called the Alamo was simply too far away from any U.S. FOBs, COPs, or other coalition friendlies to provide any level of assurance.

There were other reasons to remain uncomfortable and hyper-aware of their surroundings. Unlike many other instances where MP units had forged effective working partnerships and even solid friendships with their Iraqi counterparts elsewhere, the IPs in Karbala remained suspicious and stiff toward all U.S. soldiers assigned to their PPHQ. Despite all their sincere efforts to reach out to the IPs, the atmosphere remained strained and was growing tenser by the week for reasons that the Wolfpack MPs could not fathom.

Nonetheless, there were a few perks and positive aspects. The Internet connections at the Karbala PPHQ were perhaps among the best in Iraq, allowing the soldiers to have frequent contact on mostly reliable connections with their families back in Germany and the United

States during their limited hours of down time. The MP ready room on the second floor of the police station had overstuffed couches and easy chairs and nearly a clubhouse atmosphere, despite all the weapons and antitank missiles within easy reach.

A friendly local Iraqi teenager who they called Mike Jonez would bring them fresh bread and red, white, and blue cans labeled KARBALA COLA from the city, and many of the Wolfpack MPs enjoyed helping him brush up on his English language skills. There were card games of Spades, and the soldiers were very pleased over the almost finished, newly installed Western-style toilet, sink, and shower (only one of each, yet it would be much better than sharing a single hole in the floor) inside the otherwise dilapidated building.

Most of all, the soldiers of the 127th MP Company and 377th PFAR knew they could rely on each other, with the alienation by the IPs and otherwise tense atmosphere of KPJCC only driving them all closer together.

The MPs included some real characters, including Staff Sergeant Jesse Hernandez, one of King's team leaders and best friends. Their families lived in the same building back in Germany and their young children played together regularly. Recognizing his natural professionalism, staunch dedication to each one of their soldiers, and ability to not only listen but instantly apply all lessons learned, King thought of Hernandez as one of the most reliable and talented NCOs he'd ever worked with. Sergeant Gregory Betkijian was another top-performing Wolfpack team leader, wiry Staff Sergeant Travis Wyrick a dependable although sometimes stonefaced squad leader, and King's driver, Specialist Daniel Lyon, pretty much served as his right-hand man.

As for their platoon leader, First Lieutenant Nathan Diaz, King felt like they might as well have been married for all their hours working side by side or in tandem while staying in nearly constant communications around the clock. Unlike King, Diaz had spent some of his personal time reading about Ashura and was thus vaguely aware that it was an important Shi'a festival. Regardless, their regular briefings as given by the S-2 intelligence shop—the real pros, who were charged with alerting them to any possible threat—never raised the issue, so Diaz gave it little more thought.

On Sunday, January 14, 2007, King, Diaz, and seventeen of their MPs returned to Karbala for another weeklong shift alongside a dozen PFAR soldiers, led by twenty-five-year-old Lieutenant Jacob Fritz.

Taking up guard positions at the front gate, back gate, on the roof, and just outside the entrance of the police headquarters building, the Americans got the eerie feeling that the Iraqis inside the compound posed more of a threat than the people in the streets outside. The situation morphed from tense to openly ugly that evening when two of the MPs guarding the back gate of the compound were approached by an Iraqi Police officer who announced, "U.S.A. bad, Iraq good" and threw bread at them. Another pounded his fist into his palm while sneering, "Tomorrow. Tomorrow."

King and Diaz stepped up security inside the compound with random dismounted patrols, instructing the MPs to be on the lookout for any suspicious objects or behavior. They also met with the IP colonel in charge to express concerns regarding the obviously deteriorating IP attitudes. The colonel in turn confronted the Iraqi Police who had threatened the MP guards, but they laughed it off while claiming they had just been joking around.

A couple of days later PFAR's platoon sergeant, Sergeant First Class Sean Bennett, pulled King aside to tell him that he had the feeling that something very bad was about to happen. Yet there was little they could do about their suspicions, other than to continue their police mentoring assignment as best they could while also filing daily situation reports with their commanders, reporting serious unease and a clear need for fortifying their tiny security force at the compound.

That same night King, Betkijian, and Lyon were patrolling on the roof of KPPHQ when they observed a small light moving around an abandoned building outside of the compound, about a block away and—from their vantage point—only partially obscured by a ratty palm tree growing in someone's backyard. The upper floors of the building overlooked their compound. Two and a half years earlier insurgents had opened fire on KPPHQ from that position in an attack quickly thwarted by U.S. Marines who happened to be at KPJCC at the time. Both the Wolfpack and PFAR soldiers had long suspected that the building was still used as a makeshift watch station by insurgents.

Looking through their rifle scopes they could just make out what appeared to be the face of a cell phone moving slowly through the darkness. It was apparent that someone was indeed observing the police headquarters building. And undoubtedly watching them as they watched. They immediately called battalion headquarters at FOB Iskan to report their observations and also alerted the IP commander who was on duty.

The next morning King and Diaz led the IP colonel up the crumbling stairs to the roof. Picking their way around large piles of dirt and construction rubble, concrete blocks, water tanks, and the countless electrical cables that snaked everywhere across the roof, they pointed out exactly where they had seen the apparent cell phone. Since they were not authorized to conduct dismounted patrols outside the compound themselves, the colonel said he would send his own IPs to check the building out. Maybe, maybe not, they thought to themselves.

January 20 was an exciting day for Captain Brian Freeman from the 412th Civil Affairs Battalion, who had come to Karbala not only to carry out his regular duty assignments but also to finalize arrangements for an unofficial personal mission: sending an eleven-year-old local Iraqi boy and his father, Abu Ali, to the United States. The boy desperately needed heart surgery and hospital care that simply weren't available in their own war-torn country. Freeman and his wife Charlotte, who he'd seen only a few weeks before while on leave in California, had been working for many months to compile all the necessary paperwork and medical records. They also had been in regular contact with the Gift of Life International to help raise funds for airfare and many other expenses.

When Abu Ali came to see him at KPPHQ that Saturday, Freeman was able to tell him, with help from an interpreter, that yes, despite daunting odds and multiple bureaucracies, their U.S. visas had been approved! The wonderful news was almost too overwhelming for the desperate father, who could only thank him again and again through the interpreter. Someone fished out a camera and took several pictures of the two men with arms draped over each other's shoulders, capturing the joyous moment that would literally change a young boy's life for the better forever.

That evening, after Abu Ali left, Freeman returned to the office he shared with PFAR Lieutenant Fritz on the first floor of the KPPHQ building, the first room off the hallway just inside the main entrance.

Like the MPs and PFAR soldiers, Freeman was extremely concerned over the security situation and hostilities radiating from the IPs. Only steps away, Specialist Johnathan Chism and Private First Class Shawn Falter were fully armed and standing guard from their Humvee parked just outside the main entrance doors—and to the right of them across the courtyard, a half-dozen PFAR soldiers were lounging in a small barracks building. Other PFAR soldiers and MPs were in the communications room right next door, just on the other side of the wall from Freeman and Fritz. Over a dozen MPs were packed into the ready room on the second floor, while two MPs were manning the compound's back gate from a Humvee equipped with a .50 cal. Yet Freeman had never been able to shake his uneasiness the entire time that he'd been in Iraq, particularly while in Karbala.

King was upstairs in the ready room instant messaging with his wife. It had been a terrible tension-filled week so he was glad that his MPs could relax just a little in these precious few hours of downtime. Specialist Jason Crosby, the platoon's medic, had just come off guard duty and entered the room. At about twenty past six they all heard gunfire outside, yet that wasn't at all unusual, since the locals just outside the walls were always celebrating something by firing off gunshots.

But seconds later, *BOOM,* an explosion rocked the building. The

MPs immediately sprang up, scrambled into their body armor, snatched up their weapons, and poured out the door to race into their assigned defensive positions on the roof.

Yet King and MP team leader Sergeant Shane Warsop instead sprinted to the back stairwell, ran down the stairs, and cautiously opened the rear exit door with only one thing on their minds: to get to the MPs who were guarding the back gate. Not seeing any obvious threat they ran out the door and reached Private First Class Travis Johnson and Dean Wiley while other members of the Wolfpack watched over them from inside the building. They quickly moved the Humvee to block off the back gate as bullets flew all around them. Someone threw some kind of explosive device in their general direction, and then a second one, from the other side of the wall, but luckily their assailants couldn't actually see them and failed to throw hard enough to get the explosives over the wall.

Pussies, King bizarrely thought, while at the same time knowing it was still far too dangerous for the four of them alone to secure the gate or any other parts of the compound by themselves. "Disable the .50 cal!" Warsop barked at Johnson and Wiley. "Then get in the building!" They yanked on the rear plate trigger housing and shoved down hard on it, bending the bolt-supporting rods inside, rendering it useless for any attackers who might capture it.

Knowing that Lieutenant Diaz had taken most of the Wolfpack up to the roof to defend the building, King made an error that could have cost him his life: Upon entering the building he decided to leave Warsop with Johnson, Wiley, and the other MPs and go up there alone—without taking anyone with him.

On the way upstairs King saw, and had to walk past, the IP general, colonel, and several IPs. None of the Iraqi Police seemed even remotely concerned about the chaos, and they certainly weren't doing anything to help secure the building. They were just casually standing around, and at the sight of them King instinctively knew that they represented a serious threat. He didn't say anything to them while hurrying past, now conscious that any one of them might shoot him dead right there on the spot—while knowing he had to warn the rest of the Wolfpack, check on their safety, and find out what was really going on.

It was in the hallway that King then saw a senior IP colonel laughing on his cell phone. Laughing. Their eyes briefly met before the colonel looked away. It was in that instant that King knew—without any remaining doubts—that the IPs had sold them out to the insurgents. He fought the rippling, twisting fury within himself, fought his twitching trigger finger that so wanted to shoot the colonel in his laughing face. Yet there was not a second to spare: He had to focus on getting to his MPs. He crabbed sideways past the colonel, careful not to expose his back.

Upon reaching the roof King checked his MPs and their positions, counting heads and mentally noting who was there. Notably missing was Hernandez, who'd been in the communications room with the PFAR soldiers on the first floor. Hoping to better conceal their positions, Lieutenant Diaz shot out one of the floodlights there on the roof, and King shot out a couple more as well as at least one of the tall streetlights down below on the compound grounds. Now it was so dark that King then tripped on one of the many cables that haphazardly lined the roof, then called out warnings for everyone to watch their step.

Suddenly a huge explosion at the front of the building shot flames, smoke, and assorted Humvee parts up over the second-story roof as the MPs ducked down for cover. Diaz was knocked down flat on his back but wasn't injured.[5] Oddly, King wasn't even startled, instead thinking, *This would be a good time to check on Hernandez and all the PFAR soldiers downstairs.* Within the same minute a second explosion went off about thirty feet from the building. The Wolfpack assumed they were being mortared.

King grabbed one of his team leaders, Sergeant Joshua Taylor, saying that they had to get to the communications room. They left the roof and entered the darkened building to descend down the crumbling narrow staircases while repeatedly shouting, "Coalition Forces!—*Imshee!*" (Meaning "Get away!") The building was filled with acrid smoke and debris.

Upon reaching the first floor they saw PFAR Specialist Johnny

Washburn standing guard in the hallway outside the communications and officers' rooms. At first glance through the smoky gloom it appeared that both doors had been blown off. The lights were out so King and Taylor used flashlights to navigate. King stuck his head into the communications room to ask PFAR Platoon Sergeant Bennett, who was manning the radio, if help was on the way. Bennett replied that he did not know (there had been no reply to his call) but said they needed help from the MPs on the roof right away.

King was turning away, preparing to run and get the MPs off the roof, when he heard a weak unsteady voice coming from the darkness somewhere between him and Bennett. "Sergeant, I'm hurt bad. I need help," Hernandez croaked. For just a millisecond King froze, recognizing the voice while trying to process the enormous pain carried within it, instantly knowing his friend was in a life-or-death situation.

King turned and ran to the stairwell with Taylor hot on his heels. He yelled "*MEDIC! MEDIC!*" as loud as he could, throwing his voice with all his might up the flights of stairs. All 275 pounds of Specialist Crosby must have flown down those stairs, as it seemed that only seconds later the muscular six-foot-two medic raced to his side and King rushed him into the communications room.

They found Hernandez lying on the floor against a stack of cases of MREs with bones sticking out of his shattered left forearm and obviously very serious shrapnel wounds to his abdomen. A pasty gray grimace of pain fell like a shadow across his face. A grenade had exploded inside the room, somebody reported. Crosby had left his medic bag at the casualty collection point in another building, so King whipped out his Chitosan bandage and asked MP team leader Sergeant Joshua Taylor to find more, then started ripping up a stray ACU top into strips for more bandages.

Hernandez asked them to tell his wife that he loved her and to tell his son he was sorry. This struck King with a nearly overwhelming wave of fury at a situation so bad that his ever-reliable, incredibly tough team leader and friend would be reduced to even thinking about giving up. "Get those thoughts right out of your head," he hissed. "You're going to see your wife and son again!"

Bennett still hadn't moved away from the radio although it was clear that he had also been wounded in some way. Bennett suddenly said that the two officers, Captain Freeman and Lieutenant Fritz, weren't in their room next door. They were . . . missing. Their laptops were also gone from their desks, while their body armor remained in their room.

It was then that King and everyone else understood that the missing officers had been kidnapped—although there was no time to immediately deal with that horrific realization when their own positions in the building remained unsecured and while Hernandez and a number of the PFAR soldiers might bleed out without their full attention in the next few minutes.

Lieutenant Diaz and Squad Leader Wyrick had entered the communications room after bringing the rest of the MPs down from the roof, and King asked them to seal the entire building off from the inside since there wasn't any way for anyone to tell what hostile forces might still be within the compound's walls. As Diaz, Wyrick, and the Wolfpack established a secure inner perimeter, King and Taylor ran to grab more M-240B ammunition from the second-floor ready room, while their interpreter Ali took off to retrieve Crosby's medic bag from the casualty collection point.

Meanwhile, Crosby turned his attention to patching up PFAR Staff Sergeant Billy Wallace, who had already lost a lot of blood from shrapnel wounds to his chin, armpit, and calf.

Upon returning, King led the injured Bennett out of the crowded communications room to a safe spot out in the hallway; Betkijian took Bennett's place at the radio. Unable to hear anything on the radio themselves, Betkijian and King quickly fired up a laptop and contacted battalion using the semisecure Army Knowledge Online instant messaging service. 1-501st Battle NCO answered back, assuring them that medevac and air support were on the way.

King then turned his attention back to Bennett in the hallway, helping him remove his body armor and fleece jacket to reveal a bone peeking through a gigantic fist-sized hole in his left bicep—but no bleeding. The shrapnel that hit him had effectively cauterized the terrible wound. Bennett cursed out of shocked astonishment as King helped him sit down. "Give me a fucking cigarette!" Sergeant Warsop quickly lit a Newport and passed it to him. Crosby hurried over and applied a Chitosan bandage to the arm as Bennett held on to King's leg as if his life depended on it.

After helping Bennett to get his armor back on, King, Taylor, and Washburn were finally able to begin the desperate search for Captain Freeman and Lieutenant Fritz. They hurried upstairs to the IP general's office but didn't have an interpreter with them. "Where is Captain FREEMAN? Where is Lieutenant FRITZ?" they asked, but the IP officers shrugged their shoulders and otherwise communicated that they didn't know where they were. The IP general met King's eyes as he indicated that no, he didn't know where the missing officers were, either.

King knew in his heart that the shifty-eyed general was lying right to their faces, and wanted to grab him by the throat and beat whatever truth out of him. *You son of a bitch,* he thought, while fighting to restrain himself. Precious minutes were better spent on finding Freeman and Fritz than getting into a physical altercation with a traitor of the worst kind. As they were leaving one of the IP colonels told them, "Roof. Roof!" King indicated that they'd already been up there and didn't find the officers. They then went to the second IP colonel's office, but his guards indicated that he wasn't there and refused to let them in.

They raced back up to the roof to double-check. The missing officers weren't there.

When they got back down to the communications room Crosby was loading Hernandez onto a litter and told King that he wanted to administer morphine but didn't dare because of his severe abdominal wound. Sergeant Taylor and a couple of other soldiers left to secure the helicopter landing zone located about a city block away across the compound, with help from a few members of the Iraqi Army. Hernandez abruptly rolled over onto his injured side, vomiting. Someone said he was puking up blood.

For the first time that night King met a virtual wall of cold, dark, helpless, paralyzing fear welling up within himself. For a split second he imagined a world without his friend Hernandez, the ghastly thought that Jesse would die in this Iraqi hellhole. Then he recognized that falling apart and surrendering to that fear now could well be the death of them all. He had to get hold of himself. With a mighty mental push King shoved the potentially deadly fear away, out of his body, out of his mind. Replacement thoughts: *Hernandez is going to make it, we simply have to get him to the landing zone, we'll get him to a hospital, and then after that he's going to be okay.*

King stepped out into the hallway, where Billy Wallace was sitting on the floor with his face in bandages, unable to speak. He would need assistance getting to the landing zone. Knowing Wallace was a very religious man who led prayers before every mission and frequently spoke of "Father God," King put a hand on his shoulder and told him that Father God had his back and that everything would be fine. Wallace squared his shoulders a bit with a look of renewed confidence that went a long way in reassuring King.

Hole in his arm or not, Bennett didn't want to leave his PFAR soldiers. Their platoon leader Lieutenant Fritz had been kidnapped, and as their platoon sergeant he wasn't about to leave them in such a time of trauma and need. King pulled him aside and explained that with a significantly disabling wound he wasn't in any condition to effectively care for anyone, that they all needed him to get on the medevac chopper.

It took a lot of arguing but Bennett finally agreed when King promised to take care of the PFAR soldiers as if they were members of his own Wolfpack MPs.

As Bennett prepared to go out to the landing zone he mentioned that King would need some help with PFAR Private First Class Johnathan Millican. *This night is never going to end, just one thing after another,* King thought in frustration. *We've got people missing and others badly injured, now I've gotta deal with whatever this is on top of it all.* "So what the fuck happened to Millican?" he demanded. Bennett put his head on King's shoulder. "Millican didn't make it," he said.

Stunned, King went back into the communications room and shined his flashlight around the floor. And there he finally saw poor Millican laying facedown in a pool of blood with part of his head missing. With all the debris and obstructions throughout the darkened building that King had automatically stepped over, he now realized that he'd also stepped over Millican's body at least a half-dozen times during the course of the night.

To be left on the floor like that for even one more minute was unthinkable. Numb but determined to have the young soldier treated with dignity, King grabbed a wool Army blanket and rolled Millican's body into it. Also aware of the bowed heads in the room as other soldiers witnessed his struggles, he knew that while nobody could bring Millican back now, the lives and minds of those around him could be irreversibly scarred forever within the next few moments. Forcing his mind to focus into the one central reality—the safety and welfare of the living MPs and other soldiers around him—that had been keeping him sane throughout that terrible evening, King tried hard to be as careful and respectful as possible. It was nonetheless a horror for them all.

Bennett, who still hadn't left for the landing zone, at that point remembered where the body bags were stored deep in a cabinet there in the communications room. Sergeant Betkijian helped to get Millican's body, now mostly shrouded in a familiar Army blanket, into the bag. They gently folded his arms across his chest. Wyrick then zipped up the bag as everyone silently paid their respects to a twenty-year-old who everyone there remembered mostly as an always cheerful, always funny Southerner who had been PFAR's favorite young comedian.

It was time to get both Bennett and Millican to the landing zone while the medevac chopper was still waiting with severely wounded Hernandez—there was no point in unnecessarily pushing the power of Billy Wallace's prayers and Father God's patience when seconds still mattered. It was time to again refocus on the living, not yet on those missing or dead.

King, Vargas, and Wyrick lifted the bag and made for the landing zone on the opposite side of the compound. They could see a blown-up car and burning Humvee near the casualty collection point where Crosby was hunkered down waiting for them. King yelped as he stumbled into a hole in the ground and twisted his ankle, hearing it pop and nearly dropping Millican. They struggled on, finally reaching the landing zone, where the aid and litter team led by Washburn took over the task of getting Millican's body into the chopper.

King crouched down and quietly asked Crosby about Hernandez's condition. Crosby said he'd patched him up well enough to make it all the way to Germany if necessary, although the medevac was first taking him to the Combat Support Hospital in Baghdad, where Wallace and Bennett would also be treated.

When the helicopter lifted off King hobbled over to the barracks building, located off to the side roughly between the landing zone and PPHQ, where Bennett's PFAR soldiers were holed up. It was the first opportunity to account for all of them, but there were only seven PFAR soldiers there when the head count should have been nine. It was the first time that anybody realized that Johnathan Chism and Shawn Falter, who had been on guard duty outside the PPHQ main entrance when the compound was attacked, were not accounted for. They were . . . missing. Knowing that officers Freeman and Fritz had been kidnapped, it occurred to King that the two soldiers may have been taken as well.

Everyone gathered up their sensitive items, weapons, and ammunition and headed to join the others at PPHQ. The PFAR soldiers relieved the MPs at the inner security perimeter positions so that the Wolfpack could start loading trailers for the long trip out of Karbala. Two PFAR soldiers guarding the hallway stopped King to ask where Millican was. Emotionally drained, he gently told them that Millican didn't make it. The soldiers bowed their heads for a dozen seconds before pulling themselves back together to focus on their security duties.

At long last help arrived, in the form of a military transition team (MITT) as well as an Iraqi Army platoon that secured the compound's outer perimeter. With the premises finally secured, King and the MITT team master sergeant began searching for the missing officers and PFAR soldiers. They checked the barracks and the grounds between there and PPHQ, without result. A second MITT team arrived with the Iraqi Police Hilla SWAT unit and a few Special Forces operators. The Special Forces detachments (known as ODAs) led all soldiers who weren't on guard duty on a thorough systematic search of the entire compound.

It was then that one of the ODAs pulled King aside to report that the four missing soldiers had already been found miles away—and that they were all dead.

King and the other surviving soldiers did not yet understand that they had just survived one of the most sophisticated attacks in the entire Iraqi war.

While they were at their laptops in the MP ready room at just past six, a commando assault team had driven into the compound. They were disguised as friendly American security contractors, wearing ACUs, carrying M-4s and M-16s, and driving SUVs that were carefully outfitted to appear identical to those used by real contractors. Speaking in English, they had ordered the Iraqi guards at the compound's outer perimeter to lay down their weapons and let them in. The Iraqi guards simply complied without any resistance.

According to an Iraqi Police officer who was watching from a distance, the drivers of two of the SUVs positioned themselves to watch over the gate and interior entryway, while four or five other vehicles drove up to the PPHQ building—where Specialist Johnathan Chism and Private First Class Shawn Falter were on guard duty in their Humvee near the front PPHQ entrance. Five commandos got out of their vehicles, calling out greetings to them in English, while heading to the front door. Falter got out of the Humvee to check them out as three more disguised commandos were getting out of their SUV. One of the commandos suddenly pulled out a handgun and shot Falter in the back. Falter, who was wearing body armor that almost undoubtedly saved his life at that point, fell down as a second commando jumped onto the bumper of the Humvee and shot Chism.

These were the shots that King and the Wolfpack had first heard while they were sitting in the ready room on the second floor, and had thought were nothing more than celebratory gunfire.

Inside the communications room Hernandez, Bennett, Wallace, Millican, and Washburn had suddenly heard a short burst of automatic gunfire coming from inside the building. Their door started to open; Bennett grabbed the door but it was too late since someone shoved the muzzle of an AK-47 into the room. Wallace joined Bennett in trying to shove the muzzle back out but the attacker on the other side opened fire, spraying the room with bullets. Millican had taken position on one knee with his M-4 ready to shoot through the door, when someone tossed a grenade into the room.

They all saw their buddy Millican now lying on the floor, dead. Then they heard an explosion next door in the officers' room. Their door was kicked open and Wallace caught a brief glimpse of a man dressed in an Iraqi Army uniform. Wallace dove for the door to slam it shut but again caught the muzzle of an AK-47, which sprayed bullets for a couple more seconds.

A massive explosion in the hallway then ripped the door off its hinges and showered the room in shrapnel. Shrapnel hit Wallace in the chin, armpit, and calf; Hernandez in his arm and abdomen; and Bennett lost a chunk of his bicep.

The commando team—which now had custody of Chism and Falter (both likely wounded but still alive), as well as Lieutenant Fritz and Captain Freeman—blew up two Humvees as they left the compound. Parts of one of the Humvees showered around King and the other MPs who were still up on the roof. Ammunition for the .50 cals that had been left behind in the Humvees cooked off, sending bullets off everywhere and leading the MPs to assume that the attack was still in progress.

At 1930 (7:30 P.M.) the insurgent assault team raced five of their SUVs through Iraqi Army Checkpoint 21J in the small town of Al-Mahawil, heading for Hillah. Three men who had been loitering near the checkpoint for hours in their parked cars shouted at the Iraqi soldiers to hold their fire, claiming that the SUVs had Israelis and Americans in them. The soldiers arrested them for attempting to assist an apparent getaway.

Iraqi security forces were now pursuing the fleeing vehicles, and the commando team was undoubtedly feeling the heat. They were about to get caught red-handed.

Yet at 2000 hours some Iraqi Police officers found the five SUVs abandoned on a dead-end road just outside Al-Mahawil. Two had been left with their doors open and keys in the ignitions, causing the vehicles door alarms to emit ding-ding-ding warnings. Worried about possible explosive devices, the police backed away and called for help. An Iraqi Army unit and the Hillah SWAT team arrived at 2037.

They then discovered Falter's body on the ground in front of one of the SUVs, with his armored vest open. He had been shot twice in the chest and once in the head. Chism and Fritz were found handcuffed back to back in the rear of the same SUV. Fritz didn't have a shirt on, and Chism's vest had been opened. They too had taken double-shots to the chest and one each to the head.

Captain Freeman, who had also been shot in the head, was still breathing. An ambulance rushed him to the closest medical facility at FOB Reo in Hillah, but he died on the way.

It would take a while for investigators to piece together what happened, yet it was quite plain that members of the Iraqi Police and Iraqi Army had not only made the attack possible but also actively participated. The commando team had carried M-4s and M-16s, yet it was an AK-47 muzzle that had fired into the communications room. Wallace had caught a glimpse of a shooter who was wearing a brown-and-black camouflage uniform, the same uniform worn by the Iraqi Army.

The three people loitering in their cars were arrested for aiding the fleeing attackers. Of the three men arrested for aiding the escape at Checkpoint 21J, one turned out to be a second lieutenant with the Iraqi Police, and another was a Mahdi Army local official.

Investigators also checked out a group of fifteen or twenty men wearing purple and black camouflage that had arrived at the compound earlier in the day. They claimed to be an Iraqi Police element from Baghdad that had come to discuss Ashura security issues with the PPHQ's Iraqi general. Some of them photographed secured areas, and while some left later in the afternoon, a number of them remained. An Army report would eventually conclude that they served as an advance unit for the commandos who would carry out the kidnappings.

There was also reason to believe that local residents had been warned to stay away that day. The friendly young gopher Mike Jontz didn't show up as usual, nor did the carpenters who had been working on the new bathroom and other projects on the second floor of PPHQ. The barber shop and small grocery store that normally stayed open until late at night just outside the back gates mysteriously closed early. And about ten minutes before the attack PFCs Travis Johnson and Dean Wiley found that someone had unlocked the back gate.

But who sponsored and trained the commando team responsible? U.S. reconnaissance satellites would eventually find a full-sized mockup of the entire Karbala Provincial Joint Coordination Center compound that had been constructed at the Fajr Garrison, a Qods Force training facility in Ahwaz, Iran. The Qods Force, an elite branch of the Iranian Revolutionary Guard Corps, serves the role of organizing, training, equipping, and financing foreign Islamic revolutionary movements[6]— including the Mahdi Army and the League of the Righteous (Asaib al Haq).[7]

In a CNN interview Major General William Caldwell confirmed that the KPJCC mockup in Iran had been used to train the commandos and otherwise plan the January 20 attack.[8]

On March 20, 2007, U.S. forces managed to capture Qais al-Khazali, the head of the League of the Righteous and a former advisor to Moqtada al-Sadr, along with his brother Laith and a senior Hezbollah operative named Ali Mussa Daqduq. It was during this raid that they found a twenty-two-page memo detailing the planning, preparation, approval process, and conduct of the Karbala attack, according to General David Petraeus.[9] Brigadier General Kevin Bergner, the spokesman for the Multi-National Force in Iraq at that time, would also state that the memo showed that "Qods Force had developed detailed information regarding our soldiers' activities, shift changes, and fences, and this information was shared with the [Karbala] attackers."[10]

During their interrogations, "Both Ali Musa Daqduq and Qais Khazali state that senior leadership within the Quds force knew of and supported planning for the eventual Karbala attack that killed five coalition soldiers," General Bergner said.[11]

On May 18 U.S. forces near Sadr City attempted to capture yet ultimately had to kill Azhar al Dulaimi, whose fingerprints had been found in Karbala, and was by then believed to be the tactical commander who had led the commandos on January 20.[12]

Then, on May 29, 2007, the League of the Righteous kidnapped British contractor Peter Moore and four of his bodyguards from the finance ministry in Baghdad, and issued a demand that the Americans immediately release the al-Khazali brothers and Daqduq.

In June 2009 the U.S. military did in fact release Laith al-Khazali: "As part of a reconciliation effort between the government of Iraq and Asa'ib al-Haq [the League of the Righteous], the decision has been made to release Laith Khazali."[13]

Then, on December 31, 2009, the military released his brother, Qais al-Khazali. After 946 days of captivity, the League of the Righteous finally released Moore. His four bodyguards had been murdered and Moore himself had been subjected to many months of torture.[14]

To this day Mike King is very proud and pleased that valor awards were given to PFAR soldiers, yet bitter since none were approved for his MPs who had performed so well in a night of bloody horror against overwhelming forces that had taken literally everyone—including entire governments—completely by surprise. Not a bitter or negative man at heart, he still felt doubly betrayed by the Iraqis he was committed to support as well as the political maneuvering that led to at least two assassins being later released for political reasons, who are now free to kidnap and kill again.

17

LOSSES . . . AND GAINS

On March 8, 2007, with the backing of senior military police officers on his staff, General Petraeus sent a formal request for 2,200 more MPs to be dispatched to Iraq as part of the surge. The request was approved with alacrity by Secretary Rumsfeld and seconded by President Bush.

Petraeus told media that he "did not see the need for more combat troops" in addition to the 21,500 on the way, but was eager to have the additional MPs. Most analysts were preoccupied by the debate over the surge strategy itself and missed the meaning of adding the equivalent of two MP brigades to the fight: In Petraeus's view the center of gravity was shifting from kinetic warfighting to police operations that would instill a law-and-order environment in the country.

It was a momentous shift that went largely unnoticed.

On the first of April, 2007, Sergeant Jesse Shambo was returning with his squad to FOB Muleskinner (whose name had been changed to Rustimayah) from a routine training mission at the Iraqi Police district headquarters at al Aziziyah. They were a unit from the 759th MP Battalion, the 984th MP Company. Without warning they were hit with what was later discovered to be a five-array explosive formed penetrator device. Five massive explosions aimed at the side of their vehicle shot molten metal and shrapnel throughout the truck.

The shock knocked the truck off the road, set it on fire, and rolled it four times. The interior burst into flames. Everyone in the truck was trapped inside and badly burned until soldiers were able to drag them free. The driver, specialist Michael Cameron, lost a leg in the attack. Shambo suffered traumatic brain injury, a broken arm, and shrapnel wounds through the left side of his body. He was immediately medevaced back to the U.S. through Germany.

For Shambo, his war was over.

Three months later, on May 7, Phillips woke up to a ringing phone. He was in Baghdad in his hootch in the Green Zone. Garrity was on the line. He was now executive assistant to the deputy undersecretary of the Army. Garrity carried bad news. Colonel James Harrison, who Phillips had convinced months prior to defer his retirement and accept a deployment to Afghanistan, had been killed in action the day before.

Guilt weighed heavily on Phillips, who felt an inescapable sense of responsibility for urging Harrison to stay on active duty. It was the low point of his year. "I lay awake the rest of the night," he remembered. "I did a lot of soul searching."

Quantock, in charge of Task Force 134, took on the daunting task of dealing with tens of thousands of detainees held in detention centers that stretched from Camp Bucca near Basra in the south to Camp Cropper near Baghdad, to Abu Ghraib, and northwards to Taji. Under Quantock's control was a dog's breakfast collection ranging from hard-core criminals, al-Qaeda foreign fighters, Sunni insurgents, former Saddam gunmen, Mahdi Army fighters, and a growing mob of semiliterate unemployed young men who drifted to the various factions out of economic need or quasi-religious fervor.

Till this point, the pressing mission was to get these people off the battlefield and keep them out of the fight. Quantock assessed the reality of the situation: We can't confine most of the male population of Iraq. He recognized that the religious-based factions were essentially snake oil salesmen. They sold their particular aberrant version of Islam to men who couldn't read the Koran, handed them a weapon, and pointed them in a particular direction. Even more insidious was the distinctly unholy alliance that had metastasized between the religion-based factions and criminal gangs. In 2007 there was little or no differentiation: The expedient solution was to put them all in cages.

The first priority, Quantock realized, was to separate sheep from goats. The largely ignorant foot soldier pawns needed to be removed from the hard-core pool of foreign al-Qaeda fighters, Mahdi Army leaders, unrepentant Ba'athists, criminals, and Sunni organizers. Each of the latter would be dealt with under judicial or war-crimes proceedings. But as long as the groups were mixed, the ordinary joes would be increasingly radicalized and used to create internal disturbances. Detainee riots had characterized the installations, particularly at Bucca and Taji, since 2006.

Quantock wanted the criminals tried in Iraqi courts and, if found guilty, slammed into an Iraqi prison. Al-Qaeda fighters along with Mahdi Army and Sunni leaders needed to be interrogated by joint Iraqi-coalition intelligence personnel. Afterward special courts would decide their fate. In a parallel operation he saw the vast numbers of foot soldiers as an untapped resource. Quantock directed that dynamic reform programs be initiated to see how many could be salvaged.

Education was a major part of rehabilitation. *These guys can't read even the Koran, the book that was motivating their actions,* Quantock thought. He initiated an aggressive literacy program—all detainees held in the larger general population would learn to read. Instructors were hired and classes begun. Next it was vital that the detainees realize that what they were hearing from the Islamism radicals was not the only version—or even the majority-accepted version—of the Koran. He had his staff find imams who preached a moderate version of Islam and had their work printed and distributed throughout the facility, along with teaching that in order to be a good Muslim a man didn't need to be a suicide bomber or a violent jihadist.

While working on the motivational side Quantock concomitantly took a hardheaded approach to economic realities. If a man is illiterate, unskilled, and unemployed then he is easy prey for any radical cause or criminal recruiter that comes down the road. The literacy side was working. On the economic side, it was essential that prior to release back to society the detainees possess sufficient skill sets to make a decent living. The brighter and more ambitious were offered a range of semiprofessional skills like bookkeeping, accounting, business management, and communications. With this knowledge they could reasonably compete for entry-level jobs, or in many cases take a shot at starting a small business.

Others who leaned to the hands-on were put through vocational training in carpentry, masonry, electrical, plumbing, and general construction skills. In a country with thirty-five years of neglect and destruction people were screaming for these services.

The reforms quickly showed promise. Simply isolating the instigators quieted the place down considerably. The education program was accepted with alacrity. Iraqis are not from a stupid culture; they prize learning, and take pride in being self-sufficient. Men who had previously been shoved around like human flotsam and jetsam finally had the opportunity to stand with pride and care for themselves and their families. By being literate and schooled in a less violent form of Islam they could still be good Muslims—especially essential in the hyperemotional Shi'a faith—and not be lured or coerced into jihad.

A metric that makes sense—recidivism—showed that graduates of the combined programs returned to the fight at a dramatically lower rate than had been observed previously. Convinced that the program was effective, coalition and Iraqi forces processed thousands of lower-level men through the program and back out into society.

In October 2007, Lieutenant Christopher Nogle led his platoon from the 293rd MP Company in the Diyala district of Baghdad. Part of the surge, they were helping to expand coalition presence at the neighborhood level. For several days they had run into heavy enemy fire from a strong point located in a cluster of buildings. Unable to take the position, Nogle had called for air strikes, but the Apache pilots had demurred, claiming that they could not positively identify the target and were unwilling to risk hitting a civilian house.

Frustrated, Nogle and some soldiers crept to the wall protecting the enemy compound at night with cans of red spray paint. The following morning when he again called the Apaches for support, the aerial gunners were able to read the words "Shoot here" on the wall, along with an arrow curving upward to indicate the target house. Mission accomplished.

18

ROLLING WITH WARFIGHTERS AND SUPERSTARS

Today it is a dirty, gray pile of stones and concrete, barely distinguishable in color from the nearby desert or in content from endless rubble piles of war damage that pockmark the rest of Samarra. For centuries the mosque had towered over central Samarra, reflecting glory back to the sun with rays from its golden dome. Even non-Shi'as considered it a wonder of the world. For the Shi'a community—a majority of the population in Iraq and Iran—it was the holiest of shrines.

Whenever Lieutenant Colonel Brian Bisacre, commander of the 728th Military Police Battalion, headquartered thirty or so kilometers north of town in a desolate outpost known as Camp Speicher, visited the city—something he did often as part of his mission to build up the Iraqi Police elements in Samarra—he speculated on how and why the elegant edifice was destroyed.

The obvious answer was that rival Sunni and al-Qaeda groups were responsible for deliberately desecrating a Shi'a shrine. But Bisacre cultivates the native suspicion of a longtime law enforcement mind-set. While it was not an original theory, he leaned toward the idea that both Sunni groups and AQI were too weak and feared a Shi'a backlash too much to dare such an undertaking.

On the other hand, he wondered, who was most likely to profit from a civil war in Iraq, who had the most to gain from increasing sectarian chaos? In his mind the fingerprints on the crime scene match those of Iranian Qods Force operators and the Shi'a militia groups of renegade cleric Moqtada al-Sadr. As he told a nearby comrade, "I think the Iranians did it just to piss the Shi'a off at the Sunnis. Not that they need much provocation. If they kill their own they don't care."

Bisacre had rolled out of Camp Speicher, where in spring 2008 the 4th Infantry Division overwatched a huge area of operations (AO) sweeping from just north of Baghdad to the Syrian border and east to encompass the Kurdish territories. As MP support for the division, Bisacre's AO overlaid that of the maneuver unit commander's.

Driving Bisacre was Sergeant Trent Dyer, and manning the .50 caliber in the turret was Specialist Edward "Gonzo" Gonzales. Usually the medic rode with them but today I had his seat while he rode in another truck, and interpreter "Mike" made the fifth passenger. Given the rare opportunity, I had come to Iraq two weeks prior and embedded with MP units in the greater Baghdad area. "Come out here and see what these MP soldiers are doing!" my friend Colonel Mike Bumgarner urged by e-mail. With assistance from him and several others we made it happen.

We learned that mission emphasis had shifted from fighting to counterinsurgency. It was important to learn much more about the specific missions and daily lives of the MPs. What was really happening day-to-day?

Following the recommendation of the 18th MP Brigade public affairs officer, Lieutenant Colonel Mike Inovina, we hopped a C-130 for the ride up to Camp Speicher in the northern desert, and joined up with the 728th MP Battalion. Now we were riding out on a mission.

The squad leader of Bisacre's personal unit was Staff Sergeant Christina Huerta. Standing five foot four on tiptoes and weighing in at just a little over a hundred pounds, in a different context Huerta could be considered feminine and petite. With full battle-rattle on, 9 mm pistol slung low in a left-handed leg carry, and M-4 slung across her chest leading her squad, no one mistakes her for other than what she is: a tough NCO with high standards. "If we draw fire," she told the squad before they rolled down south to Patrol Base Kauffman, "we are going to return fire aggressively and take the fight to them."

"Make no mistake," Bisacre said, "that is one solid NCO. She isn't afraid of anything, male or female, friend or enemy, and doesn't mind who knows. Best squad leader I've ever had."

Bisacre stands medium height and has a solid, fit physique. He is square-faced and when he removes his Kevlar shows thick black hair in a high-and-tight cut. He eschews the wraparound sunglasses common in the desert for clear protective eyewear, and his penetrating blue eyes seem to miss little of interest. On the battered, fought-over streets of downtown Samarra there is much to watch.

He had arrived in Samarra this day to visit the Iraqi Police commander and a few local stations to measure progress. Unusual from the norm, Bisacre had me along as a visitor and took a moment to show me the sights, to the dismay of Doc, the medic, who was an integral part of the protection package that sticks tight to the CO. When Bisacre and I dismounted from Humvees, walked casually around the streets and took photos, Doc was beside himself, anxious for the BC (battalion commander) to remount the truck.

Pointing down the shabby street to the debris pile that was once the Golden Dome, Bisacre noted sadly that the insurgents—whichever group they were—had not been content with the first strike and had returned later to blow up one of the two standing minarets, tall, graceful towers that stood watch outside of the mosque proper from which the muezzin or prayer leader would lead the community in a call for prayer in the peculiar singsong tone characteristic of Arab culture. He mused about how beautiful it must have been in its day, touched deeply by the loss.

The possibility of a sniper loomed large that morning. Samarra is still, in military argot, considered Indian Country by the handful of American soldiers who live and operate there. Few windows have any glass or shutters over them and the dark recesses offer excellent hiding places for taking a shot. Only in movie thrillers do you know exactly where the sniper lurks. Walking the streets of Samarra with a thousand nooks and crannies, soldiers could almost feel crosshairs zeroing in.

Bagging a battalion commander would be a huge coup. Yet Bisacre was relaxed and comfortable out walking. He seemed to enjoy the freedom of movement after tight confinement behind the blue force tracker system in his Humvee. It was hot, muggy, and the air tasted grainy from desert dust. Nostrils were assaulted by the constant low-level stench of the unwashed city, but at least he was outside. Soldiers, tend to be outside people, in all senses of the phrase. His squad had automatically assumed a protective corridor around him, keeping passersby distant in a nonthreatening, but unspoken clear statement: Keep walking but don't get any closer. By 2008 the prospect of suicide bombers was an ever-present reality all over Iraq.

Doc Cardey, meanwhile, was beside himself with anxiety.

"Stand over there," Bisacre directed. "I'll get your picture with the ruins of the mosque in the background." After considerable nagging from Doc, Bisacre reluctantly remounted his command vehicle and successively visited several IP stations in various stages of repair—the war damage around Samarra was significant and largely unattended. JDAMS—special laser-guided bombs—and other precision munitions had taken out entire buildings; Ba'ath Party headquarters and Fedayeen strong points had been leveled. The postwar insurgency knocked down a lot of what remained.

Bisacre's mission was to train up Iraqi Police to assume increasingly greater levels of responsibility and this day, as on all others, his focus was on that goal.

Making the already daunting task much more difficult is the fact that police stations are a primary insurgent target. They are typically understaffed by lightly armed, poorly trained men of suspect motivation. Even more tempting to insurgents is the psychological value of taking down a station or a handful of IPs. The government can't protect you, the message becomes, and we can hit you whenever and wherever we want. Several stations had been overrun here in Samarra by the Jaish al-Mahdi Army (JAM).

In one particularly vicious attack, JAM brought a white Toyota pickup to the gates of a major station after softening it up with a torrent of RPG, small-arms, and machine-gun fire. Mounted in the truck bed was a huge Soviet-designed .51 caliber machine gun, firing bullets big enough to smash through concrete walls. Barely large enough to contain the recoil from the weapon, the truck bucked and lurched, but was still stable enough for the gunner to spray and spray belt after belt of rounds into the defenseless station, literally crumbling the building into dust and debris. Few of its occupants, trying to fight back vainly with small-caliber pistols, survived.

Yet even in this environment of constant death and destruction, Bisacre is continually surprised by the number of men who step forward, volunteering to join the Iraqi Police. He is worried not that the recruits are unavailable, but about the bureaucratic backlog that has resulted from trying to rebuild an entire Ministry of Interior from scratch. Even at this date only rudimentary personnel-screening procedures are in place. Many of the recruits, Bisacre and others fear, are JAM or AQI plants who will leak intelligence about operations or on occasion turn rogue and attack their comrades or, worse, American and coalition soldiers.

As always logistics has become the long pole in the tent. At one stop he met a jocular, exceedingly polite Iraqi Police chief who was literally building a station from rubble. The chief apologized profusely for not being able to offer more than a perfunctory glass of chai, and it was clear that while highly motivated, he and his skeleton staff were faced with an impossible task.

"We need everything," he told Bisacre frankly. Though his face smiled, the deep worry lines in his face reflected his realization that basic survivability is at stake here. His station, if it can be called that, is composed of a couple of dilapidated trailers, surrounded in part by concrete Jersey barriers. "Look around you," he suggested to the American MP commander, sweeping his arm to point out the mess, which is all too apparent even to a casual visitor, and stunningly inadequate to someone like Bisacre who sees tactically.

"We are completely unprotected. My men want to do their jobs but we have nothing." He shrugged. "If we could just have some . . ." He stumbled for the word but managed to make clear that he would like the Hesco barriers that proliferate around strongpoints in Iraq. These barriers—simplicity itself—are huge burlap, wire-reinforced sacks that hold sand, dirt, rubble, or anything to provide substance. Stacked side by side and layered up they provide instant protection from small arms, RPGs, and larger caliber weapons. Considering the availability of lots of rubble on the streets, it is often a practical way to address two concerns with one fix.

"And weapons. Many of my men are still unarmed. How can we be real policemen without badges and pistols?" By now the chief openly pled his case.

Bisacre was polite and supportive, but spoke carefully, not wanting to over-promise or raise expectations unduly. He promised to bring these concerns up in his next meeting with the overall chief, whose office he had visited previously.

Leaving the pathetic excuse for a police station, Bisacre gnawed a lip in anger and frustration. He knew full well that if JAM attacked with any seriousness the station wouldn't last a minute. It was a hopeless, defenseless position. Yet here was one of the most motivated IPs he had met, a man struggling mightily to perform a thankless task in the face of overwhelming odds, who through it all was unfailingly polite and never without a smile. *All he needs,* Bisacre thought bitterly, *are the tools to do his job.* He pledged to himself to raise it with the local IP general but already could imagine the mindless bureaucratic fumbling that would ensue as a result.

He and his battalion could do the job in a couple of weeks. But that was not the mission. The task confronting him—and the hundreds of MPs throughout the country—was to push, cajole, encourage, motivate, and train the Iraqis to the point that they could do it themselves. Everything the chief and countless others like him needed was already in the system, Bisacre knew, it was just a question of forcing the system to function properly.

It was, Bisacre concluded, a shit mission.

Frustration is the name of the game in Samarra, as in much of the rest of Iraq.

Bisacre directed his driver to take a tour of the city before he visited the U.S. outpost, named Patrol Base Kauffman after a soldier killed years earlier. The IP general had discussed the results derived from emplacing huge, sixteen-foot-high Texas barriers (some wag commented that they were Jersey barriers on steroids) around a volatile Samarra neighborhood. With the barriers lined side by side with only two narrow openings for pedestrian or small-vehicle traffic, the neighborhood looked like a prison from the outside.

Though they first thought the barriers would confine and suffocate, residents now find them liberating. Prior to their installation, suicide bombers drove explosive-laden cars or small trucks right into the neighborhood, detonating them in the marketplaces. Citizens recoiled in horror as their families and friends were blown to pieces or terribly maimed.

Those days were over. A VBED (vehicle-borne improvised explosive device) could detonate on the outside, even parked closely to a barrier, and the neighborhood would not be harmed. Not only was it a physical relief, but it was a liberation of the mind. For the first time in months, the neighborhood was calm, the economy was prospering, people were resuming normal lives.

Authorities had fabricated special ID cards for residents of the neighborhood. This allowed IP guards at the entry points to intercept infiltrating JAM operatives and arrest them. In a neighborhood terrorized by intimidation, protection rackets, kidnapping, and robbery, there was now relative peace. There had not been a targeted assassination inside for several weeks or more. Even local community politics were thriving.

The neighborhood, standing across the street from the ruins of the Golden Dome mosque, was a microcosm of what could happen to the country as a whole if sufficient security could be put in place. Instead of physical barriers, as effective as they were in this small case, that role was to be assumed by Iraqi security forces. All of them—the army, police both national and local, border police, even traffic police—working together to build a combination of local and regional law and order, could effectively thwart the nefarious external infiltration of terrorists and deprive internal dissidents of the anarchic environment they required to thrive.

Next on Bisacre's schedule was a visit to his people. Pulling into

Patrol Base Kauffman gave Bisacre a new meaning to the words "living ugly." The patrol base is sited just alongside the Tigris River on the eastern, or city side. Across the river, parallel to the bridge bringing traffic in from MSR Tampa, a large dam creates a broad expanse in the Tigris that spills over into lush green marshes and affords irrigation for desert farmers. When rolling in from Tampa, the contrast from monochromatic, flat desert to intense green almost hurts the eyes.

Just downriver from Saddam's hometown of Tikrit, Samarra was a Ba'athist playground of sorts. The dictator had a palace or two alongside the river where he reportedly engaged in hunting and fishing. Migratory waterfowl found it an inviting stopover as they made their annual north-south voyage.

The patrol base, on the other hand, looked like a place that smart ducks would avoid but in which snakes, spiders, and rats would thrive. PB Kauffman looked like the type of ramshackle, tossed-together frontier station that would have housed an Army bivouac during the Geronimo Wars in the American Southwest. Well, on second thought, maybe not that fancy. Nasty as it was, it occupied a tactically sound position—"key terrain" in military parlance—hence the decrepitude was shared by American and Iraqi soldiers. In clouds of ubiquitous dust, the five-truck convoy passed through battered steel gates and was met by Captain Frank Pescatello, who was in charge of the patrol base and a colocated joint security site (JSS) manned by a combination of Iraqi Police, National Police, and U.S. Army, primarily MPs.

At PB Kauffman, soldiers lived in appalling conditions. Desert dust was ubiquitous, layering the outdoor exercise machines (wherever they go, soldiers will put an effort into a makeshift gym before attending even to comfort items like messing and latrine facilities) to the point that the black and stainless steel equipment resembled stone artifacts from the museum of Mesopotamian history. You half expected to see a Nebuchadnezzar-type character with tight braids and loincloth step out and start bench-pressing.

Tension showed on the faces of the soldiers manning the PB. Pescatello walked Bisacre around the dilapidated compound, noting that the unit got shot at almost every day. "Sometimes snipers," he said.

"Last week RPGs." Bisacre frowned and nodded. Just weeks prior he had to relieve the commander of Kauffman for poor performance. He had hand-selected Pescatello as a replacement and told him to get the place squared away. Following a relieved commander was a tough act and Samarra was a steep learning curve, but Pescatello was solidly in charge.

As crappy as it was, Bisacre knew, the patrol base was the only coalition toehold in Samarra. That also meant that this shabby camp by definition became a prime JAM target. In addition to the police-training mission, the site was the sole point of coordination between Iraqi security forces and coalition elements operating in the area. Knocking Kauffman out would be tantamount to winning Samarra. So mission requirements forced him to put soldiers in a shithole and expose them to continuous danger. He hated doing it but it was necessary.

Bisacre and Pescatello grimly walked the perimeter, protected by a hodgepodge of Hesco barriers, shipping containers, and the remains of the mud wall that originally surrounded the site. From the flat rooftop Pescatello pointed across the road that led from the Tigris bridge to the city. "Most of the fire comes from there. The IA [Iraqi Army] is supposed to be housed there but most of them are probably JAM members, so we figure that's where the attacks originate."

In addition to manning the JSS—a system designed to coordinate battlespace among coalition and Iraqi Security Force elements—the MPs run regular police training team missions out to the stations that Bisacre had just visited. During those visits Bisacre had asked—with apparent casualness—if they were receiving regular visits from members of the patrol base team. When told that they showed up several times weekly, Bisacre nodded and went on to the next question. Like every good commander he lived by the dictum of checking details and verifying assumptions.

Pescatello looks surprisingly like actor Bruce Willis. He is big and solid with a shaved head and the face of a fighter who has taken a couple of punches and given a few more back. He dominated the room. Pescatello gave Bisacre a situation briefing, running his hand absentmindedly across his shaved pate. The key topic quickly shifted from operational actions to logistics. MP frustration with the tortuously slow reform process of the Ministry of Interior on down was apparent at all ranks across the board.

Like many commanders in Iraq with a similar mission, Bisacre was steamed over the fact that what he was seeing was actually an improvement over what existed previously. He hesitated even to glorify the process by calling it a system. In his eyes it was not organized enough to warrant that label. Iraqi officers up and down the MOI chain held on to supplies as if they were personal property. Relatives, friends, fellow tribe members, those who gave sufficiently important gifts—they received support. Others, regardless of need and organizational requirements, went home empty-handed. The rule of thumb in Iraq was painfully clear: If you don't have personal contacts to get you material, you are screwed.

Commanders in the field, and staff at Phoenix Base under General Phillips, had worked diligently to change the process. Measuring gains in inches, not miles, they all recognized that what they were attempting was a sea change of a basic culture. They had taken on a daunting task but were nonetheless determined to do the best they could in a less-than-perfect environment.

On the run down and back on MSR Tampa, as on every trip outside the Speicher wire, Bisacre and his Iraqi-American interpreter, a U.S. resident named Michael, played a constant game of "who's really in charge here." Michael, once they rolled, sat in the right rear seat of the Humvee, directly behind Bisacre, out of the line of sight. He would quietly unfasten the double seat belt that he found restrictive and bury his nose deep in a paperback book of Sudoku games, pencil quietly scribbling numbers in the blank squares.

Bisacre, as the guy responsible for the safety of his personnel, would patiently ask, "Michael, got your seat belt on?" With a grunt acknowledging the order, Michael would grudgingly fumble with the dual belt system while keeping his eyes focused on the elusive numbers. "He hates to wear a seat belt or his Kevlar," Bisacre explained.

"I've got to stay on his ass constantly about it. Hate to lose him in a rollover. He's a temperamental cuss, but a great interpreter."

Like a lot of Iraqis, Michael is solidly built, with a spreading mid-section that indicates a love of food. Iraqis in the chain of command often mirror the old Sicilian proverb of "a man with a belly" to indicate a wealthy, powerful individual. Conversely, others are whip-thin and wiry, tough as tanned camel hide, and look like they could have just stepped out of the desert. Unfortunately body type alone does not distinguish who is on the take and who is honest, or who will fight and who will hold back.

Interpreters are an odd bunch, and, like other civilians in the war, often underappreciated. They die at a much higher rate than soldiers, being especially lucrative targets for AQI or JAM, whose leadership paints them "traitors to Islam and Iraq." Some, recruited in Iraq, have sent their families to live in Europe or the United States from fear of reprisal. Such attacks are frequent and often fatal. One of the more enlightened programs instituted by the United States is that when interpreters who are not U.S. citizens finish an extended period of duty and wish to apply for citizenship in America, their applications go to the head of the queue and are treated positively. Many commanders spoke of tearful, emotional departures as interpreters who had earned their citizenship the hard way were finally on their way to their new homes.

Surprisingly, a large number of interpreters in Iraq are women, more than a few relatively young and attractive. While most dress in civilian field clothing on missions—although Phillips insisted that his female interpreter don an ACU uniform so as not to differentiate her from the other soldiers—many wear tight jeans and snug T-shirts back in garrison, drawing attention (desired or not) from soldiers who are long into the puritanical deployments that mark today's Army standards.

There are a few stories involving sexual liaisons between interpreters and commanders, all of which, when discovered by higher command, ended painfully for the participants. More than one field-grade officer has had his command or staff position curtailed and been sent home with an unsatisfactory fitness report because of raging hormones. General Order Number 1 violations—whether alcohol-, sex-, or drug-related—are a quick ticket back to the States and out of military service.

How effective are the female interpreters? That question—in male-dominated, female-suppressed societies like Iraq and Afghanistan—needs to be explored. For the most part, reports are that they are as effective as male counterparts, for the same reason: ability to work with people and to function well in both languages. Commanders said they did not perceive a diminution of respect or willingness on the part of Iraqi counterparts to work with women. Or maybe the senior Iraqi officials were just good poker players.

Staff Sergeant Ronald Cardey, known universally—as most Army medics are—as Doc, talked about his experience riding with Bisacre. "We were rolling home when we ran into a traffic jam. Mine-clearing equipment ahead of us on MSR Tampa slowed things down. We were creeping along and I was watching the median outside my window. I noticed that all the shrubbery was pretty dried out and dying. No big deal, we're in the desert. Right in the middle was this really nice, green shrub. I thought it was funny, why was this one alive and the others dead? As we crept up beside it I started to say something. Well, it was an EFP [explosively formed penetrator]. Then it blew. Fortunately the guy who made it screwed up or it would have wiped out the whole Humvee. Rod, the driver, got knocked around but was still conscious. Tommy, the gunner, was wounded in the leg.

"I was screaming 'Go, Rod, go, go!' while trying to treat Tommy's wound. He kept telling me not to cut his uniform. Hell with that. I sliced his ACUs with my scissors. So I'm bandaging him up and the CO has Rod stop the truck and jumps out. Christ, what am I going to do? I check Rod quickly, he had facial cuts but the Kevlar and goggles mostly protected him. Then I jumped out and ran around the other side where the boss was walking around.

"I went nuts, yelling at him, 'Get back in the truck, sir. Get back in the fuckin' truck!'

"Here I am jumping up and down and he just turns quietly and looks me in the eye and says, 'Doc, this isn't the first time I've been shot at. I'm checking my soldiers, now calm down.' Not pissed-off or anything, just doing his job and telling me in his own way to do mine. He was impressive."

Later Bisacre confirmed the story, cracked a grin, and drawled, "Doc gets a little carried away worrying about me sometimes."

Whenever he visited inside a police station in Samarra, Bisacre removed his helmet and body armor and relaxed with the Iraqi Police (IP) officers. It served two purposes. Primarily it was a tangible gesture that he felt secure in their presence, that he trusted them. Also it was more comfortable.

Not Doc. He stayed in full battle-rattle the entire time, posting himself close to the door in case someone came in with hostile intent. Or, in the unlikely event that one of the IPs turned rogue, he was prepared to stop anything quick. Such things had happened at Karbala and elsewhere. American soldiers' lives were lost by IP betrayals. In Doc's mind, the price for keeping one's guard up was cheap compared to the alternative.

Salman Pak was notorious. It was here that the ruthless terrorist group Ansar al-Islam had set up a training camp. At the camp jihadis came from around the world to learn skills in spreading poison gases like sarin and ricin into mass subway attacks and how to hijack aircraft with knives. Two mock-ups of fuselages of aircraft were found, along with reams of documents, when the nearby camp was secured after a pitched battle with U.S. Marines in April 2003.

The Ansar al-Islam camp was reportedly opened by terror mastermind Abu Musab al-Zarqawi shortly after the Taliban fell and he fled Afghanistan seeking protection from Saddam Hussein.

It was late April 2008, the third evening with the 95th MP Battalion. I had been on one patrol and had spent the better part of a day interviewing soldiers around various units on FOB Rustamiyah. My handler, Sergeant First Class Todd Busch, had scheduled me for more interviews tomorrow but I was getting antsy and felt FOB-bound.

At Lieutenant Colonel John Bogdon's invitation, I dropped by the screened veranda outside his single-story concrete quarters that evening for "near beer" and cigars. As other officers and senior NCOs dropped by, I quickly realized that this was part of a nightly winding-down ritual that Bogdon encouraged. Not only did it allow the extroverted Bogdon a chance to let off steam, but more important for the commander, it provided an informal bitch, complain, and suggest session for his junior leaders and staff. A time when hair was let down and opinions flowed freely.

"We're surrounded on three sides by an Iraqi garbage dump," Bogdon explained, gesturing with his large cigar. "Several square miles of garbage surround us. The Iraqis burn everything—garbage, plastic, tires, metal, wood, cardboard, general crap, you name it, they burn it. And it burns constantly, night and day."

For the past couple of days the constant pall of smoke that overlaid the FOB was shocking. The smell was so noxious that at one point it induced nausea. "On the really bad days," Busch offered helpfully, "it's plain hard to breathe." The smell penetrated the three-story building that housed small individual rooms. Even powerful air conditioners—which turned the room into an icebox compared to the raging heat outside—failed to scrub the air sufficiently to remove the awful odor. You didn't have to be an environmentalist to wonder what toxins were present in that air.

"Every soldier who serves at Rusty has a letter added to his medical file when he leaves," Busch said. "It states that if he ever has respiratory issues in the future chances are good that they originated while he served here."

An added bonus for the toxic air was that when the sky filled with smoke and dust, JAM insurgents knew that counterbattery radars' capabilities were degraded. Consequently they picked those times as ideal for shooting rockets and mortars into the FOB. Given the constant burning garbage and brisk wind, the FOB got more than its share of incoming.

"Take cover, take cover!" the mechanical voice—activated automatically when the radar picked up incoming rockets and mortars—would shout. At that point, you followed the FOB SOP: first drop to the ground wherever you happen to be. Wait for the first explosions. If you're lying flat chances of shrapnel hitting you are reduced. Unless it's close; then you're toast. Immediately after the first rockets impact, jump to your feet and dash to the nearest bunker. In the first few days I'd had lots of practice perfecting my technique. Over the next week I'd get really good at it.

"One nice thing," Bogdon groused over his cigar, "is that you know when you smoke one of these things, that's the best air you're gonna get here."

Captain Elizabeth Cain was on her second tour, having rolled over the berm on Operation Iraqi Freedom (OIF) 1 while attached to the 3rd Infantry Division. With flaming red hair pulled tight into a military bun, the energetic Cain commands the 54th MP Company, one of Bogdon's subordinate units. Of medium height and build, Cain runs a tight ship. Many of the NCOs in her unit remarked positively on her organization and leadership skills. "The captain knows what she's doing," a senior NCO said. "We may get in the shit, but we won't get there by screwing up."

As the conversation unfolded, Cain discussed the following day's mission down to Salman Pak. Just south of Salman Pak was a huge swampland, once home to a particularly unique ethnic group known as the Marsh Arabs, and densely populated by an ecological cornucopia of wildlife including exotic wading birds and rare species of fish and mammals.

Saddam Hussein had drained those swamps, blocking water flow and diverting it into his pet projects as part of punishment for the independent Marsh Arabs, who were not enamored with the man nor with his Ba'ath Party. International organizations had declared the water redistribution an ecological crime. Now, slowly, the CPA and new Iraqi government were liberating the water and the Marsh Arab population and trying to restore the damage done by Saddam. It would be a long, difficult undertaking in a country with many competing infrastructure priorities, but it was at least a start on making things right.

Early in OIF, Marines attacked the terrorist camp near Salman Pak and fought a pitched battle there. Embedded with the Marines, former Lieutenant Colonel Oliver North reported on stacks of documents describing how best to attack subway systems with sarin and ricin gas, and how to take over a civilian airliner with knives.

Over the years, as tactical units and MP convoys rolled through its streets, Salman Pak developed the reputation as a shooting gallery. "When we were tasked to go to Salman Pak," Cain told me later, "we always went loaded for bear. We knew we were in for a fight."

As Cain discussed the next day's mission with Bogdon, I interjected a request. "Can I ride with you tomorrow?" Cain was visibly less than thrilled with the idea.

"Well, it's kind of late to add someone . . ." She fidgeted, finally deferring to authority. "If the battalion commander says it's okay, then you can."

Bogdon was off on another subject so I waited for a break in the action. "John, Captain Cain says that if it's okay with you I can roll with her tomorrow. How about it?"

"What's on your schedule now?" he asked, slightly annoyed to be distracted from his discourse.

"Just interviews here on the FOB. It would be a good chance for me to see some operations." I wasn't quite begging but it was getting close.

"Sure," he said. "Sounds like a good idea to me. Liz, make it happen, okay?" Bogdon then resumed the subject he had been expounding upon before I interrupted.

Cain is a good soldier. She wasn't thrilled by the idea but now agreed to make the best of it. "Meet me in my office about 0730 and we'll get you set up."

As we did a final equipment and vehicle check, Cain directed me to a seat. "Ride in the left rear of my truck," she said. "Six months ago I would have asked that you not be permitted on this mission. I think it far too dangerous for someone who doesn't have to be there and I wouldn't have wanted responsibility for your safety."

As we headed south, Cain told me of past battles.

"We knew that every time we rolled into Salman Pak we were going into a fight," she said. "IEDs, EFPs, VBEDs, ambushes, you name it, they threw it at us. Mostly AQI elements, but some JAM also.

"We have made such progress bringing along the Iraqi Police that we work with, that once the AQI is pushed out by maneuver elements and Iraqi security forces they are capable of keeping and maintaining order. The people want to live in a peaceful, secure environment and AQI brings repression and destruction. When ordinary citizens realize that their future is with the government and that the police are there to protect them not hurt them, then they turn on AQI and the bad guys have no place to hide."

The city was not clear by a long shot, Cain said. "If you look at the map you'll see a bend in the river just south of the city. That's where the AQI and Sunni insurgents are based." South of Salman Pak, winding its way to the Persian Gulf, the Tigris River makes an extraordinary bend in which the river forms a deep pocket. That area was crammed with AQI and Sunni fighters.

"The maneuver brigades are looking to reduce that pocket as we speak," Cain said. "As soon as they kick enough of the bad guys out we'll be down there to help the police rebuild and restore law and order. But for today, we're not going there."

We pushed down through Salman Pak, quiet this morning with the markets starting to draw customers, toward the ancient city called the Arches by soldiers. This was the ancient ruin of Ctesiphon, a major city of the Parthian Empire, already a century old by the time Christ walked the earth. It was conquered and defeated four times by Roman legions, overcome by Muslim warlords in the eighth century, and source of one of Scheherazade's songs in *One Thousand and One Nights* as she entranced her captor to avoid dishonor.

How odd it was to drive in modern, up-armored Humvees past standing ruins of a towering Parthian Empire archway, called Taq Kisra, dating from the sixth century, in the midst of the desert. The walls stood at least forty feet high, carved to resemble the façade of a pillared temple but solid stone. The elliptical arch stands virtually unscarred a bit higher, between two sets of walls.

The ruins of Ctesiphon tell us a story: We are not the first soldiers to muddy our boots in Iraqi soil. Back when this was the Babylonian Empire and wondrous gardens hung from the principal city, foreign armies marched north and south across the land. Some cultures leave a lasting imprint; all who venture into this desert leave their blood that soaks into the sands, and their bones bleaching in the sun after being picked clean by vultures.

What is going to be our legacy in this ancient land between the rivers?

Maybe better than a lot of people think. As we rolled back north through Salman Pak Cain let out a happy cry. "Look at that, on the right." She pointed. A mustached, thick-bodied man, in Iraqi Police uniform, strode down the median. He wore a broad grin and waved back frequently to civilians in the marketplace who greeted him.

"That's the chief of police, General Adman," Cain said in surprised wonder. "He isn't even carrying a weapon. A few months ago he would have been assassinated, gunned down on the spot. What a transformation!"

Cain interacted well with the Iraqi general. Both obviously had built up a relationship of mutual trust. It was clear that the general enjoyed the visit and from his remarks had great confidence in Cain's ability to advise and assist him in their mutual mission.

Most of their conversation was focused on specific issues: the level of AQI activity in the city and surrounding area, the chronic shortages in the logistics systems and how to expedite requisitions and deliveries, recruiting and training new policemen, attitudes of the civilian population, manning checkpoints, detainee handling, and a long list of other topics.

The conversation was free-flowing and frank, with comfortable joking and sidebar discussions. Exactly what one would expect to see between colleagues, albeit in a dangerous business.

"You have to be careful, *saidi* [a term of respect]," Cain said. "I saw you walking down the street earlier. You need to have a body-guard and a weapon."

"This is my city," the general laughed. "If I cannot be safe here than neither can my people. I walk among them alone to show that they are safe here. I am not worried."

Several members of the general's immediate family had been killed by al-Qaeda in attempts to intimidate him, scare him away from the city. The chief, like many of his fellow Iraqis, was hard as nails inside and refused to be bullied into submission. The terrorists don't have a chance of frightening a guy like this.

We stopped at the southernmost IP station in the city. As we walked in, we stepped past piles of sand and gravel, sidestepped a worker mixing concrete, and ducked so that we would not get splat-tered from paint by workers on ladders. "This station is undergoing a total renovation," said Sergeant First Class Stephen Mudge. A Plym-outh, Massachusetts, native and career soldier, Mudge is optimistic about the changing situation. He leads the squad that is based with the IPs and lives at the station.

"I like living down here with the IPs. We're closer to the action and get way better intel than if we went back to the FOB every day."

He admits that life in Salman Pak is dangerous. "We get shot at by AQI pretty regularly," Mudge said. "They also like to use deep-buried IEDs against us. Every so often a sniper will take a pot shot, but most of their weapons are non-scoped so they have a pretty small porch." This refers to al-Qaeda use of iron-sighted weapons—without tele-scopic sights—thereby giving the shooter a much shorter effective range to engage a target.

"They test us all the time," Mudge said. "They learn from us; we learn from them. It's a game. The last attack a few weeks ago was a free-for-all. Fortunately all small arms with some RPGs. The tower there got hit more than a hundred times. But we didn't have casual-ties to speak of on our side. The IPs fight a lot better when we're here with them. Can't blame them for that."

Mudge is happy with the expanding Sons of Iraq program, the Petraeus-backed plan to reward former insurgents with pay and jobs.

improving their professionalism daily," noted Lieutenant Colonel Daryl Johnson, the 716th MP Battalion commander. "This isn't a game of major victories, just steady progress. Sometimes we take a step back, then the next day we have to push for two steps forward."

In the Milk District of Abu Ghraib, where five years before Sergeant First Class Abigail Vantichelt and her squad had been fighting for their lives, the expanded police presence, continually monitored and encouraged by the MPs, has seen a return of the old marketplace, reopening of businesses, and scenes of civilians walking the streets to shop and conduct business. A visit to Mayor Shaker's office revealed lines waiting to see him on what could only be described as routine and largely prosaic requests. The forty-something mayor gestured to encompass his constituency. "Without the police presence on the streets and neighborhoods we could never be meeting and living like this. When Saddam was here this was an oppressed neighborhood. When al-Qaeda was present my people would hide in their homes, fearful of their lives. Now we are building a new Iraq."

19

THE POWERHOUSE MPS

Dak is one tough soldier. He weighs in at about a hundred pounds and has intense brown eyes that stare laser beams through you when he concentrates. He has been an MP for his entire adult life and has three hundred combat missions in Iraq to his credit.

When last deployed Dak had a specialty few other MPs could match: He would wait silently outside the back doors of buildings other soldiers had entered through the front for a search-and-clear operation. If anyone came out the back door—"squirters," his fellow soldiers called them—then Dak would dash after them, run them down, and capture them without firing a shot. Amazingly, no one ever escaped his clutches when he was on the chase.

Even knowing that Dak was on an operation—for he quickly got a reputation among the Iraqi insurgents—caused more than one enemy fighter to give himself up and plead for mercy.

Dak is a German shepherd, a fully qualified military working dog. While in Iraq, Dak and his human partner, Specialist Chris Bond, became an integral part of the maneuver unit charged with clearing suspicious houses. On one occasion the unit air-assaulted into a known insurgent-controlled village. Moving deliberately through the villages—clearing buildings, house by house—soldiers developed a standard operating procedure (SOP). While they burst in the front door and poured through to clear a house, Dak and Bond slipped around the rear and watched for enemies trying to flee.

The SOP paid immediate dividends.

Dak—in the dead of night—ran down a squirter and nabbed him by the upper arm. Bond, M-4 at the ready, rapidly followed, jumping debris and junk piles that littered the yard, dodging obstacles, and scanning for other insurgents through the eerie green tones of his night-vision goggles. In short order he approached a screaming, blood-soaked insurgent writhing on the ground. Dak, ever alert and ready to pounce if the man got to his feet, sat beside him, pieces of bloody flesh dangling from his muzzle. Bond called for soldiers and a medic to assist.

They figured, on examination, that the man must have resisted Dak, tried to fight him and to pull away from those inch-and-a-half-long canines. As a result, a good portion of his triceps had been torn away.

It quickly got to the point that when Bond and Dak were spotted outside a building insurgents would reverse direction and head back inside even if American soldiers were crashing in through the front. Dak's reputation was such that they would rather take their chances dealing with a gun than face that dog.

Military working dog (MWD) handlers, while justifiably proud of the multiplier effect that a dog team can bring to the fight, are quick to point out something that makes them a unique battlefield weapons system. An infantryman who spots a target may raise his weapon and engage it. The same thing happens with a dog team. But what happens if the scenario changes, and, as could happen, a child suddenly darts out of a house or alleyway?

Once that bullet is fired it is gone forever. An attack dog, though, is a guided, controlled weapon. Handlers say that dogs are "a bullet we can call back." This trait of instant and complete control over the dog, according to Staff Sergeant Lee McCoy and his fellow dog handlers, affords them a special role in the kinds of urban combat that the U.S. military fights today. Nor is this capability coincidental. Even in a full sprint, lunging into an attack, an MWD can be stopped on a dime by a voice command. Commands are practiced, rehearsed, and repeated, often daily, so that in time dog and handler became a smooth team.

In the same way, Dak and his new handler, Specialist Chris Reed, train daily to go downrange. According to McCoy, who is only half joking, Dak is training his new handler well. It is established practice within the MWD community to place the more experienced dogs with the newest handlers, and vice versa. The end results, all are convinced, are stronger man-dog teams.

Dog handlers are a special breed, pun unintended. They uniformly grouse—with some apparent justification—that they are underappreciated by other MPs and are last in line when it comes time for promotions. Most are MOS 31-B, the largest military police specialty group. There is talk about creating a separate MOS 31-R for dog handlers, but handlers have mixed emotions because it would narrow the field too much, thereby further limiting promotion opportunities. They are convinced that if a soldier seeks quick rank, the dog handler occupation is not the place to find it. Promotions come slower, they believe. McCoy and his team accepted such constraints. With them it all comes down to two things: love of the job and love for the dogs.

It has to be love because the headaches are so great, especially when traveling. Unlike the old cliché, getting into a combat zone with a dog is definitely not "half the fun." Sergeant Jason Alber lugged eight duffle bags loaded with enough gear for an entire year: dog chow, specialized combat gear for him and the dog, canine medical kits, comfort items, uniforms—every required and conceivable item the team would need. He dragged this mountain of bare essentials through civilian airports until they arrived at the replacement depot in Kuwait.

Just getting Eva, his specialized search dog, a gentle, black Flathair retriever, through TSA screening was a huge chore. Alber had to convince skeptical screeners that Eva was authorized to be there in the first place. They wanted her to travel in a kennel. "No way!" Alber insisted. He patiently explained that she was not a pet but a military working dog—a four-legged soldier—on the way to war. After endless wrangling he finally won the point.

Even in the waiting area simple tasks become nightmares. The two travel alone, so no one is there to watch over gear if he has to grab a snack or relieve himself. He plans for a potty break for Eva before entering the terminal. But when faced with a flight delay or long layover he has to take her outside the terminal and repeat the painful screening process all over again.

On a military base like Kuwait's Ali Al Salem replacement depot, life for the dog team is also difficult. Some people who share the sixteen-man tents aren't comfortable with a dog's presence. When it comes time to go to chow, guards at the dining facility try to keep the dog outside.

When Alber and Eva finally got to Bagram they were both worn out, and their deployment had barely begun. Standing forlornly outside of the terminal, sand blowing cold in their faces, Eva's tail and ears drooping as she cautiously looked around, Alber wondered what he was going to do. All about him was a confusion of people coming and going, vehicles jamming in and leaving. Utter chaos, with everyone preoccupied with their own problems and tasks. It looked like a mile to get to the nearest building to ask directions to their receiving unit, and he had no assistance with his bulky baggage.

Suddenly a white Toyota pickup truck pulled up, with a big, bearded man leaning out of the window. "Hey, dog guy!" he called. "Hop in." Eva's ears perked up as she tentatively wagged her tail. Alber almost felt like wagging his tail too as he had some help loading all the gear into the back.

Alber had met his Special Forces unit and was taken care of from then forward. He found that the special ops units worked frequently with dogs—particularly in sniffing out caches of hidden explosives and weapons, and detecting buried IEDs—and fully appreciated the team's capabilities.

This characteristic has become a critical component in combating an enemy who uses guerrilla tactics, and the Special Forces community recognized their value. In contrast to attack/patrol dogs, these breeds, like Eva, primarily from the retriever family, are specially trained to make use of their extraordinarily acute sensory characteristics. With the super-refined nose that characterizes retriever breeds, they are especially useful in detecting explosives and drugs.

The downside is that they don't intimidate anybody.

Sometimes the Special Forces guys chided Alber about Eva's gentle disposition. "That dog ain't gonna bite anybody." Here was this sweet, friendly pooch with big long eyelashes who begged for attention and wouldn't maul anyone. Alber patiently outlined the difference: "Eva spots the contraband, she doesn't attack. She's not a bite dog," he explained.

After Eva began to unearth buried IEDs and caches, the teasing stopped. Instead, team members began to ask questions about capabilities and how best to employ the dog. And to slip her snacks.

Alber has already had combat tours to Afghanistan and Iraq. He and Eva were on the Iraq deployment together. Like many handlers, Alber insists that the dogs were happiest when deployed. Downrange they live with the handler—Alber used to pull Eva into his bunk at night to sleep beside him. Contrast that to being back on a military base where dogs are kept in kennels and only see handlers during the day.

Sergeant McCoy had a similar relationship with Spaulding, his chocolate Lab, on their Afghanistan deployment, also with a Special Forces unit. Like a lot of his breed, Spaulding was happiest when he was out in the field working with McCoy. Afghanistan kept them both very occupied.

On a mission in Afghanistan, the Special Forces unit and dog team air-assaulted into a suspected Taliban village with the mission of finding hidden weapons and explosives. As soon as the village was cordoned off and secured the search began, and yielded almost immediate results. Inside one of the mud-floor buildings Spaulding alerted. Digging revealed an enormous explosives cache. Searchers uncovered a hidden site with more than 4,500 pounds of homemade explosives, mostly ammonium-nitrate-based. The Taliban could have constructed a lot of deadly car bombs and IEDs out of that material.

Dog handlers may work either as attack/patrol or special search dogs (SSDs) depending on vacancies and need. Because the behavioral differences between attack/patrol and special search dogs are enormous, making the transition from SSD to bite dog is a huge undertaking. Regardless of assignment, they are all on duty for one purpose: to improve combat efficiency.

In both Iraq and Afghanistan, IEDs have become the insurgents' weapon of choice. While the Department of Defense is spending much time and resources in defeating these weapons, special search dogs have proved especially effective. Handlers affirm that dogs have saved hundreds of soldiers' lives by their efforts in both the attack/patrol function, and especially sniffing out IEDs.

How does a dog alert a handler to the looming presence of explosives or an IED? Years ago they were trained to bark, but over time it was determined best to have them assume a relaxed posture when they find something. So handlers train them to sit or lie down when they discover a suspicious substance. To the dogs it doesn't matter if it's explosives or drugs. It's all a game of find and reward. Usually handlers reward them by giving them a ball to play with after they find a cache.

Sergeant David Ricks, who spent a combat tour in Iraq with Storm, a female Golden/Lab mix, pulled a red ball out of his ACU trouser cargo pocket. A simple trinket like this is all dogs work for. That, and the love and affection of their handlers. Handlers are trained to work with their canine battle buddies in a playful manner, making serious training into a game for the dogs. They love to work—they are happiest when out exercising their skills—but the work is purposely designed to make it an enjoyable experience for the dogs.

MWDs are well cared for. They eat Science Diet (carried on field operations by handlers, along with a bowl and adequate water supplies), have frequent checkups by military vets, and can be treated by their handlers in emergency situations. All MP dog handlers are trained not only to render first aid to fellow human soldiers, but to be able to do the same for their dogs.

Indeed, at the kennel they maintain a small but well-stocked clinic and have regular visits from the on-base vet. The star attraction at the clinic is a well-designed medical training aid manikin known as

"Rover." ("Kinda lame," Specialist Chris Bond said with a self-effacing grin.) Using Rover, dog handlers are taught how to insert an IV, apply a tourniquet, clear airways, stop bleeding, and do all the other first-responder actions necessary if the dog is wounded. Using the very sophisticated manikin, soldiers can actually feel a pulse, get immediate feedback on whether the IV is inserted properly, and perform any other function they may be called on to do in combat.

Sometimes in the field, soldiers need to be made aware of the dog's limitations as well as capabilities.

One day Sergeant Ricks was working a ten-kilometer stretch of Route Irish over a four-day period when he was attached to an infantry unit in Baghdad. It was high summer, blazing hot. Ricks carried standard battle-rattle of more than seventy pounds. Plus he was carrying food, water, and gear for Storm. As they went house to house in the burning sun they uncovered several devices. So far the patrol had been worthwhile. On several occasions Ricks had to stop the grinding pace of the search. He needed to get Storm in the shade for a rest. He was worried that the dog was wearing out and needed to recharge her batteries. Dogs are just like people: If their physical condition deteriorates, so does their combat effectiveness.

Dogs, again like humans, are subject to all types of stress. One of the handler's jobs is to be alert for the signs of it. It might mean the difference between life and death. Heat, cold, fatigue, anything that might degrade the dog's capabilities could endanger them both. One point dog handlers have to make with maneuver units to which they are attached is firm: When on a search with a unit, the unit must understand from the beginning that the dog runs the show.

On a tour in Afghanistan, Staff Sergeant Mike Pierce handled a special search dog that became severely affected by post-traumatic stress disorder (PTSD). One day his dog had found the first IED but missed the next one. After they passed it, the device exploded, badly frightening the dog, who then jumped into the back of a Humvee about twenty yards away. Pierce reported that it was as if the dog just said, "To hell with it." He'd had enough.

In Afghanistan especially, the Taliban and al-Qaeda have also begun to target dogs and handlers because of their effectiveness. They have placed booby traps especially designed to kill dogs. The enemy is inventive and cunning. Over time, antidog devices are going to become common. Accordingly, handlers are learning to be increasingly alert. If the enemy adjusts, so will they.

Wild or feral dogs in Afghanistan are also a threat. Pierce found that wild dogs were extremely hostile to the military dogs. When on patrol they would bark, lunge, and occasionally try to attack, particularly if they roamed in a pack. On one mission he was working with another dog team he heard a shot and inquired what had happened. "Had to shoot a feral dog," was the terse reply over his radio.

Typically in Afghanistan, while riding with Special Forces on patrol, the dog and handler are out of the trucks and on the road at the first inkling of danger or even suspicion. This means that while they find the IEDs they are also exposed to the first shots in an ambush. McCoy reported that when the Special Forces thought that they were getting close to contact they would pull the team back into the trucks for better protection.

Pierce, who had also worked with Special Forces in theater, agreed, but was quick to note that he and the dog make "big targets." Also, the dog teams typically have a much shorter span of view, being focused on what they can see on the ground in front of them. Hence it is essential that while they are up front of the group that the rest of the soldiers keep alerted to the overall battle scenario. Soldiers refer to this as "situational awareness."

Rarely is the dog the first one hit. The casualties in a dog team almost always are handlers. Perhaps because the dogs themselves—though hated by the enemy—make a smaller target and can find cover more easily than a larger human.

On rare occasions a handler can adopt his dog when it comes time for the dog to retire. McCoy noted that dogs will at some point in their working lives just decide to call it quits. This is an accepted outcome. At that point the military tries to find them a good home. This is much easier done for the retrievers, who are always family oriented. Attack/patrol dogs, on the other hand, have to undergo a special detraining program before they can be released. In not all instances are the dogs and handlers rotated simultaneously. Some dogs prefer the field and stay deployed longer, with new handlers rotating. This can be a good thing as long as the dog is willing and eager to work, because it becomes a real expert in its area. Once a dog seems to be tiring, however, it is rotated back to the U.S.

Dak, Storm, Spaulding, Hatos, Bodo, Eva, Falco, Frank, and their battle buddies are prepared to deploy yet again into harm's way. Americans can be confident that these soldiers are up to every facet of accomplishing their missions.

Lalonde is big and solid. Physically he looks like he could easily tear someone apart, but with his wide brown eyes and friendly face many would find him almost huggable. Years ago he was described by Lieutenant Colonel Tom Lombardo, who crossed paths with him in Djibouti, Horn of Africa, as a "shy young pup."

No, First Sergeant Chris Lalonde isn't a military working dog, he's just handled them for the entire twenty years of his career, a record in the Military Police Corps. Big, strong, and solid, his youthful visage belies the stark fact that he has spent the latter years of his career either preparing for imminent combat or engaged in active fighting. He is proud of his accomplishments but doesn't brag. And he growls at his old friend Lombardo's reference to his ever being shy; a natural propensity to exercise stealth must never be mistaken for shyness.

Lalonde had originally been a K-9 specialist in a previous tour with the U.S. Marine Corps. Out of sixty Marines who applied, only two, including Lalonde, were selected for the school. He ended up working the 1994 World Cup tournament with a bomb dog, a Belgian Malinois named Boris. After this assignment he didn't reenlist. When Lalonde realized he'd made a mistake, the Marines had no specialty that interested him, nor would they reinstate his rank or allow him back with dogs.

The recruiter had given him two job options he didn't want— Lalonde picked a third: He joined the Army, had his rank, and was accepted as a dog handler. He recieved his set of Army orders within two hours. Yet retribution from a traditional Marine family was harsh: His father didn't speak to him for two years.

By 2003 Lalonde was deployed to Iraq as part of a special operations unit in the first of what would be seven return tours. As the insurgency grew and al-Qaeda poured resources and fighters into the theater, his role focused on killing and capturing high-value targets identified through highly classified intelligence processes and by secret informants.

In the dawn hours following one particularly harrowing mission Lalonde cleaned up, went back to his room, and prepared to sleep. Unit members worked reverse cycle in Iraq: operate at night; sleep during the day. As was customary, Fasco, who did the last two tours with him, hopped up on the bed with him and plopped his big head on the pillow. Lalonde, trying to catch some sleep, was appalled: Fasco's breath, normally "doggy," was nauseatingly fetid—and blowing right into his face.

Lalonde looked hard into his dog's mouth. To his shock he discovered pieces of human flesh imbedded between Fasco's teeth. Disgusted, he dragged both of them off the bed, snatched up his toothbrush, and began to energetically brush Fasco's teeth. ("I just pried his jaws open, lathered up the toothbrush, and went to town. He'll let me do anything to him.") After a thorough brushing and rinsing, satisfied that Fasco's mouth was finally clean, the pair crashed. Another day downrange.

Lalonde is troubled by some of the combat he saw for years in Iraq. "We were always on 'kill-or-be-killed' missions," he remembered. "Every time we went out we knew someone was going to die: one of them or one of us. Night after night. After awhile that stuff builds up inside and plays with your head."

Seeking counseling, the tough first sergeant was assigned an Air Force lieutenant colonel psychiatrist who was preoccupied with seeking solutions in Lalonde's childhood experiences. "You are depressed," he ruled, putting Lalonde on an increasingly long list of depression medications. "I was taking a dozen pills a day," Lalonde said. "And none of that crap was helping."

Finally one day Lalonde had enough. "Look Doc, I had a good childhood. That isn't the problem. It's all those tours to Iraq. That's the damn problem. And, I'm not depressed!" He now works to address his PTSD issues more independently with the unwavering support of his wife, Jolene.

Having his family around helps a great deal. "My kids are great. They are still pretty little and love to play on Fasco." He keeps Fasco at home with him, and despite his deserved reputation as a fierce warrior, the dog is a happy pet with the children. "My kids climb all over him, pull his tail, tug on his ears, and he just tolerates it. Imagine, a trained military working dog putting up with all that! But let someone come up to the house and he's alert and guarding the place. I don't have to worry about an intruder ever breaking in and hurting my wife and kids."

20

BITTER FRUITS OF CORRUPTION

When the subject of an investigation knows that the cops are coming after him, the situation gets dangerous for those law-enforcement officials. When that subject is a powerful, well-connected police official himself, especially in a place in which summary action is common, then you can bet that he will invoke violence to try to thwart that investigation. In December 2009, law enforcement professional (LEP) Tom Anderson found himself in that unenviable position.

Anderson, a diminutive, feisty former cop with a wicked sense of humor, who was assigned as a LEP advisor to first the 709th MP Battalion, then the 95th MP Battalion in Gardez, Afghanistan, had been hot on the heels of Afghan Police General Sayeed Aziz Wardak for weeks. He was steadily collecting evidence of alleged gross corruption and dereliction of duty in an effort to put Wardak behind bars or at least out of a job.

The LEP concept is simple: Since an honest, fair law-and-order environment is necessary in a counter insurgency fight for the civilian population to have a sense of security, then bring in the additional skill sets of community policing, investigation, and forensics to theater by hiring former policemen and attaching them to military police and other units. LEPs are recruited in the United States by civilian contractors such as MPRI, who are seeking to fill slots needed by the Departments of Defense and State.

As with any other group of people, military or civilian, the effectiveness of the LEPs depends largely on the motivation and capabilities of the individuals hired and capabilities of the units they support.

Anderson, a thirty-year veteran cop who has worked in police departments in Cincinnati, Ohio, and Coral Springs, Florida, was thoroughly skilled in his profession. He had cut his teeth investigating official corruption cases. His distaste for the apparent corruption of Wardak burned inside of him. Putting Wardak in handcuffs became a personal mission.

By 2009 anticorruption was increasingly emphasized by authorities in the International Security Assistance Force (ISAF), with some notable successes. Several lower-ranking officials in Gardez Province had already been brought up on charges, tried, and were in jail. Others around the country were in various stages of investigation. The word was out that coalition and Afghani authorities were cracking down. It was, in the estimation of Anderson and the 709th MP Battalion commander, Lieutenant Colonel Rob Dillon, time to go for the bigger fish: Wardak.

Anderson knew that it was a risky business: When a foreigner operates against an established authority figure in a country like Afghanistan, and especially a closed community like Gardez, word gets around. Retaliation is the order of the day, and in the hyperviolent society of the Pashtu tribal lands, finding compliant gunmen to assassinate someone, even a foreigner, is an easy task.

As far as Anderson was concerned, a target had already been painted on his chest. He believed it was not a question of *if* Wardak would take direct action, he believed, but when and how. So Anderson and his associates were caught up in a deadly game: Could they remove Wardak before he killed them? They were feverishly working to collect evidence before Wardak could take steps to counter their moves.

On the morning of December 21 Anderson and a LEP colleague, Tom Carter of DynCorps, a twenty-year-plus veteran of the Atlanta PD, planned to attend a regularly scheduled meeting at Police Provincial Headquarters (PHQ) in downtown Gardez with General Wardak presiding. PHQ supervised police operations in the entire Paktia

Province and it was a lucrative sinecure for Wardak. His behavior was so egregious, according to Anderson, that during a simple walk through downtown Gardez, Wardak would extort money from local merchants even while accompanied by his American mentors.

"Wardak would tell them, 'Give me money or I'll have my police shut your business down,'" Anderson recalled. "Right in front of us! It was disgusting. And that was just the tip of the iceberg. He was involved in contracting scams, kickbacks, faked payroll reports, pay-offs from the Taliban, drugs, you name it."

Anderson and Carter arrived early, driving over from FOB Lightning in DynCorps pickup trucks. It was a routine meeting, but tension had been building as Wardak was fully aware of the ongoing investigation into his affairs. Despite the mutual distrust, Anderson and Carter expected that the pretense of good relations would persist and that Wardak would perform in his usual flamboyant manner while holding a lengthy meeting.

Wardak typically held court like a minor prince, demanding on fawning praise from subordinates who spent endless hours reading from handwritten reports. After they'd been read in toto, reports would then be handed directly to Wardak, who placed them in a large binder. The general seemed to collect the reports with the alacrity that hobbyists collect stamps. His behavior at meetings was predictable: He relaxed and joked, removed his coat and hung it over the back of his chair, and placed his automatic pistol and cell phone on the table throughout the meeting.

But on the Monday morning of December 21 the atmospherics were radically different. From the moment he saw Wardak that morning Anderson's police instincts kicked into full gear. "Something was suspicious about his body language. The hair on the back of my neck just went up." He told his colleague, "Wardak's up to something." Carter had picked up a similar vibe and was equally disturbed. "Watch him," he replied.

Anderson expected that the new U.S. officer who ten days ago had assumed command of the 92nd Military Police Company, Captain Marcus Perez, would attend also. Unlike his predecessor, Perez viewed

PHQ as high-value asset. Perez had been pushing Wardak to agree to a 24/7 American MP presence at the station, a move that Dillon, Anderson, and Carter strongly supported. But Perez got push-back from Wardak, who saw the initiative as far too much oversight on his operation.

When it came to assistance for financing projects or obtaining equipment, Wardak was happy to accept. Having Americans looking constantly over his shoulder, however, was unacceptable. Perez persisted. Wardak seemed anxious to discourage Americans from settling in too close for comfort. He continually tried to deflect the subject whenever it was raised.

Anderson contended that as the events of that day unfolded, Wardak likely saw a chance to resolve American interference in his corrupt operations in a single bold stroke: He would eliminate the most troublesome stones in his shoe, Anderson and Carter, and by so doing discourage casualty-adverse American military leaders from willingly housing soldiers in his compound.

Though new to command of the 92nd MP Company, Perez, a native of Cleveland, Ohio, was an experienced officer. He was eager to see just what his soldiers could do when tested. In a somewhat unusual move, Perez had been named to replace the captain who had originally commanded the 92nd MP Company back in Bamberg, Germany, and deployed with it. The captain had been transferred in mid-tour. So Perez had not met the members of his company nor had he the opportunity to train with them prior to their June 2009 deployment six months earlier. Perez and his soldiers were unknown quantities to each other, like new dogs meeting and sniffing one another out. Neither knew what to expect when the inevitable crisis erupted.

In the Military Police Corps, as with other Army units, new commanders are evaluated by soldiers and noncommissioned officers, just as the reverse is true. These are at best dicey situations. Success in combat is a matter of mutual trust and confidence that normally takes time and effort to build. No one in any unit really wants to make these kinds of judgments for the first time in combat. It happens, but is stressful at best.

Not that Perez was shy about his intentions to take full command of the company. He is a big guy both in frame and self-confidence, standing six foot three and weighing in at 220 pounds ("I'm down from 280 when I played defensive end for *the* Ohio State University"). Some soldiers, accustomed to the disengaged, ineffectual leadership of his predecessor, interpreted his style as arrogant and egotistic. Nevertheless, Perez had been around the block. He was thirty-two years old and had already served in Iraq and was on his second deployment to Afghanistan. He had not come here to win a popularity contest but to perform his mission and lead soldiers in combat.

A key part of the 92nd MP Company's mission was to train Afghan police to the point that constant coalition presence would not be necessary. Perez, well-schooled in law enforcement techniques and the philosophy of the importance of rule of law, was determined that his unit would accomplish that mission. Though just arrived, he had learned of Wardak's duplicity from those who had been around longer, including Anderson and Dillon. Perez saw Wardak as an obstacle to instilling a genuine law-and-order environment to the community and was committed to removing the Afghan commander or at least tightening the leash on his activities. Colocating a squad of MPs at PHQ—a technique that had proven effective in Iraq and elsewhere in Afghanistan—seemed like a good starting point. Perez was determined to make that happen.

For his part, Anderson was happy with Perez's aggressive attitude, contrasting it positively to his more passive predecessor. He thought that Wardak had been allowed to run amok far too long. He was all for the idea that housing U.S. soldiers alongside Afghani counterparts would not only expedite training and mentoring of the policemen but would help rein in Wardak.

On arrival by pickup truck at PHQ, Anderson and Carter watched Perez pull a convoy of MRAP vehicles into the compound and dismount. Perez had just dropped off a squad of MPs at police Precinct 1, a short few blocks away from PHQ. That squad, from 92nd Company's 3rd Platoon (Enforcers), was under leadership of Staff Sergeant Donald Lowery, originally from Salem, Illinois. Soldiers at Precinct 1 lived and worked closely with their Afghan Police counterparts and had trained them in a combination of basic soldiering skills and essential police work for several months.

Lowery and his squad left the FOB at 0800 aboard Perez's personal security detail (PSD) squad's vehicles and headed to Precinct 1. The squad lived there with their Afghani policemen for days at a time and did not require MRAPs. They had grown quite close to their counterparts and developed a rare level of mutual trust and affection. The thirty-three-year-old Lowery had been in the Army for eight years, and an MP for the last two. As a field artilleryman he had two deployments to Iraq, including his first in 2003–2004 when fighting had torn the country apart. This was his first experience in Afghanistan and his first deployment in an MP specialty.

By chance there was an unusual amount of coalition activity in the area that Monday morning. A two-vehicle convoy of Special Forces soldiers from the Operational Detachment A (ODA) located on FOB Thunder (adjacent to FOB Lightning), pulled out onto Route Idaho, the primary road through Gardez, headed west.

At the same time a four-vehicle convoy from the 92nd's first platoon was on a mission even farther west of Gardez. As part of this mission the convoy was alerted as an additional duty to act as a quick reaction force (QRF) in case any local unit came in contact with the enemy. As was standard operating procedure, all units had radio contact, if not with each other directly, then with the battlespace owner, in this case the 92nd Company (call sign at the time "Rock Solid") and with the brigade combat team from the 82nd Airborne Division ("Avalanche").

Perez remembers that back at PHQ, when Wardak called the meeting to order he acted nervous, preoccupied, and anxious to leave. Wardak repeated the phrase, "Today Gardez city is going to be attacked." Unlike at all previous meetings, Wardak was frowning, not smiling. He did not remove his coat nor place his cell phone on the table. Carter leaned over and whispered to Anderson, "Something's getting ready to happen."

"Whatever it is, I think we're fucked," Anderson replied with characteristic cyncism.

About that time, Wardak's administrative officer, Colonel Wali Jan, whom Anderson also suspected of complicity in the corruption investigation, entered the room, whispered something in the general's ear, and left abruptly. Without further comment, Wardak pushed his chair back and fled the room.

"Let's get out of here, now!" Anderson told his partner. Rising, the men motioned to Perez, who also stood. At that point they could see Wardak's truck in the courtyard below abruptly pull out of the PHQ compound.

The Americans spoke briefly and checked their weapons. "I think we're about to get hit," Anderson told Perez. Simultaneously they raced out into the parking lot, yelling at their drivers to get the trucks started. Perez dashed down a series of steps and ladders to reach his people waiting in the lower parking area. He alerted his soldiers for possible action while Anderson and Carter assembled their pickup trucks. They ordered everyone to load up and leave at the same time. "If we get hit, we want to be together for support," Anderson said.

By leaving early, the Americans had disrupted Wardak's schedule. The meetings normally lasted two hours or more, this one just a few minutes. According to Anderson, this was just enough to prevent the hit team from getting their act fully coordinated, and forced them to initiate contact precipitately.

Meanwhile, they had observed Wardak's personal truck, with the general inside, dash out and behind the governor's house, which was located behind PHQ compound out of the line of fire. "The sonofabitch is running," Anderson told his people. "Get ready, here it comes!"

When Anderson and Carter's first truck began to exit the driveway on the side of PHQ perpendicular to the main frontal road they came immediately under small-arms fire from AK-47s from an estimated two or three shooters.

"When we left early they only had the shooters who were already in place," Anderson remarked. "Given more time they could have brought up the RPG guys, then our first vehicle would have been destroyed and we would have been cooked."

Immediately, scattered firing broke out from several locations.

Minutes later a large explosion rocked the town a couple of blocks away. It was later determined to be from a motorcycle-borne VBED. Other explosions began to go off around the relatively small area of central Gardez.

As soon as the DynCorps trucks came under fire, several shooters in a building under construction across the street from PHQ opened up on the 92nd MP Company soldiers mounting MRAPs in the parking lot. Perez and his PSD squad were now engaged in the fight.

The time was about 1000 hours. A short distance away at Precinct 1, Lowery and his squad suddenly heard shooting. "It sounded like at least a thirty-round burst from a heavy machine gun, a PKM maybe," Lowery remembered. "We don't train our people to shoot that way. We train Americans and Afghani Uniformed Police to shoot eight-to-nine-round bursts. So I knew right away it was coming from the bad guys."

Lowery ordered his squad to "get your gear on!" and sent several soldiers up to the roof to gain situational awareness. Private First Class Eric Atar, a lanky twenty-one-year-old Texan from Dallas, climbed up the northeast guard tower of the precinct carrying his squad automatic weapon (SAW). From the adjacent roof, his team leader, Specialist Jimmy Salazar, twenty-two, from Long Beach, California, spotted gunfire coming from a three-story building across the main street from PHQ. The building, intended to be a hotel, was under construction. The steel I-beam structural members were in place but the façade of the building was incomplete and fully open except for a large pile of lumber in the southwest corner of the building.

"Light him up with that SAW, Atar!" Salazar called. Atar began to pump steady bursts of automatic-fire 5.56 mm rounds at the building. By now the squad at PHQ was returning fire, the Afghan Army and Police were mostly "spraying and praying" magazines of AK-47s on full auto in the general direction of the hotel. "'Nothing happens in Gardez' my ass!" Salazar shouted to his battle buddy Private First Class Aguilar, while firing at the building.

Lowery and Anderson later reported that gunfire and explosions had broken out in isolated spots across Gardez. "How much gunfire came from Taliban or bad guys and how much from ANAs or AUPs opening up is hard to say," Anderson commented. Lowery agrees about the small-arms fire. "But most of the explosions were a combination of IEDs, grenades, and suicide vests that the shooters in the building were tossing out."

Soldiers from the PSD squad—directly across from the partially constructed building—do not recall hearing fire other than from the building. Given their proximity to the building and high volume of return fire, especially from Afghanis firing full auto, it is not surprising that they were deafened to any shooting other than in the immediate area.

Lowery, unaware that any other U.S. elements were in town ("We were used to being by ourselves") radioed company headquarters requesting a quick reaction force join them. Several minutes later he heard the distinctive roar of MRAP engines. "How could they have gotten here so fast?" he wondered.

Perez's MRAPs relocated from PHQ to the lower compound closer to the fight. Along the way, he dashed by Precinct 1 and Lowery's squad. While moving through the streets, gunners, for inexplicable reasons, had ducked down in the turrets. "Why aren't they up there shooting?" Salazar shouted in frustration.

Perez later said that he took his vehicles to check on the status of the squad at Precinct 1, and to instruct Lowery's people to "stay put." Lowery acknowledged the visit but does not recall receiving such orders. Atar said that about thirty minutes into the fight the commander appeared at their location but he did not overhear the exchange between Perez and Lowery. Videos of the incident taken by soldiers in the fight show the MRAPs roaring past the precinct, and the gunners were indeed down in the turrets not engaging the enemy or watching for danger.

The relocated vehicles parked—rear troop doors opening toward the target building—in the lower PHQ parking lot closer to the target building. Soldiers exited and began to return fire. Perez, who had apparently jumped out before they got into the parking lot, was livid that they parked in such a manner, because every time a soldier entered or exited a truck he or she presented a target to the enemy. Most of the casualties—and they were slightly wounded, none serious—according to Anderson were from fragments and ricochets from this tactical error.

"They weren't shooting accurately," Perez said, referring to the enemy. "They were firing way high, holding weapons over their heads and pulling the trigger. So when I recognized this I moved down to the street level and felt confident walking around there organizing the fight."

By this time the two ODA trucks that were coincidentally passing by were engaged and pouring mini-gun fire into the building. One Special Forces soldier leaped from a truck and fractured his kneecap and tore a medial collateral ligament in the fall. Like the small bullets from the SAW and from M-4s, the mini-gun rounds were ineffective in penetrating the pile of wood behind which the shooters hid.

The 1st Platoon squad west of Gardez was alerted to return. "A normal twenty-minute trip took them about five minutes," said Aguilar. "They really had the pedal down."

Lowery, either ignoring instructions from Captain Perez to stay put or having never received them—the issue is clouded—organized his American soldiers and AUPs into a coherent force and moved toward the battle by a maneuver called "covered bounds." One section gave covering fire while the other moved, then the latter section advanced while the lead element covered them. Lowery was impressed. "They moved great. We worked through the alleyways and streets smoothly and no one got hurt." All the training they had done seemed to be paying off as the Afghans moved quickly and professionally into the fight.

After crossing a few blocks Lowery's squad was picked up by the four PSD MRAPs and moved to PHQ. They took up a position on the lower level of PHQ, firing at point-blank range, less than two hundred meters distant, into the enemy position on the third floor. Aircraft were overhead—US F-16s, French Mirages, and a Predator drone. Perez was talking to his commander throughout the fight while the 82nd Airborne Division colonel, Avalanche 6, watched live video feed from the drone. "I'm walking on the corner," Perez said.

"I see you," replied the colonel.

As the fight dragged on past minutes to an hour and more, concern for "unnecessary" property damage began to trouble Avalanche 6. He instructed Perez to diminish the volume of fire being put out against the enemy. Perez, agreeing, complied and persuaded the ODA to cease fire with the mini-gun. Some present said that Perez had originally called for an airstrike against the building but his request was denied given the location inside Gardez.

Other soldiers report that one of 92nd Company's squads had engaged for a while with .50 caliber machine guns, weapons also prohibited by ISAF commander McChrystal's published rules of engagment from being used in an urban area. Regardless, for an extraordinarily long time by combat standards, three hours plus, coalition and Afghan forces were firing light ammunition—5.56 mm and 7.62 mm—against the enemy, who had an ideal covered and concealed position. The lightweight bullets simply could not penetrate the lumber. Now heavier rounds were prohibited, many think irrationally.

"It's bullshit," Anderson observed. "American soldiers and Afghani police are being shot at for hours, the bad guys are tossing grenades and explosive charges from the building. No one is in the building, and the civilians have all run away. But our guys are still not allowed to end the fight with sufficient firepower."

At some point late in the fight, which lasted from three to three and a half hours, Lowery ordered his men—U.S. and AUPs—to fire M-203 grenade launchers at the enemy. "We aren't stopping them with what we're using," he told his soldiers. "Go to the 203s." Standing on a parapet built into a building wall, ducking behind Hesco barriers, Lowery's squad and enthusiastic AUPs began to aim M-203 rounds—40 mm grenades that have a bit more power than a hand grenade—at the third floor of the half-completed hotel.

"I was in charge of the safety and welfare of my soldiers as well as the AUPs we advised," Lowery said. "This fight had gone on for too long in my best judgment and was getting nowhere. We were increasingly risking friendly and civilian casualties. We had line of sight to a target with no civilians around. I made what I thought was the best call to take care of the friendlies. We just had to end it right then and there."

Within minutes Lowery was slightly wounded in the face by bullet fragments and debris shot up from one of the Hesco barriers. When he saw blood gushing on the ground from his face he shouted to a soldier standing beside him, "Am I okay? Am I all right?" Reassured, he continued, but when the bleeding wouldn't stop he was eventually dragged down off the wall by Sergeant Edward Dillard, his assistant squad leader, a twenty-seven-year-old MP from Miami, Florida.

Perez, angered by the use of M-203s without his express permission, snapped orders on the radio to cease their use. Meanwhile, the AUPs tried bravely, but futilely to clear the building. "The AUPs had made a couple of attempts to clear it. They were enthusiastic but disorganized," Perez noted. At one point he had to physically remove AUP General Dustiger from the fight for his own safety.

"The general was in the lead, attacking the building and holding his AK over his head and spraying. He was too valuable for that nonsense, so I pulled him back into PHQ," Perez reported.

"General Dustiger is a good guy," Atar affirmed. "He was right in the thick of things, fighting to get into the building. He's honest and trying to control this corruption, not like Wardak. He leads by example."

Perez decided to take the attack to the insurgents with MPs. He pulled together two "stacks" of soldiers—six-man teams designed specifically to hit the building and clear it—to attack the building and take out the insurgents. Perez designated himself number two man in the lead stack, with Atar and his lethal SAW leading the way up the stairs. Squad members Dillard, Peterson, Dickey, and Bakken were also in the stack. Grenades kept exploding off the side of the building ("It was like those guys had an endless supply," a soldier noted) and the AUP still poured large volumes of badly aimed suppressing fire at the target.

Perez secured a flash-bang grenade from the ODA. As the stack pushed upward and AUPs shouted something about a suicide bomber in the area, grenades tossed by the shooters on the third floor exploded around them. Bullets struck from every direction. Specialist Bakken, a female member of the stack, received slight wounds from shrapnel. Members of the following stack began to drag wounded out of the way. On order the stack pushed quickly, relentlessly up the stairwell.

When they got to the top Perez tossed in a green smoke grenade first ("It almost hit Dickey in the hand," Atar reported), then followed with the flash-bang. Perez gave the order to assault.

"I was afraid at first," Atar said. "But then I just wanted to get up that tower. The adrenaline was pumping hard." As the stack crashed onto the third floor a chaotic scene awaited them. Danger was every-where. Who knew how many shooters were alive up there just wait-ing for them to present themselves as targets?

"When I crashed into the room," Atar reported, "one guy was lying dead on the floor about the middle of the building. Out of the corner of my eye I saw another guy bring his weapon around. He was the one hiding behind the lumber. I hosed him down with a burst from my SAW and hit him five or six times."

The insurgent went down. Perez's MPs quickly cleared the build-ing. When the second insurgent, the one shot by Atar, was discovered to be still alive even after taking rounds to the head, stomach, leg, and both shoulders, soldiers were amazed.

"I thought, what do I have to do to kill a guy with this thing?" Atar said.

Afterward, everyone involved agreed that the outcome was as good as could have been expected. Some reports were of up to five shoot-ers, and noted that three may have escaped by posing as civilians. Perez was convinced that there were only two shooters. "One guy was killed by 7.62 fire and he was lying out in the open when we en-tered the room," Perez reported. "PFC Atar neutralized the second one. As far as I'm concerned that's all that were up there."

"When I think back on it," Atar commented, "there are a bunch of things that could have gone wrong. We could easily have had a blue-on-blue [fratricide] incident with so many people shooting. The guy who was still alive when we broke in could have got me or someone else. Fortunately none of my buddies got shot."

When soldiers discovered that one shooter was still alive, medics immediately began to work to keep him alive. After bandaging his extensive wounds they carried him on a stretcher down the narrow stairwell to evacuate him to a nearby military hospital on FOB Thunder. "His arms kept flopping off the stretcher," a soldier noted. "We strapped them across his body." The shooter was eventually evacuated to Bagram and survived the fight.

Atar remembered MPs clearing civilians from the surrounding area after the fight as the search commenced for unexploded ordnance and the possible presence of other, hidden insurgents. "One MP carried an old woman out of a nearby house on his back," he said. The Afghani police quickly snatched up any weapons found on the site. "We wanted one for a souvenir for the unit," Atar said, "but they wouldn't give any back."

"It was a real celebration back at Precinct 1," Lowery recalled. "They had got ahold of some goats and lamb, cooked up big pots of rice and vegetables, and made dinner for all of us. They were really proud and pleased as to how they performed that day. And we were proud of them, too."

Anderson thinks that the suspected assassination attempt along with the joint success of the AUPs and coalition forces working together marked the beginning of the end for Wardak's empire. "He was pulled up to Kabul not long afterwards," Anderson said. At first the reason given was "reassignment" but later it was clear that even the corrupt leaders in Kabul had more pressure from ISAF than they wanted. Wardak was placed under arrest and the Ministry of Interior prosecutors were busy building a case against him. He is still awaiting trial.

At the end of the day on December 21, 2009, all of Wardak's initiatives backfired: The investigation was accelerated and U.S. Military Police established a semipermanent presence at PHQ. Wardak was replaced by his deputy, General Dustiger, who by all appearances was a dedicated law enforcement officer, courageous and committed, who would give the province the kind of leadership it needed.

The following day the 709th MP Battalion commander, Lieutenant Colonel Rob Dillon, had just finished congratulating Lowery for doing a good job. Lowery's face was bandaged from shrapnel wounds.

But Perez was unforgiving of Lowery for using the M-203. In what came as a terrible shock, Perez broke up the squad. He relieved Lowery of his duties as squad leader and sent him into virtual exile at a remote combat outpost at Chamkani, deep in the Hindu Kush mountains where a squad from 92nd MP Company has permanent presence. A few days later Dillard was also relieved and downgraded to a team leader, ostensibly for writing some bitter comments about the situation on a poster in his B-hut room.

A controversy developed between Lowery and 92nd MP Company leadership. Lowery thought he had legitimately earned a Purple Heart for wounds, but both Perez and 92nd Company's first sergeant disapproved the request.

Third squad—indeed all U.S. presence—was removed from Precinct 1. "The Afghanis couldn't understand," Lowery said. "Here we had this great success and then we were pulled out. They took it as a personal criticism for doing good. 'Why are you leaving us now?' they asked me. I didn't have an answer for them."

The removal of third squad from Precinct 1 was "planned long before I took command and had been announced," Perez maintained. "The events of 21 December had nothing to do with my decision to pull that squad out. Basically they had done a good job and were needed somewhere else." Lowery recalled that the first time he heard about them being removed from Precinct 1 was days after the firefight.

Unit morale and cohesion suffered throughout the remainder of the tour. Many soldiers identified more with their platoons from that point forward. At the basic soldier level the feeling was so toxic that one said, "Our company commander hates us."

Into this mess stepped the two writers.

II

GOBSMACKED: A DOWNRANGE REALITY CHECK

21

GRINDING IT OUT

You can talk, read, ask questions, and conduct interviews. But to learn the truth, nothing beats boots on the ground. In spring 2008 I went to Iraq for a month. Two years later we were both able to embed in Afghanistan for two months in the spring of 2010 and one month in the fall. This section deals primarily with our direct observations from the war zone and the amazing people we met there.

We had written about the exemplary actions of soldiers in both theaters of war. Now we wanted to go to the point of the spear—in eastern and southern Afghanistan—to observe firsthand the day-to-day operating tempo of deployed military police units. It was important to see how "ordinary" soldiers were interacting with and training their counterparts.

We were hosted by the 95th MP Battalion, the same unit that Gordon had embedded with in Iraq in 2008. During our three-month embed in Afghanistan we spent time with the 92nd MP Company, the 615th MP Company, the 630th MP Company, Bravo Company of the 151st Infantry (Indiana National Guard), and the 504th MP Battalion comprised of the 170th MP Company, 202nd MP Company, 720th MP Company, 552nd MP Company, 54th MP Company, and a special detachment advising Provincial Headquarters. Along the way we met soldiers and civilian contractors from all specialties and components.

By this time in the war, focus had shifted to strict counterinsurgency operations with large emphasis on training, coaching, and mentoring the Afghani Police. All operations we accompanied were driven by the goal of "having an Afghani face" on them, hence we were able to observe close-hand the results of that training and understand the soldiers' interpretation of their role. One of our first embeds was with the 92nd MP Company. Before we even got settled we heard stories about the December 21 firefight and picked up rumblings of discontent. We were placed with the third platoon—comprising the remnants of Staff Sergeant Lowery's squad—and discontent turned into open hostility.

When Captain Perez decided to pull the squad he sent them somewhere else other than downtown Gardez's Precinct 1. That "somewhere else" turned out to be Combat Outpost (COP) Zormat, west and a bit south of Gardez, a forlorn outpost built, literally, on a septic field. A sad collection of trailers and B-huts, Zormat sits on an open plain adjacent to a small but key Paktia Province town. The water table—despite the altitude—is very high. Dig down a foot or so and you'll hit water. Each B-hut had between six and twelve inches of stagnant water beneath it. You can smell the stink rising up from the floor of your room. "Come warmer weather," a LEP assigned to COP Zormat said, "and the water is black with mosquito larvae." That this kind of obvious health hazard is permitted for American soldiers and civilians in a malaria-endemic country is a scandal.

Zormat had been a Russian base camp during the Soviet war. On their way out the Soviets deliberately salted the earth in a biblical display of hatred for the population, contaminating the soil with tons of salt spread over scores of acres in order to ruin it for future agriculture and grazing. Looking at masses of salt leaching from Hescos and working its way up the sides of B-huts gives credence to the allegation. Foot patrols outside of Zormat cross acres of land that can barely support tough weeds, proof of the effectiveness of Soviet revenge.

Third Platoon Sergeant First Class David Ronje, on his fourth deployment, led his platoon minus third squad well in combat maneuvers (his third squad under Sergeant Franzac is stationed at Gardez).

TOP LEFT: Aftermath of the 9/11 attack: Then-Colonel David Phillips's Pentagon office suite was struck directly by a hijacked aircraft. When he and his senior NCO entered the flaming wreckage all they were able to salvage was a canvas-covered American flag from Phillips's office. "I carry it with me to each new assignment," Phillips noted. "It is a stark reminder of why we are in this war." *(Courtesy of Brigadier General David Phillips)*

RIGHT: He's every bit as tough as he appears: Master Sergeant "Mike" Stillwell on patrol in Iraq. Stillwell flew to Bagram, Afghanistan, in the early days of the war to assist with managing the overwhelming load of captured enemy fighters. *(Courtesy of Master Sergeant Mike Stilwell)*

BOTTOM LEFT: She pulled her patrol through a deadly firefight: Sergeant First Class Abigail Vantichelt, with great courage and perseverance, fought her way out of a nighttime ambush in the dangerous streets and alleys of eastern Baghdad. Here a student at Fort Wood's advanced noncommissioned officers' course, Vantichelt is now in Gardez, Afghanistan, with the 92nd MP Battalion. *(Photo credit: Chris Fontana)*

TOP: What IEDs do to trucks: Destroyed HUMVEE that Sergeant Jesse James Shambo rode in Iraq when he was seriously wounded. After that, Shambo's war was over. *(Courtesy of Staff Sergeant Jesse Shambo)*

LEFT: Fighting on the deadly, dirty urban battlefield: Sergeant Jesse James Shambo prepares for another mission in Iraq, 2004. On an earlier mission Shambo spotted a group of fifty insurgents just as his patrol rolled into a brutal ambush in Diyalah. For several days the MPs wondered if they would be able to hold out against the waves of attackers. *(Courtesy of Staff Sergeant Jesse James Shambo)*

RIGHT: "Send me!" The first soldier lost when the 16th MP Brigade (Airborne) deployed to Iraq, Staff Sergeant Wentz "Baron" Shannerberger insisted that he leave his desk and be given a platoon. "I need to be out there with the soldiers," he told his commander Colonel David Quantock. Awarded the Silver Star for heroism, Shannerberger's experience alerted him to danger and kept his unit from driving deep into an insurgent ambush kill zone. *(Courtesy of Major General David Quantock)*

TOP: "Just get it done!" Then-Colonel David Quantock led the 16th MP Brigade (Airborne) during the violent Mahdi Army insurgency in Iraq for fifteen months. He initiated the tactic of "shadowing" Coalition supply convoys with MP patrols, thwarting insurgent ambushes or punishing any enemy who attempted one. *(Courtesy of Major General David Quantock)*

LEFT: He's tougher than he looks: Sergeant First Class Gary Watford in the 92nd MP Company tactical operations center in Gardez, Afghanistan, in 2010. This day no one is whispering in his ear, "Shoot that Afghani guard!" *(Photo credit: Chris Fontana)*

RIGHT: Airborne all the way: First Lieutenant Alvin Shell in Iraq. Horribly burned in an ambush by a raging fuel truck fire, Shell saved his platoon sergeant's life and almost lost his own. When told by his commander that he was a hero, Shell replied, "A hero is a sandwich. I'm a paratrooper!" *(Courtesy of Major General David Quantock)*

TOP: "The Alamo" at Karbala, Iraq, 2005: Sergeant Jesse Hernandez and First Lieutenant Nathan Diaz before the deadly attack that resulted in the kidnapping and assassination of four U.S. soldiers. *(Courtesy of Master Sergeant Michael King)*

BOTTOM LEFT: Homecoming: After a long, bloody fifteen-month deployment to Iraq, David Phillips brought his 89th MP Brigade back to Fort Hood, Texas. During the long absence, Dawn was unofficial leader of waiting spouses, many of whom had understandably difficult times with the adjustment. *(Courtesy of Brigadier General David Phillips)*

BOTTOM RIGHT: Learning from the best: First Sergeant Michael King, survivor of the terrible Karbala incident, stands before some of his new trainees at Fort Wood, 2009. A key point in training new military policemen is that combat veterans constantly teach their hard-won knowledge to soldiers-in-training, most of whom will be deployed in a year. *(Photo credit: Chris Fontana)*

TOP: Rolling with the 18th MP Brigade operations officer: Lieutenant Colonel Tom Lombardo and author Gordon Cucullu prior to a mounted patrol in eastern Baghdad, April 2008. Lombardo, later a battalion commander at Fort Leonard Wood, is one of the more cerebral and dynamic modern officers and a founding board member for the Valhalla Project. *(Photo credit: Lieutenant Colonel Michael Indovina)*

BOTTOM LEFT: When Apache pilots need guidance picking a target: The previous night First Lieutenant Christopher Nogle led a patrol to paint directions on a troublesome target that helicopter gunships were reluctant to strike because they "lacked positive identification." That day the problem was resolved. *(Courtesy of Captain Christopher Nogle)*

BOTTOM RIGHT: Battle buddies: First Sergeant Christopher Lalonde and Military Working Dog Sergeant Major Fasco spent many long nights raiding terrorist hideouts in Iraq. "When we went out we knew someone was going to die. One of them or one of us," Lalonde said. *(Courtesy of 1SG Christopher Lalonde)*

TOP: Defeating IEDs: The medieval appearance belies the effectiveness of a device attached to the front of the lead MRAP in convoys. Designed to roll over and detonate buried IEDs and electronically counter others, the mine roller attempts to shift the odds. Unfortunately Taliban and al Qaeda bomb makers adjust to U.S. tactics and we continue to lose soldiers. *(Photo credit: Chris Fontana)*

BOTTOM LEFT: No regrets: Staff Sergeant Donald Lowery, Third Platoon, 92nd MP Company, ordered his soldiers to use their M-203 grenade launchers to stop a three-and-a-half hour firefight in downtown Gardez on December 21, 2009. "The fighting had gone on too long," Lowery said. "I was worried that one of my soldiers would be killed. We had to stop it so I ordered up the 203s." Lowery was later relieved by his commander for the decision. *(Photo credit: Chris Fontana)*

BOTTOM RIGHT: Checking the area for danger: PFC Jennifer Manning, 1st Platoon (Crusaders), 92nd MP Company briefly scans the rooftops while preparing to search female residents of a suspect compound during a "knock and search" operation south of Gardez, Afghanistan, April 2010. MPs strictly observe protocols for dealing with women, always worried that one could be a male terrorist in disguise. *(Photo credit: Gordon Cucullu)*

TOP: Ready to roll: 95th MP Battalion's Command Sergeant Major Henry Stearns and commander Lieutenant Colonel Duane Miller prepare for a mission through the dangerous Khost-Gardez Pass to inspect a remote Afghani Police station in May 2010. *(Photo credit: Chris Fontana)*

BOTTOM LEFT: Who is that masked man?: Afghani Police often conceal their identities when on operations to protect their families from Taliban reprisals. Joined on the search by the 92nd MP Company, police inspect all possible hiding places for weapons and explosives while resident chickens scratch and peck around them. *(Photo credit: Chris Fontana)*

BOTTOM RIGHT: Details matter: Sergeant First Class Tony Rosado, 1st Platoon, 92nd MP Company, caught in a rare private moment in April 2009. A good platoon sergeant monitors every detail from vehicle readiness, weapons maintenance, mission planning, and soldier morale. The priority order Mission, Men, Yourself is drilled into army leadership from the inception of training. *(Photo credit: Chris Fontana)*

TOP: Downtime: Sergeant Nick Olszewski lifts Specialist Jarid Matthews while the personal security detachment of the 95th MP Battalion takes a break at FOB Gardez, Afghanistan, 2010. *(Photo credit: Chris Fontana)*

BOTTOM: Break time from training: 95th MP Battalion soldiers train Afghani police on essential law enforcement techniques such as searching suspects, entering and clearing a room, and protection of evidence. Authors Chris Fontana and Gordon Cucullu flanking Captain Ryan Goltz, with Specialists Emily Vautaw and CJ Rich at lower right. As per ISAF rules the interpreters face has been concealed to protect his identity. *(Photo credit: Specialist Dontrell Dailey)*

Rather than drive the kilometer or so to the police station Ronje leads soldiers on foot patrols to and from. "It's better for them because they get to see the villagers up close and vice versa. Also we don't scare Afghanis as much when they get to see us as people rather than behind huge armored vehicles."

Ronje was largely mute about the action in Gardez. "I was on R and R back in Germany at the time." But he has to manage the poor morale and bitterness that resulted. "The rules are nuts," Specialist Shawn Potts is quick to say. "General McChrystal says 'Don't kill Taliban because that just makes more.' So we're just supposed to be targets for them? It's crap that we can't use the weapons we have."

The old military tradition of beginning operations in the predawn hours is still alive and well. Wakeup was at 0330 on the morning of Saturday April 3, 2010, for a premission briefing at 0445 on conduct of Operation Pistol.

The planned operation as was explained to us the previous evening was relatively simple. "We're going to surround this large qalat [a traditional compound constructed of mud]," explained First Lieutenant Michael Barnhart, leader of 1st Platoon (Crusaders), 92nd Military Police Company, while pointing to a spot on overhead imagery. "Then we'll go in and search for weapons and explosives."

"Will we blast a wall out and storm the place?" Chris asked with obvious anticipation.

"Uh, no," Barnhart said with a whimsical smile. He held up his clenched right hand and motioned it back and forth. "We'll knock." And that's where the complexity began.

By spring 2010 it was firm coalition policy that operations had to have an Afghani face on them, preferably with Afghan National Army (ANA) or Afghan Uniform Police (AUP) taking the lead. Since these kinds of cordon-and-search operations were a primary police function, that meant that the local Gardez Police Headquarters would be heavily involved. Accordingly Barnhart and his platoon sergeant, Sergeant First Class Tony Rosado, had invited AUP General Dustiger over for dinner on the night before the operation to explain the operation concept and gain his enthusiastic participation. Dustiger had been appointed as police chief of Gardez Province after Wardak's removal.

Later that night the MPs met in the B-hut headquarters of 92nd MP Company. A couple of noncommissioned officers brought some Styrofoam clamshells of chow from the DFAC along with sodas to wash it down. Barnhart and Rosado laid out maps and aerial photos of the target qalat and two nearby secondary targets. Dustiger had already agreed to the plan and had offered to task additional AUP assets to the mission. On the following morning, the AUPs would mount a significant presence.

Dustiger is somewhat typical of some of the younger, up-and-coming Afghani Police leaders. He stands of medium height and sports a well-groomed, British-style mustache that matches his salt-and-pepper hair color rather than the full beard of some Afghanis. His woolen, blue-gray police uniform is impeccably tailored, insignia polished and gleaming. He carries a Glock pistol strapped tightly to his narrow waist. Barnhart and Rosado were satisfied that if Dustiger told them that he would bring all of his assets to the fight, then he was as good as his word.

By 0440 almost everyone who was supposed to attend the final operation briefing had crammed themselves into the headquarters B-hut. Body armor, weapons, and radios added to the congestion. Rosado, his forehead wrinkled in concentration, ran down the roll call for the platoon then checked on outside support. Two U.S. Air Force combat controllers reported in, as did an artillery forward observer NCO. The 81 mm mortar squad from the Vermont Army National Guard Infantry unit on Forward Operating Base Gardez came in late, and that visibly irritated the normally sanguine platoon sergeant. He was about to get even angrier. "EOD?" called Rosado, raising his voice in his reference to the Explosive Ordinance Division bomb removal experts. "Where's the EOD guys?"

"They called last night at 2200 and said that they weren't coming," Barnhart said with an air of resigned frustration. When he's stressed, the slightly nasal Maryland accent comes out in the Gaithersburg native. During the initial operational briefing the previous evening the EOD rep, a junior NCO, had not only been present but brought with him a list of requirements he somewhat arrogantly insisted upon. By abruptly pulling out of the mission EOD aggravated the entire group.

"If we find anything on site we'll call them to come out," Barnhart said.

Rosado rolled his eyes and let it slide, but Sergeant Allison, a tall, lanky blond team leader standing nearby growled, "Now if we do find something we'll friggin' have to wait three or four hours for them to get off their asses and out to us."

Rick Hatfield, an experienced LEP, was steamed. Angrily he shifted the mass of his body armor on his large frame. "The whole purpose of this op is to find explosives and weapons. If anybody ought to be there it's EOD."

"Never mind," Barnhart said patiently. "We will run the operation without them." Frankly, at this stage of events the platoon leader had little choice but to push on. The Afghan AUPs were energized and they would shortly have close to forty policemen and six trucks loaded and ready to go. Battlespace owners and others in the chain of command were on alert. Aircraft were already flying. According to the Air Force combat controllers, a pair of Apache attack helicopters and two F-15 Strike Eagle fighters would shortly be on station. Preplanned artillery was coordinated.

Everyone was ready to rock and roll except EOD. Their absence, irrational as it might be, was insufficient reason to scrub the operation. Barnhart would have to work without them.

Within minutes the MRAP convoy of heavily armored super trucks— led by an MRAP with a medieval-appearing roller device extending from its front bumper to trigger any pressure-plate IEDs before the truck hit them—rolled out of FOB Gardez on schedule, turned west on Route Idaho, and collectively roared down to Provincial Head-quarters. Before the convoy even turned left onto the divided road-way that paralleled PHQ boundary, evidence of Dustiger's enthusiasm was clearly visible: A score of AUPs were on the streets blocking and directing traffic, and almost a dozen green Ford Ranger pickup trucks with AUP insignia lined the roadway with Soviet-style PKM machine guns mounted in their beds.

At least fifty AUPs lounged around or loaded cans of ammo into the trucks. A few smoked, but not as many as if they had been Iraqi Police. AUPs, when they do smoke, tend to puff on hash (occasionally laced with opiates), not tobacco. Today, most appeared sober.

"All elements remain in the vehicles," Crusader 6, Barnhart's call sign, announced. "Stay put in the trucks: Do not dismount. We'll be rolling soon." At that point he and Rosado got out of their MRAPs and went to locate Dustiger.

For any veterans who might worry that the Old Army philosophy of "hurry up and wait" has been overtaken by modernity, be of good cheer. As the diesel engines idled the reinforced 1st platoon watched through narrow MRAP windows as AUPs milled about outside. The platoon interpreter, Mike, had been called for right away. About forty minutes later he remounted our truck carrying two *naan*-bread-wrapped objects that vaguely resembled Italian calzones. "Want one?" he offered generously.

Chris politely declined. It was still too early in the morning for her to consider what the locals tried to pass off as actual edible food seriously. I similarly declined since I'd managed to down a quick pack of cereal before rolling out of Gardez; any remaining appetite was promptly killed by the repugnant odor emanating from the mystery meat present in the one that Mike was munching.

About twenty minutes later Dustiger was finally spotted walking to his truck. "Let the AUP vehicles mingle with ours," Barnhart ordered over the radio. It was almost precisely 0900.

The mass of vehicles rumbled south out of Gardez. Our target qalat was about seven to ten miles away over rapidly deteriorating roads. Everyone knew from the briefing that the last few hundred yards to the target would be little more than donkey paths through some wadi beds.

MRAPs give the expression "rides like a truck" new meaning. Each small depression or hole in the road felt like a crater, and the big ones bounced even tightly-strapped-in passengers from sidewall to overhead. By the time the AUP elements leading us recognized that the initially planned route was impassable due to recent heavy rain and an alternate route was chosen, almost an hour passed. If any AUPs were spying for the bad guys they certainly had ample time and opportunity to phone ahead on their mobiles to alert anyone at the qalat and compromise the mission. Still, there was always the possibility the Taliban might be caught by surprise.

"This qalat is large," Barnhart had alerted his team. "One of the biggest I've ever seen." As the trucks pulled up, some surrounded the far side of the qalat and were positioned to block any attackers while also having eyes on two adjacent, smaller qalats. These trucks were from Franzac's squad, on loan from 3rd Platoon. The base element, under Rosado, established a command post, while the 81 mm mortar team set the baseplate and tube nearby and laid the weapon in on possible targets. Barnhart led the main element—including, of course, Dustiger and his AUPs—near the front entrance.

Barnhart stands slightly below medium height, with piercing blue eyes, a sharp nose, and a slow but frequent grin. His shoulders are about as broad as he is high, so that he carries the excessive combat load demanded by today's Army, plus some. Barnhart decided to have an M-203 grenade launcher mounted beneath his M-4 rifle, and so carries ammo for the 203 as well as a dozen magazines for the M-4 plus his M-9 Beretta pistol and several 9 mm magazines for it. Add a radio, water, smoke grenades, first-aid kit, knife, combat helmet, armored vest, and other gear; he easily pushes an extra hundred pounds on his body.

"The LT can fool you," Sergeant Allison, who works out with Barnhart at the FOB Gardez gym, noted. "He does incredible numbers of pull-ups. He'll strap ninety-five pounds to his waist and do pull-ups."

Barnhart dismisses that as an exaggeration. "I only did one repetition with ninety-five pounds," he said. "Usually I do my reps with just sixty-five pounds." Barnhart is a Ranger. He will not remove his gear or even sit for the entire day, staying on his feet and moving among the soldiers and AUPs, constantly checking, coordinating, or simply observing.

Already as the trucks pulled up and unloaded, a team of Apaches roared overhead circling the qalat and surrounding area, not threatening directly but alerting anyone with bad intentions that help was available if needed.

The standard operating procedure for one of these searches goes somewhat like this: A combined AUP-coalition presence knocks on the door—literally. They then explain to whomever answers that they want to search the premises for contraband weapons and explosives and any sign of foreign fighter or Taliban occupation. The senior Afghan AUP then presents the owner or his representative with a paper to sign agreeing that it is okay for them to search, and further denying the presence of war-related material or personnel.

Dustiger was apologetic but firm in his dealing with the owner, a fairly tall, large-boned, heavyset individual in loose-fitting Afghan clothing with the ubiquitous white pillbox hat firmly planted on his over-large head. He wore a short, full black beard. His body odor would stop a charging rhino. None of the Afghans appeared to notice.

From inside the walls the qalat—which looked quite imposing externally with eighteen-foot-high brick and mud walls—was stunningly large, running approximately two hundred meters in length and seventy meters across. "It has twenty-four rooms," Mike the terp said, pointing to the far side of the qalat where rooms had been constructed along the length of the wall. The far wall had been built especially thick so that rooms jutted from it; there was also a second story, which appeared to be storage space, and a rampart along the crenellated wall.

"It's going to take a helluva long time to search this big sonovabitch," said Sergeant West, brushing past to get on with the task.

"The real owner is not here," Mike informed us, pointing to the large Afghani talking with Barnhart and Dustiger. "This is one of his seven sons who live here with their families. This is a rich qalat." By Afghani standards, perhaps, but little inside seemed to affirm that supposition. Room floors were covered with threadbare carpets. Most rooms were cluttered with tin pots, cooking utensils, bric-a-brac, clothing, quilts, and nondescript junk.

Though enclosing a huge interior space—more than three acres—

little had been done to improve it. A few tiny mud-formed domes with small entrances served as roosts for a handful of skinny chickens that scratched around the hard-caked, gravelly brown soil. A small plot against the near wall covered with manure and fenced with junk wood barely contained a nanny goat and her scrawny jet-black kid. A low brick wall marked what appeared to the stunned survivors of a half-hearted attempt at a vegetable garden. Clearly, whatever made this qalat "rich," it wasn't agriculture production and livestock husbandry.

The search, supervised by Hatfield and a squad leader, moved at glacial speed. Procedure called for the owner to accompany the search team while MPs photographed everything along the way. "There used to be complaints that we were stealing their stuff," Barnhart explained. "So now we take lots of photos and insist the owner goes with the search team. Plus they can't say later that we planted something on them."

Why not use specialized search dogs when seeking out explosives and weapons? The standard reply that "Afghanis don't like dogs, and we don't want to upset them," makes little sense. Mangy stray dogs are everywhere, a lot more offensive than properly cared-for professional military working dogs. Then Afghanis probably are not overly fond of either AUPs or Americans going through their qalats, either, but put up with it because of security conditions. A good SSD would have combed the qalat with speed and thoroughness that could not be matched by human search techniques: pick up, look under; slide over, look behind. Nevertheless, other than with Special Forces and some maneuver units, dog teams are rarely used by MPs.

While teams searched, Barnhart controlled the immediate disposition of troops on the ground while Rosado monitored the overall situation from the temporary command post several hundred meters distant.

Rosado, with olive skin and a full head of black hair that he later shaved bald in a vain attempt to beat the heat, stands about medium height and weight. The sixteen-year veteran hailed from Killeen, Texas, son of an Army dad. He likes to keep things calm and reasonable with his soldiers, but on occasion his brown eyes can flash anger.

Today, he was sanguine. Even lacking EOD presence, things were proceeding according to plan.

The Apache pilots continued to fly protective circles over the area, one bird only several hundred feet off the ground, the other far higher in an overwatch position. Rosado reported that when the Apaches first appeared several men fled the main qalat headed on foot for the secondary and tertiary qalats two hundred yards away.

The search yielded nothing significant. The absence—without apparent good explanation—of most of the men was taken as suspicious behavior, but insufficient in itself to initiate further action. Everyone in the qalat had been searched, including the women. Female MPs are essential for this work.

Specialist Jennifer Manning, a turret gunner, was tapped for the search duties. She is slightly built, pixie-like blond 20-year-old MP from Greenfield, Indiana. Her normally aggressive potty-mouth and hell-raising demeanor contradict her freckled-faced, friendly appearance. Despite paradoxical looks and mannerisms, Manning is a professional. When the job is at hand she automatically shifts gears, checks her personality at the door, and accomplishes the mission. Today she had been tasked to frisk Afghan women, and promptly began.

The owner designated a room where Manning took the women, one by one. The lone Afghani Police woman present—covered head to foot in a sky blue burka—accompanied Manning and each subject into the room with a camera, again to protect coalition authorities from charges of inappropriate behavior. "Even with just the three of us in the room," Manning said, "the women never show their faces. They'll giggle, laugh, and chatter, but remain covered." This means Manning and other female MPs have to do a thorough pat-down type search. Manning donned light blue surgical gloves.

"Women hide things under the garments in odd places," Manning reported. "They have small cloth bags on strings hanging over their shoulders worn under the armpit beneath their burqas, so I have to look hard to find it. Usually it contains nothing more than ID cards, money, or some papers, but it can be hard to find. Now that I've done a lot of these searches I know where to look." Increasingly a problem has been that Taliban or foreign fighters dress like women in order to take advantage of coalition and AUP reluctance to touch them.

"If one of these women is a guy in disguise," Manning said, "I have to be prepared for that eventuality. So I'm armed with my rifle and pistol, plus I've got two guys guarding outside the door. So far we haven't found any like that ourselves, but we have to be alert for the possibility since it's happened too many times before. They know how we work and are constantly trying to find ways to get around our tactics."

As the search progressed, several soldiers grew disgusted. "Look at the size of this thing," Specialist Cruise said. "There are more places to hide stuff here than we could ever find." Hatfield, taking a break in the process, was more optimistic. "It's big," he agreed. "But if there is anything here, we'll find it."

Meanwhile, Barnhart's radio crackled with a call from Rosado. Three Afghani men were stopped outside by AUPs. They were driving suspiciously slowly past the qalat and did not have a good reason to be there. The AUPs apprehended them and brought them to the MPs for questioning. "Bring them in, HIIDE them, and have the terp question them," Barnhart directed after he rogered the message.

Compared to the three men inside the qalat—older, fatter, dirty, and disheveled—these three were young, well-groomed, and dapper. One, with a lean rodentlike face, wore reflective designer sunglasses and smart clothing. The second was a fresh-faced handsome young man who assumed an air of faintly amused innocence. The third was a beefy, taller, round-faced individual with porcine, furtive eyes. After a few minutes of questioning by MPs and AUPs, with the terp handling translation, Barnhart directed a team to record their biometric data for inclusion in the national data base that the coalition is building.

Team members use a device called Handheld Interagency Identity Detection Equipment (HIIDE) to catalog individuals.[1] The $10,000-a-unit minicomputers are able to obtain data including fingerprints and iris scans, and come with facial recognition software that imprints a person's identity into the overall system known as Biometric Automated Toolset (BAT) that stores tens of thousands of profiles into a national system.[2] The purpose of the system, in use both in Iraq and Afghanistan as well as other troubled areas such as America's southern border, is to assemble a sufficiently large identity base so that if a person in question attempts to surface at another location using an assumed identity, the system will detect the imposter. Soldiers frequently complain of "false positives" from HIIDE but agree that it is a necessary tool in countries where aliases and false documentation are the norm.

After the HIIDE process was complete the three individuals were released. They wasted no time getting back on the road.

The two U.S. Air Force combat controllers walked outside the qalat. The Apaches were near bingo fuel level (just enough to get them back to base) and were to be replaced by two USAF F-15 Strike Eagle fighter jets. A distant roar followed by a low-level pass let everyone know that fast movers were on station. The day that had begun cool and dry turned hot and breezeless. As the F-15 banked in the distance it was silhouetted against slate-gray clouds from a storm gathering strength over the nearby Hindu Kush mountains.

About this time I went outside and stood near the Air Force controllers observing their actions controlling the aircraft. A foot-wide ditch used to drain sewage from the qalat separated us.

Without warning an AUP—one of Dustiger's security squad—came up from behind me on his way to the qalat. Though he had ample room to pass he shoved me hard in the direction of the ditch and passed by with a muttered curse and hard glance.

"What the hell was that about?" asked the senior USAF controller. "Arrogant asshole," added his companion, spitting tobacco on the ground. When Chris mentioned it to Jen Manning later she offered, "I would have put a boot up his ass." Given Manning's default disposition, that was almost certainly true. It helped that she was well armed while I had no weapons, no doubt further inducement for the AUP to take advantage.

Shortly thereafter the search moved to the second and third qalats. Both were markedly smaller than the primary target, and only the second was inhabited. After lengthy posturing from the owner, a heavyset man probably in his sixties who used a cane while walking with a pronounced limp from what appeared to be a painful hip, the AUPs and MPs commenced a search.

Under a tin awning stood a brightly painted several-hundred-gallon-capacity tank trailer. One of the AUPs from Dustiger's security squads, a clean-shaven individual in his late thirties with a quick, broad smile, tried to search it. Earlier he had given us a demonstration on how the grenade launcher functioned on his AK-47 assault rifle and had proudly reloaded a grenade, so we knew it was lethal and set to go.

After tapping with his rifle on the side of the tank trailer to determine if liquid was present, he tried vainly to remove the large round cover on top so that he could peer inside. It resisted his attempts to remove it, so he then inserted the muzzle end of his AK—with a bullet in the chamber and a round in the grenade launcher—under the lid in an attempt to pry it open. "Maybe this would be a good time to get some distance," I mentioned to Chris and a few soldiers standing nearby. The lid didn't come off but the weapon didn't fire either, so all concerned considered it a net plus.

After a negative result on qalat number two, the party walked to the third qalat. En route I stepped hard in a ditch and severely bruised my left thigh. With no water—none of the search party anticipated that this was going to drag on for hours—and drenched with pain-induced sweat, I sprawled on the ground to catch my breath.

Meanwhile Barnhart's radio came alive: "Be advised," Rosado warned, "that twenty to thirty Taliban driving white Toyota trucks and on motorcycles are headed from the southeast to your location."

Great, thought Chris. *What a moment to get into a fight.* "You can roll into that ditch, sir," Specialist Cruise pointed, "and be safe there." Obstinately I refused to go into a ditch. Chris became increasingly concerned. "I can't carry you so you've got to man up and walk out of here," she insisted. "Get up! Let's get out of the open, into the qalat, right now—get up!" In time, without Taliban encouragement, I did.

In some ways the third qalat—under construction with stacks of mud-and-straw sun-dried bricks stacked haphazardly alongside piles of clay in the courtyard—was the easiest to search. At least it wasn't stacked with furniture, rugs, and family paraphernalia. Unlike the other two qalats this one did not have a new well in the center, a feature that marked just about every qalat and many roadside villages in Paktia Province. Clean water, properly considered an essential, had been a key infrastructure project from international development agencies, and judging from their presence was at least a visible success.

"We need to search this one thoroughly," Cruise announced. "Sometimes they like to use these to hide weapons and explosives, thinking that since nobody lives here yet we won't bother with it." But again, searchers drew a blank.

"This is what it is," Barnhart said, motioning for his men to begin to move back to the waiting perimeter of trucks. "Sometimes we find stuff; more often we don't. A few weeks ago we found a large cache of weapons and explosives in qalats just like this. Today we came up empty. But by getting out here with the AUP we're accomplishing several goals. We show a presence to the civilians, let them know that we're concerned with their security. That's important. Also we are in reality training the AUPs. We show them how to conduct a reasonable search, gather evidence, deal with people, and, when we find contraband, how to conduct a forensic investigation and process evidence. If we were living with them we could train them better and have more influence. But we've got force protection responsibilities at the FOB and that keeps us from doing it. So even if it's been a tiring and boring day, we got something done."

Unlike in films or according to popular ideas, most of the work of war—particularly the kind of war in which popular perceptions are at stake—is repetitive, exhausting, and often boring. It is necessary work, taken with the ever-present risk that someday it will all blow up in your face—literally. It is what MPs do in a counterinsurgency environment.

22

THE WILD EAST

Lieutenant Colonel Duane Miller's PSD (personal security detachment) squad at FOB Lightning is happy. Private First Class Duntrell Dailey is running around with a broad grin on his face. Corporal Curtis Kimball has a tight smile. Sergeant Nicholas Olsiewski is bustling everyone to get the trucks ready, mount weapons, double-checking to make sure that extra ammo, MREs, water, and night-vision gear is loaded. Lots of kidding and enthusiasm; soldiers ragging on each other. The sun is still a couple of hours away from rising. The atmosphere is electric.

Mission of the day: travel up the Khost-Gardez Pass to inspect various Afghani Police stations and checkpoints. Everyone expects that we'll get into a fight. Civilians might not always understand the soldiers' mind-set. Think of it as the motivation that drives firefighters to run into a building while everyone else flees. Soldiers are trained to get close to and defeat the enemy, not to avoid contact. "We came here expecting to get into it," Olsiewski said. In effect, they are ready and eager to test themselves against the best the enemy can field.

It's Sergeant Olsiewski's first time running a fairly complex operation. He briefed it over the secure phone system the night before to the battalion commander, who we'll pick up this morning at the regional training center. Ski is excited, while more than a bit nervous. Lots of rank looking over his shoulder now, and he wants to get it right.

The 95th Battalion MRAPs form the core element, while Sergeant the trek, are tied to the sides of the bundles. They watch the passing convoy with innocent curiosity. Riding on the very tops of the humps are the small children and babies. Each is dressed in bright silk and, like the young animals, tied in place. They look like tiny aristocrats mounted on stately camels. Give them a couple of more years and they will be leading the flocks.

Hours drag. The road is one constant lurch and drop into potholes; careening over rocks. Someone called out that we're now passing Combat Outpost Wilderness on the left. This is the deepest coalition presence in the K-G Pass. The 92nd MP Company has soldiers who rotate through here, and the 101st has an artillery unit and some infantry based with them. One advantage of having Allison's squad leading the way is that they know the road out to here fairly well. Beyond Wilderness, it's essentially new terrain for everyone.

Perhaps a half hour later we finally pull into Waza Zadran police station. The facility hugs the mountains in a small, relatively flat bowl beside a subsistence village. On the surrounding high ground stone-mud observation posts placed for optimal fields of fire provide expanded force protection against attacking Taliban. The station is large and permanent-looking. A Hesco-protected mud-and-stone wall, broad parade ground with some trees struggling against the elements, and a roomy headquarters building along with outbuildings for police barracks, kitchen, and storage.

Fatar, with Miller by his side, made an inspection, questioned the policemen, and looked over the camp. Fatar clearly didn't like what he heard: Police were not eating properly, have pay issues, and rarely train. It appears that the local commander is embezzling funds earmarked for their welfare to line his own pockets. This is common practice, but Fatar, according to Miller, is determined to put a stop to it. From all accounts he is honest. He backed his words with action, heard everyone out, then turned to the local commander and relieved him on the spot. His replacement would come from Gardez in a few days.

On a slight rise, near the corner guard tower, sit two modular latrines. These were provided to the police by the coalition. Stearns, Chief Warrant Officer Smith, and a couple of NCOs drifted up that way to relieve themselves. Appalled by the condition they returned, green-faced.

In his earthy manner Stearns summed up conditions: "They filled the toilets with shit and rocks. Then they filled the urinals, then the sinks, and finally covered the floor. Nothing to do with those modular latrines now but soak them in diesel and set them on fire."

The chief grabbed his camera to document the mess. We watched him lean into the building—no doubt holding his breath—while snapping shots. A report will be passed up the chain but it is unlikely any action will result. Basic sanitation is still unknown among many Afghans. And in a land with minimal access to toilet paper, many use rocks to wipe themselves with instead.

The run back to Gardez is uneventful. Soldiers are proud of the operation but disappointed. The gunfight they desired will have to wait till another day.

There is a sense of urgency that permeates the MP mind-set in Afghanistan. Though loath to criticize the Obama administration directly, everyone concerned voices the same worry: "We know what we need to do and are doing it. But it won't get done anytime soon. It will take lots of time, more than eighteen months."

Miller and his staff at the 95th MP Battalion exemplify the larger quandary. They understand their mission: train up the police forces in the eastern region of Afghanistan so that they can be responsible for a law-and-order environment and local security when coalition forces draw down. This presumes a functioning Ministry of the Interior, but that is someone else's mission.

Miller has to make the assumption—otherwise he would be intellectually hamstrung—that the someone in question in Kabul will be successful. He has an identifiable counterpart, Fatar, knows the Afghani chain of command, and has a certain ability to put pressure on the logistics system to produce, even if he has to back-door the process through higher headquarters. Organic to his battalion he has at hand a staff of officers and senior noncommissioned officers who came to

Afghanistan prepared to "train, advise, coach, and mentor" opposite numbers at the hub of all police activity, the regional training center.

So why isn't it going faster? The simplest answer, "this is Afghanistan," sounds flip but carries deeper implications than its surface meaning: Nothing happens quickly here. At the root of the culture is a strong, almost visceral resistance to change. In corporate America we hear "We've always done it this way." In rural America we hear "My granddaddy did it this way." In Afghanistan we hear "We have done it this way for centuries."

Afghans have a vision of a mythological past in which a strict, well-understood social and economic order resulted in health, wealth, and prosperity for all. There was no sense of nation or even wider region, but a comfort zone that included tribe, family, and most of all, faith. Only the appearance of a foreign army bent on conquest was sufficient catalyst to bring the tribes together, nevertheless still maintaining respective ethnic identities; Pashtu, Dari, Tajik, or other.

Today Americans and NATO types are the foreigners. We are outsiders insisting that the old ways need to be discarded for more efficient, more humane Western-style skill sets. We bring in young officers to sit beside forty-year-old counterparts who have more than two decades of fighting under their belts and wonder why the Afghanis resist advice. It is not that the thirty-something Americans can't offer a lot. They can, and try. But they collide with a cultural imprint that sees change as threatening, foreigners as distasteful infidels, and anyone outside of their tribe as a potential enemy.

Nevertheless, Miller is convinced that progress is being made. At least on the surface, he is correct. Many of the Afghanis, though not quick to accept advice, have recognized the innate efficiencies of some practical Western methodologies. Basic police procedures like fingerprinting, handcuffing, and systematic searches produce immediate perceived benefits and are generally accepted once demonstrated and practiced. Unarmed combat techniques and shooting skills are appreciated. Even crime scene investigation gets a nod.

Other actions that seem self-evident to Americans are inexplicable in the Afghani mind. Soldiers are taught not to handle IEDs after locating them. Afghanis enthusiastically jump in and try to defuse or remove them, often with fatal consequences. An Afghani police officer in Zormat has lost most of the use of his eye as a result of fiddling with an IED. Yet he is praised by his fellows and superiors alike for having uncovered and defused twenty-three such devices until his luck ran out.

At Chamkani, the Afghan security guards employed by the Special Forces detachment responded to a call from local Afghani Police that they had recovered an IED, a 105 mm rocket round. Three ASGs hopped in a pickup truck, dashed to the station, and were happily returning to their compound. One drove, the other was a passenger, and the third sat in the bed and cradled the 105 mm round between his knees.

The truck hit a bump. The man in the back, cousin to the driver, evaporated in the explosion. The driver was concussed, and the passenger had a piece of his skull blown away.

The MPs, then part of the 92nd MP Company, who manned a site across from the Special Forces, received a frantic call for assistance. "Our medic is in the field. Do you have anyone who can help?" The MPs, all trained in combat lifesaving skills, responded in force.

"We only need six," said the Special Forces soldier at the compound when the entire platoon showed up.

Sergeant Joshua Turner and his buddy dealt with the casualties directly. "I was working on the driver," Turner recalled. "He was conscious, and frantic when he learned that his cousin was dead. It was all we could do to restrain him." The other MP soldier assisted with the more critically injured passenger. "He literally held his hands on the side of the ASG's head to keep his brains from running out." Remarkably, after stabilizing him as crudely as they could, the two men were medevaced to a hospital and both survived.

Worse than the flagrant disregard for even elemental safety standards, a bane of most primitive societies where accidents are ascribed to the temper of a vengeful god, is the blatant corruption that metastasizes in Afghanistani and Iraqi cultures like cancer. Miller acknowledges that this may be the toughest nut to crack. "It's been so much a part of their system for so long that many don't even recognize it as wrongdoing."

Particularly with the assistance of some of the law-enforcement professionals, great progress has been made at rooting out some of the most egregious offenders. Tom Anderson and his team at least got Wardak removed, though at the time of this writing he has still not been brought to formal trial. "It's many of the lower-level guys that are a problem," Anderson recalled. "Highers-up like Wardak made them pay for their positions. They don't make enough salary so the only way they can repay the original debt and make a living is to be on the take."

Skimming policemen's salaries, charging them for things like food and ammunition that are issued through the system, and extorting protection money from local merchants is seen by some police commanders as a normal way of life, not a crime.

Exacerbating the situation was the suspicion that one of President Hamid Karzai's relatives was the largest drug kingpin in Afghanistan, and the certainty that the Karzai administration is corrupt. Mining contracts awarded to Chinese companies in 2010 smacked of huge payoffs and kickbacks, and the administration's hands-off-the-opium attitude leads to no other conclusion. With the leadership of the country so openly corrupt, for Miller and others at the muddy-boot level to try to force change is a Sisyphean exercise at best.

The bottom line for officers like Miller is that they are not in position to change or influence the greater system or overall policy. They have been given a mission to complete and are doing everything in their power to complete that mission while keeping soldiers as safe as possible. It can be frustrating, is always demanding, and is rarely satisfying. But it is their mission and they will succeed in their small piece if at all possible.

Since U.S. soldiers are in place only for a year or so at a time, the accepted methodology is incremental and goes like this: Perhaps I won't be able to do everything I want to accomplish, they think, but I can do at least a part of it, perhaps a major component of what is necessary to overall success. If I can do that with my soldiers and leave the situation better than I found it, then that in itself is a version of mission completed.

23

TAKING IT TO THE TALIBAN

Afghanistan observers will affirm that the past five years of emphasis on building the army first left the police forces neglected, fending to their own devices. And for far too long corruption, venality, nepotism, purchase of positions, and tribalism were hallmarks of the various police agencies. "We're working to change that," said Colonel Kevin Palgutt, who escaped his native Buffalo, New York, four days after he finished high school more than thirty years ago to enlist in the Army. After a stint as an enlisted man and a degree at Florida State University he became a military police officer and has remained in the corps since.

His position as advisor to the Minister of the Interior for law and order in Kabul places him squarely in the forefront of all reforms that are ongoing or scheduled to happen with the Afghani Uniformed Police forces. Palgutt has to think strategically and act tactically. With rarified NATO oversight and no shortage of wise pronouncements and guidance emanating from Brussels and Washington, Palgutt is the guy who has to convince an egotistic, irascible (do they come in any other models?) minister of the interior that the courses of action he suggests are best for Afghanistan, the coalition, and—probably of primary importance—to the minister's career and longevity.

If you think of Afghanistan as being a few years in progress behind Iraq, and many people do, then the position Palgutt occupies is analogous to that of General David Phillips when he advised the Ministry of Interior in Baghdad in 2007–2008. Like Phillips and quite a few MPs, Palgutt comes in size "tall to extra tall," and works hard to maintain a trim physique. He credits the impetus to focus on the AUP mission to a primarily NATO initiative brought to fruition in November 2009. "The NATO desire to kick off the NATO Training Mission in Afghanistan—NTMA," Palgutt said, "provided the glue to bring a previously fragmented effort together."

All NATO countries have a piece, according to Palgutt, but "not all of them are paying their dues." Part of his job is to give ammunition to those who are busy pushing NATO to fill the positions to which it has committed. Out of frustration the United States is considering filling those positions on a "temporary" basis. One reason is to build on rising momentum. The other is the political clock in the background steadily ticking down the days until President Obama has said he would begin a U.S. withdrawal.

Precipitate U.S. pullout would be, in Palgutt's words, "frustrating." When the president visited Karzai in March 2010 it created a "sense of urgency" to a situation that had already been showing "changes for the better" in the previous ten months. "There are lots of positive trends and we are seeing them here," Palgutt affirmed. "But if we try to move too fast—to get things done against a political deadline—then things might not get done properly."

Sustainability—or the possible lack thereof—obviously bothered Palgutt. "We're not going to be finished with this project in eighteen months," he stated flatly. "It took a major effort over several months to get the Interior Ministry to approve personally a five-year growth plan. That was huge; a watershed moment. He has approved a comprehensive, well-conceived plan with recognizable, measurable goals. It includes the six pillars of what the Afghani Police will stand for and how they will operate. This is a major step forward and we must follow through with the time and effort to bring it to fruition. Implementation and success of this plan will permanently transform the country."

Another member of NTMA, Colonel Scott Jones, is emphatic: "It's going to take ninety to a hundred and twenty days before we even have metrics available to see progress." Allowing time for the training mission to take place is essential, in his opinion, and can't be rushed. Jones sees similarities between the situation in Iraq when focus shifted from training the Iraqi Army, which had been recruited, trained, and fielded from scratch and achieved a certain level of competence, to police. "The police are the face of the government—maybe the only one most people ever actually deal with—here in Afghanistan just as they are in Iraq," Jones noted.

By early May 2010 we were on our way out. Miller had a suggestion. "First stop by Khost and spend a few days with B Company, 151st Infantry. They're out of Indiana National Guard and are acting in lieu of [ILO] MPs." The ILO concept surfaced in Iraq during the times when MP units were hen's teeth scarce and the coalition was overwhelmed with route security, police training, and detainee holding operations. Other units as varied as artillery, infantry, or even transportation units were thrown into the gap. Some did exceptionally well and the concept moved to Afghanistan as demands increased. B/151 was pulling that mission on the Pakistan border.

When we got to the top of the steep hill that contains the OCCP (operations coordination command post)—staffed 24/7 by Afghani Army and Police as well as coalition units—we also found the headquarters for B/151 Infantry. Met by Captain Chris Crawford and First Sergeant Larry Sparks, we were immediately struck by sky-high morale, visible evidence of initiative, and complete mission focus. The soldiers were inordinately proud of the training they had given to Afghani Police, the firefights in which they had taken the fight to ambushers, and the overall success of their tour.

Their living quarters—designed by them and fabricated from plywood and dimension lumber, were the best we saw in-country. Crawford was proud of the fact that he had his own DFAC—the only other occasions we saw this were with the 108th MP Company in eastern Baghdad and after the 95th MP Battalion relocated to

FOB Justice—and we were treated to a steak dinner after Miller and Stearns joined Crawford and Sparks in an awards ceremony. Watching the broad grins on soldiers' faces as chests were pounded after pinning Combat Infantryman's Badges, Combat Medic's Badges, and valor awards was a thrilling sight.

Bravo Company had been in several firefights, most at very close quarters. We saw the site of one upon which a new police station was being constructed. "We used AT-4s when we got shot out of there," a squad leader informed us. We looked at each other with raised eyebrows, recalling how Lowery was relieved by his commander for using a much smaller M-203 round in an intense firefight in Gardez. In this unit, the commander pinned awards on their chests. Small wonder morale was high.

We rode out about mid-morning to Khost Provincial Headquarters and visited several sites, including Precinct 2, where, just two weeks earlier, soldiers from B/151 were in a TIC (troops in contact) that left two Taliban dead and several Americans wounded.

To view it at the most charitable, Precinct 2 is a work in progress. More severe critics might describe it as a pile of rubble. Somewhere between probably lies the truth.

Complicating matters, Crawford points out, are bureaucratic snarls over which Afghani government agency actually owns the land. If, for example, Ministry of Defense owns the space and another agency such as police (under Ministry of the Interior) improves the land, then fear is that the Ministry of Defense will simply demand that the improvements transfer over to their agency, leaving police to find a new site.

Dealing with such apparent trivialities in the middle of an active insurgency causes teeth-grinding frustration among coalition and Afghani officials alike.

Precinct 2 is an example. Work is progressing—we were surprised to see almost fifty laborers, and several machines, pouring concrete footers, removing rubble, and constructing walls when we arrived unannounced. A tall stone wall that was not there just a few weeks ago now stands on one boundary of the property.

Soldiers pointed out a heavily damaged, two-story small brick building at the edge of the property where at least two Taliban set up to ambush soldiers. "They opened up on us when we dismounted from our MRAPs," explained Sparks. "As we moved up to engage them we began to pick up small-arms fire from back over there." He gestured in the direction of some residences a block or so distant.

It was not known whether these were additional enemy fighters, or ANA who may have been shooting at the small building also. Typical of urban fighting in this country, much of the time you never know who is shooting at whom.

Twice Sparks's soldiers assaulted the building. They were driven back by a swarm of hand grenades. Exploding fragments buzzed through the air and wounded two to three soldiers. "Grenades were flying all over the place. Only a couple hit, and didn't do much damage." On all sides of them ANA and AUP were firing RPGs at the building. Several bounced off, others exploded ineffectually. Sparks decided, "Screw this. We pulled out our AT-4s and put two into the building. At that point we launched our final assault."

Two stacks of soldiers entered the building, one from B/151, a second from a cav unit that had been passing nearby and opportunistically joined the fight. They kicked the door and raced up the stairs, guns at the ready. Smoke and dust filled the corridor. As they sprang into the room the lead B/151 soldier saw one Taliban lying dead. A second was severely wounded. "We were just inside the room when someone in the Cav stack saw a Taliban move and fired into his chest." The shooter reportedly was a Cav lieutenant colonel who had stripped his nametape and rank from his uniform to join the stack.

Suddenly the room erupted in a terrific blast. The force of the explosion knocked soldiers about. "It blew us down the stairs and caused a couple of more people to get wounded. The enemy wore a suicide vest and it detonated when the shot hit him. Fortunately only part of the vest exploded and nobody was killed."

The fight at Precinct 2 is typical of what fighting in Afghanistan has become. Small groups of Taliban infiltrate urban areas and take a stand in a local strongpoint. Firefights last for hours, primarily because of restraints placed upon commanders regarding use of weapons. They are prohibited from employing the heavy weapons that would rapidly degrade an enemy strongpoint because of the possibility—regardless of how remote—of property damage or civilian casualties. America is now in the position that official policy has come to accept friendly losses rather than risk harming an Afghani civilian. The B/151 soldiers were positive about pulling an MP mission, something that they probably would have disdained prior to deployment. In Iraq some of the ILO units did such an outstanding job that they were later awarded the coveted MP brassard. In our eyes B/151 Infantry more than earned this honor, but it was never given.

On the last day we shared a shady bench at Forward Operating Base Salerno with Staff Sergeant Steven Ward, platoon sergeant for B/151 Infantry, from Indianapolis, Indiana. Ward recounted stories—both promising and frustrating—about his tour and interactions with the Afghanis. "We've had some major successes with the police. We have to think big picture, plan for our successor units, get things started so that they can build on them. Even if we only get three or four initiatives rolling and do them right, then by the time it's all done we'll have accomplished something big. The key is keep several programs going simultaneously and if one gets stuck, keep pushing on the others till you resolve it."

24

BLOODHOUNDS AND DRAGON FIGHTERS

In mid-May 2010, several units in Regional Command East of Afghanistan changed over. The infantry company, Bravo 1/151 Indiana National Guard, was replaced in Khost Province by the 330th MP Company from the California National Guard. In Gardez the 92nd MP Company headed back to Mannheim, Germany, when the 615th MP Company from Grafenwoehr switched out with them.

Captain Bryan Anderson, commander of the 615th, expected his unit to hit the ground running. They did not. They came in by Blackhawk helicopter. They had just arrived and were tasked to conduct an airmobile mission. His company had not trained for air assault. Suddenly their first mission in Afghanistan was to join elements of Delta Force and the Rakkasans from the 101st Airborne Division in a combat assault. "We're MPs. I told my people regardless of the mission, we can do this."

Anderson task-organized his soldiers to join the assault. Abruptly he was contacted by the Delta commander on the ground. "You've got a female soldier on our bird. We don't go into combat with females." First Lieutenant Kimberly DiFiori and some of her soldiers had been assigned that part of the mission. "I honestly hadn't thought anything about it," Anderson commented. "When we run operations we go with what we have: men, women, doesn't make any difference to us. We're all MPs." Anderson replied to the various commanders who had by now become involved: "That's the way we're supporting this mission. I'm going with what you have right now or not at all."

DiFiori later laughed about the shocked expressions on the faces of the Delta operators as she climbed into the bird. "It turned out that it didn't matter at all," she said. "We got the job done."

The captain's gunner, Specialist Cory Gage, recalled that, "It was pretty exciting. Here we were, brand-new in-country, and hadn't had any training for this, on a combat air assault. We pulled it off, though."

While the 615th MP Company continued over the next several months to pull fast-paced missions, they were still responsible for force protection in their area of FOB Gardez. On September 24 just after noon Specialist Shawn McNeill was pulling duty at the entry control point (ECP) assigned to the company. The ECP is a barren, Hesco-covered gate with a wooden guard tower nearby. Suddenly he heard shots and shouting. Long bursts of AK fire ripped the air. *Taliban!*

Local security force and Afghani Army guards sprinted past him, eyes wide in panic. McNeill charged his M-249 squad automatic weapon and dashed to the front of the ECP to fill the sudden void. Suddenly he saw five of the enemy running toward him, firing AK-47s and RPGs. He made out the suicide vests above their clothing. McNeill had trained for this moment. Bringing the SAW to his shoulder he took them under fire. Squeeze a burst, shift target, squeeze another burst. Calmly, he killed two and forced the remainder to seek cover. After what seemed long moments but was only minutes, other soldiers joined him in the fight.

This was a complex attack. Rounds continued to impact. The ECP was under fire from additional Taliban to the east. While RPGs detonated around them and suicide vests exploded McNeill remained at his post. The noise from explosions was deafening; cordite, smoke, and dust blinded the Americans. But they fought off the Taliban and held the ECP secure.

Had the Taliban fought past the ECP they would have been scant yards from a crowded DFAC. If they had burst into the tent the suicide bombers could have inflicted heavy casualties on American soldiers and civilians. By manning his post—single-handed for the first minutes—McNeill prevented a terrible tragedy. Because of his quick response and demonstrated bravery, McNeill was awarded the Army Commendation Medal with V device.

The COP (command outpost) itself is a work in progress, as are most of the remote bases. From showering in a makeshift plywood stall while your battle buddy poured bottled water over your head in spring 2010 to a fully functioning system with hot water and real flush toilets by fall, improvements have boosted soldiers' morale at this remote post. Within sight of the Pakistan border, the Chamkani area is a convenient way station for Taliban on the move and grows its own permanent cells. An MP pointed to a valley that opened up just beyond a nearby defile.

"That's where the Taliban live," Staff Sergeant Kenn Schoonover said. Previously only the Special Forces from the detachment located at the original COP ventured into that area. By October 2010 Anderson's platoon leaders and NCOs were pushing into the previously denied valley, volunteering to be a quick reaction force for Special Forces operations. In time they plan to convince Afghani authorities to open police stations, one at a time, in the area. They want to push Taliban supporters and fighters deeper into the mountains. Or back to Pakistan.

Economically Chamkani is key terrain. Daily, hundreds of heavily laden jingle trucks bring goods to and from towns in Pakistan and places like Gardez. In the recent past drivers were forced to bribe their way through Taliban checkpoints in order to make the run, or risk losing their cargo or their lives. Increasingly Afghani Police have set checkpoints along the route to serve a dual purpose: protect the drivers and cargo, and check for contraband, especially things like ammonium nitrate—a fertilizer that conveniently converts to powerful homemade explosive.

First Lieutenant Nathanael Higgins, who received his commission from the University of California–Santa Barbara in 2008, runs the platoon out of Chamkani. Higgins leads with unbridled enthusiasm, something he tries to disguise occasionally with a cynical aside. The self-described "nomad" clearly enjoys leading MPs in this mission and aggressively pushes out to engage the enemy or thwart Taliban intentions. On a small rocky promontory, little more than a terrain bump alongside the main road, Higgins and his team, including Sergeant David Pierce, Corporal Zack Enko, Specialists Ron Grass, Josh Cuervara, and Daniele Brown spent time with a ragtag group of Afghani Police who were manning a roadside checkpoint.

Pierce pointed out that the police get shot at frequently but give back more than they get. Incidents continue, but the police have not been intimidated. Day by day, the police, sometimes with U.S. assistance, improve their positions, patrol farther out into the adjacent mountains, and gain the support of a small resident populace who have begun to enjoy the results of permanent security.

On the river side of the road, just across and downhill from the checkpoint, a dun-colored, torn tent flaps in the gentle breeze. That's the new school. Several dozen children played in the rocky yard. "Permanent structures are in the works," Higgins pointed out. "For now that's where they are going. Girls on one side, boys on the other."

As happens frequently in a counterinsurgency (COIN) environment, conditions change rapidly. MP leaders are challenged to switch mind-sets from "assist" to "kill" in an instant. On a recent patrol Higgins and Afghani Police were taken under fire. He maneuvered his forces, engaged with M-203s, dislodging the enemy from hiding places, and killed a local Taliban commander. Higgins described the action as "surreal," but it typified the intrinsic ability of MPs to be sufficiently flexible and balanced to hand out school supplies one moment and bring death on those who threaten the local children the next.

"Intelligence sources," Anderson, call sign Raider 6, explained to his senior leaders, "have identified two possible locations for one of the top two Taliban leaders in the district." Tomorrow the 615th MP Company would conduct a predawn raid to capture him. "We'll get there early, pull him out of bed if he's there, and by surprise will avoid a fight." Anderson decided to turn operations planning and control over to his executive officer, DiFiori.

She will be leading her own company soon, he reasoned, and this is solid, necessary experience for her to have. But with Anderson's kinetic personality, he did not intend to sit this one out. He and his PSD squad would participate in the raid, too, assaulting one set of qalats while DiFiori led the main force against a second grouping, approximately a mile farther south on the same dirt road.

The evening prior to the raid, all elements met in the 615th tactical operations center for a final briefing. DiFiori led the briefing, issuing her operations order that thoroughly outlined the plan of movement, actions at the objectives, and handling of suspects. Additionally, in keeping with the spirit of COIN, backpacks loaded with school supplies would be carried along to distribute after the raid was complete.

We were invited along. Just before 0500 we joined the task force at the entry control point, where just weeks prior McNeill killed five Taliban suicide attackers. Early winter skies were still pitch black. The moon had long set, opening up the brilliance of the stars in the crystal Afghanistan skies. Vehicles lined the approach road, diesel engines idling. Soldiers checked weapons, communications equipment, ammunition loads, and even the location of the backpacks for the kids.

Anderson, finished with last-minute instructions, nodded to DiFiori, who issued the command. "Mount up. Let's get rolling!" In the truck, lighted only with pale red night-vision lighting, Private First Class Caleb Currie drove, Gage was in the turret, and the SAW gunner, Specialist Brett Chavarria, loaded and checked his weapon. The medic inspected her kit, making sure she had all necessary gear, and the terp donned his helmet. Good to go. We strapped in and rolled out into the dark. "We're timing this to hit both compounds simultaneously," Anderson said. "I'm still hoping we'll catch them in bed."

The convoys roared up to the compounds as morning twilight spread across the desert. No sun yet and it seemed colder. The rear door flipped open and Anderson's voice, shouting "Let's go, move quickly!" penetrated over the loud engine noise. First the SAW gunner, "Chevvy," then medic, then terp piled out. Checking his soldiers' deployment he positioned the SAW gunner by the door of the qalat and assembled a stack. "Knock, then open it up," he directed.

As we passed through the narrow opening everyone was tense. Weapons were "red"—locked and loaded—but soldiers kept fingers away from triggers as they had been endlessly drilled.

Even for an Afghani qalat this place was a mess. Trash, broken bricks, and human feces was everywhere, strewn across the unleveled ground. Near one wall a mud-roofed storage pit (a fighting position?) bumped out of the ground. Soldiers began systematically to search. As yet there was no sign of life. "Someone's coming out of that doorway!" All eyes turned to see a tall, exceedingly well-groomed man step from the living area. He wore long white Afghani garb, had no beard, and his hair was carefully combed.

Upon questioning through the interpreter the man said he had just returned from a trip to Saudi Arabia and had his passport to show it. "Walk him out to the truck," Anderson directed, "and get his vitals entered into the HIIDE system." After a thorough search, including sending Gage into the bunker under the watchful eye of Anderson, turned up negative, it was time to move to the adjacent qalat.

This was going to be a sensitive knock-and-enter. In this very qalat back in February a SEAL team on a night raid had erred badly, opening fire and killing several residents, including a man later identified as an Afghani Army lieutenant colonel. What kind of reception could we expect?

Anderson was concerned both from a security standpoint and the idea of further imposition on these people. But intel had identified this residence as a possible hiding place for the high-value target we sought that day, so it had to be done.

At that moment, a tall, older Afghani with a long gray beard approached beside a younger man. He was the owner. Listening quietly through the interpreter, he agreed that it was legal and proper to search the residence, and opened the door for us. Everyone relaxed a bit. As soldiers conducted the search, women and children exited, the kids

eager to see what all the excitement was about. The children w
barefoot despite the cold. Anderson instructed Gage to go grab
backpacks for distribution.

The elderly Afghani emerged with photos and a magazine
with more pictures. We understood that he was showing us th
tos of those in his family killed by the SEALs earlier in the year.
quite uncomfortable, but Anderson handled it respectfully an
appropriate dignity. "We're sorry we have to intrude," he told th
"We'll make this as quick as possible."

Back out on the road, word from the second objective w
ginning to filter through. The element under DeFiori had not
hended the HVT but had three of his brothers in custody. An
directed that they be brought back to FOB Gardez where they
be questioned by authorities. Meanwhile, a crowd began to
MPs handed out book packs and candy that they had stuffe
ACU cargo pockets. Afghani Police directed traffic. After an h
so a pair of Apache helicopters arrived on station and began to
"Now they get here," groused Chevvy.

One young boy, eagerly wanting one of the gaily colored bacl
that the other kids had, burst into angry tears when informed th;
were all gone. After he'd pitched a tantrum, some of the soldie
around for a few trinkets to give him. We later agreed that his be
appeared an appropriate metaphor for the attitude of the entire
try: Give us something or we'll scream and cry till we get
weren't sanguine that was the right message.

Back at Gardez, Anderson questioned the two brothers cap
by DiFiori's elements. One seemed subdued but the elder was
gant, even smirking, avoiding direct answers. Finally, in exasper
Anderson said, "You're in deep trouble," and directed that the n
flex-cuffed and turned over to interrogators. The expression ch
on his face—from arrogant to worried—as the soldier gently
first one then the other arm to the rear and slipped the plastic cu
him was well worth the pain of the predawn wakeup.

•   •   •

"Take over this city and get it under control." Those were essentially the marching orders Lieutenant Colonel John Voorhees received when told that his 504th Military Police Battalion (Dragon Fighters) was going to deploy from Fort Lewis, Washington, to Kandahar, Afghanistan, in 2010. It was clear to Voorhees that the game was changing under the guidance of General Stanley McChrystal. There were three pillars to the military side of counterinsurgency operations: kill or capture, convict, and reintegrate. These were the basics that had worked successfully in Iraq with the Anbar Awakening and were to be employed in Afghanistan—with appropriate modifications to fit with a different society and culture.

Kinetic operations were changing from emphasis on the first type of mission—because large formations of Taliban had been killed, captured, or chased from the region—to place more importance on convict and reintegrate, functions that were dependent on the Afghanis themselves to develop a law-and-order environment. While civilian advisors were working diligently to assist Afghanis with the judicial and incarceration operations, it was incumbent on the military police to train, mentor, coach, and advise the Afghani Police at all levels to learn the essentials of good community policing that would enable prosecutors to make a case that would stick in court. In order to accomplish this, Voorhees and the soldiers from the 504th were tasked to work side by side with the local police forces and instill in them both the techniques and the values associated with good police operations.

The reintegration issue, as Voorhees was aware, was not his mission. By nature this had to be accomplished at the national level. His mission was to make the Kandahar police force into an institution that would win over a traumatized community and give the population the kind of security that would allow them to live their lives peacefully without intimidation and terror.

He spent time with his predecessor unit, absorbed all of the lessons learned, and reached an inescapable conclusion: The killing part was happening. Taliban were being attrited at a steady rate. But the conviction element was missing. Due to the rules of an emerging

Afghani legal system, till recently bereft of the knowledge and power of forensic evidence, too much emphasis was placed on eyewitness accounts, and little on what in the West would be considered conclusive: fingerprints, DNA, and circumstance. He was determined through education and example to focus on the education and skill sets necessary for police to build solid, scientifically unshakable cases against captured enemy fighters and enablers.

It helps that Voorhees is a natural people person. His green eyes flash with pleasure when he meets and greets Afghanis, from the general to the private level, with a genuine *"Salaam alaikum"* and a hand over his heart. Though he pretends to fret a bit about the increasing gray strands in his close-cropped dark hair, it mitigates his youthful appearance, a useful trait in a society that respects age.

Voorhees is a quick, focused study and insists that his junior leaders open their eyes and their minds to what is going on around them. Listen, learn, analyze, then act decisively. Voorhees has a good relationship with his immediate counterpart, Colonel Faisal Shirzad, and is savvy enough to have dug into his background. Shirzad, he learned, was a Russian-trained, educated officer who fought against the mujahedeen during the civil war. This puts him squarely at odds with others involved with governing and administering Kandahar in that many of them led from the opposing side.

Keeping them focused on the mission at hand and not refighting old battles requires a great deal of patience, tact, and urging from Voorhees and others who form the American side of the security working group at the Rule of Law Center meetings. Along with Voorhees two lieutenant colonels—Mike Chandler and former Special Forces Jim Hayes—meet regularly with members of the Afghan National Civil Order Police (ANCOP), Border Police, National Defense Security (NDS), AUP, and ANA.

Gathering around an elongated, highly polished conference table at the governor's palace, the men sip bottled water and nibble candy passed around by Afghani orderlies. Shirzad chairs the meetings, which trail staff members, primarily Americans, down both sides of the table from the principals.

According to Voorhees, Chandler, and Hayes, when they first began these regular meetings, feelings around the table were acrimonious. None of the Afghanis trusted the others, information was held closely, and coordinated operations were agreed to grudgingly if at all. Working quietly and diligently to advise and mentor, the American officers provided an example of how such meetings ought to function. "They watched us, saw how we each gave a little, took a little, and reached agreement," Voorhees observed. "Pretty soon they were doing it too."

At this meeting various agencies reported that they identified four potential suicide bombers, captured two Taliban commanders, and uncovered a cache of home-manufactured explosives (HME). A bombmaker, the police commander noted indignantly, had blown himself up along with some innocents in the area. Police followed up and arrested a guy hanging around with a pistol hidden in his man-dress. The NDS representative—normally the most reticent about sharing information, as are most intelligence officers—told how they were watching suspected Pakistani intelligence agents in the area. At that point everyone around the table roundly condemned the Pakistani intelligence service (ISI) for interfering in their internal affairs. They might not agree on everything, but they universally despised and resented the Paks.

On the subordinate unit level, Voorhees pushed his Dragon Fighter companies out to the police and border stations. "We've got to get out there with the police," he urged. "Don't do it for them but show them what right looks like and back them up when they're doing it." On one of the unit's first combined U.S.-Afghani missions they rolled up nineteen Taliban suspects, found a pressure-plate trigger device for IEDs, and uncovered a large supply of HME. The following day, before the MPs could get to the station, the police eagerly went out on their own and came back with renewed confidence.

"We don't need to motivate these guys," noted Captain Andrea Acosta, commander of the 202nd MP Company on her second Afghan tour. "We can give them a lot of help with tactics, techniques, and procedures, but they are aggressive and mission-oriented. We need to help, but also to make sure we're not getting in their way." This attitude, noted by several soldiers who served in both theaters, was decidedly different from that in Iraq where the police culture was to wait in the station for a citizen to report an incident.

Denying the Taliban access and providing increased security force presence might just make the difference in converting Kandahar from a Taliban safeground to a free city. So the mission went out to the 504th's subordinate companies: Move into the surrounding farmland and orchards and establish a safe area. Concomitantly the Afghani Army would secure and clear ground, Border Police would establish blocks and checkpoints, and uniformed police would set up stations. Over time this expansion strategy would force the Taliban to consolidate farther south in Spin Boldak where operations would be undertaken to deny that area also to them.

First Lieutenant Daniel Durkin, a twenty-four-year-old Chicago, Illinois, native, led his 3rd Platoon, 170th MP Company (Ghost Riders) into the Malajat region south and a bit west of Kandahar on August 8, 2010, for what was intended to be a three-day-long cordon and search of the area. The terrain, while relatively flat, was intimidating. Pomegranate and fig orchards along with grape vineyards were so densely planted that movement by road was impossible. Only small footpaths penetrated inside the orchards. Any vehicles that tried to move into the area—and Durkin's soldiers tried mightily—were almost immediately immobilized. At that point the MPs became infantry.

The orchards were legendary Taliban hideouts. During fair-weather months, camps and redoubts were built inside the orchards, out of sight of overhead surveillance, and sufficiently removed from roads to discourage foot patrols. For decades dating back to Soviet occupation, Taliban fighters had camped safely in the extraordinarily dense groves. Afghani security forces to date had not dared venture deep into the groves without being forced to withdraw.

Now the U.S. forces were telling the Afghani security forces, "We'll go in together, clear, hold, and build. And exclude permanently the Taliban from a comfortable safe haven to terrorize Kandahar."

Initially frustrated by inability to get his vehicles into the orchards,

Durkin's platoon marched into the dense woods, following foot-paths. They reached the tiny village of Spin Kalacheh, secured it, and pushed on to Gari. Both places were supposed Taliban strongholds but the enemy had fled. Locals they encountered were poor, fright-ened, and withdrawn if not hostile. Order of battle was stacked so that the MPs entered along with elements of 4th Brigade 82nd Air-borne Division on their flanks. Canadians, using the call signs Stab A and Stab B, were to act as a quick reaction force. Behind them were elements of the Afghani Army, then Border Police, and regular police elements.

On paper it was a simple plan that was expected to take about three days to execute: Americans penetrate, engage, and defeat any re-sistance; Afghani Army then clears up any pockets of resistance; the Border Police establish checkpoints on routes entering the area; and the local police set up stations that would grow into permanent facili-ties to maintain law and order. This kind of move, according to Cap-tain Andrew Sergeant, commander of the 170th MP Company (Dragon Slayers) whose unit was conducting the operation, would create "white space" between the Taliban and the population, permitting Afghani governmental forces to establish control.

Like all plans drawn up in a headquarters distant from ground reality, this one began to unravel as soon as it was discovered that armored trucks were unable to participate in the fight.

Resistance was relatively light, but continual. Aware of the danger, MPs discovered several IEDs intended to restrict maneuvering within the orchards. Snipers fired at them from distant tree lines; mostly, as Durkin described it, "harassing fire" intended to discourage aggressive action. The platoon had no air support and was a kilometer or farther from any other coalition elements. Impeded by the terrain, the mission began to drag and the three-day goal was quickly abandoned.

Durkin had a problem: aware of the frailty of plans, he had di-rected that more than a seventy-two-hour supply be loaded on the trucks. But the trucks were a long way distant and all his soldiers had was the incredible loads they were carrying in the intense August heat and humidity. Water, always the long pole in a combat tent, was running short. Anything available was husbanded for drinking. A week into the mission Durkin thought, "We really stink."

A day after a Chinook blew a resupply to the adjacent U.S. unit ("They didn't land but dropped pallets from the air that exploded on impact. When we got there the following day the field was covered with plastic water bottles."), the MPs were finally resupplied. This time the big, twin-rotor chopper landed in the open field and the supplies were received intact. After clearing, the platoon established a base area for the police to set up a station in a field filled with cow manure. Time dragged and it was fifteen days before they were relieved in place and made the welcome return to Camp Nathan Smith.

Voorhees is pleased with the results. Nineteen Taliban were captured and a large cache of pressure plates for IEDs was uncovered. He recognized that it was hard on his people, but now is proud of the fact that both Border Police checkpoints and nascent police stations are up and running. Essentially, the MPs denied a traditional safe zone to the Taliban, and if operations progress as intended, the enemy will be pushed out of Kandahar. Concomitantly with spreading ops south and west, the local police, aided by growing community-derived intelligence, have been aggressive about finding and reducing Taliban safe houses inside the city. Regardless of the season, Voorhees thinks, there will be no place for them to hide inside or outside of Kandahar.

Meanwhile, other elements of the 504th MP Battalion were directed to establish a permanent presence at as many police stations as possible, including at province headquarters, assist the police in establishing new stations in areas deemed to be too large for existing forces, and train their police on essential elements of protecting and analyzing crime scenes. This has proceeded apace, with several new stations opening and functioning. One measure of their success has been the attempts by Taliban fighters and suicide bombers to attack the stations.

Also, the enemy is changing tactics. A new element on the streets of Kandahar is the emergence of "ghost fighters," or *cherocki,* a Farsi word designating professional assassins. A marked departure from the suicide bomber, these men ride two to a motorcycle and avoid direct danger. The back-seater is the shooter. Targets are Afghani officials and those civilians who have been seen to side with the Afghani government and the coalition.

Captain James Hannabass mentors at the province headquarters. He is acutely aware that the Taliban are winning the media war. "Any crime, especially if a policeman is murdered, is immediately jumped on by the Taliban as something they pulled off. By the time the government or the coalition responds with facts the impression of an overwhelming Taliban presence has already been made to the local citizens."

Voorhees sees the Afghani Police's greatest strengths as presence and growing professionalism. On the challenges side, he is pressing for more community policing, letting the people know that they are there to serve the citizens, not the other way around. Soon to be established in Kandahar is a model law-and-order center. It will be adjacent to the prison and be a place where prosecutors, police, forensic specialists, and representatives from the entire system will be present and working together. He sees this as a catalyst to facilitating solid convictions, maintaining a database on both common criminals and enemy Taliban, and a showpiece for the rest of the country on what "right looks like" in regard to a law-and-order environment.

Some of the soldiers who have pulled tours in Iraq or previously in Afghanistan view this approach generally as a continuation of tactics employed earlier. For others, such as 552nd MP Company (Peacekeepers) commander Captain Christopher Nogle, the different tactics required a mind-set change. His unit's mission in Afghanistan demands constant partnership with local forces. They don't see the immediate short-term gains that typified surge years in Iraq but instead are playing more of a long-ball game, building a foundation for the police that through training, mentoring, and time will produce a professional force.

Sometimes it depends on the luck of the draw and which area you are assigned. In Arghandab, north of Kandahar, Captain James "Jay" Shaffer, commander of the 54th MP Company, found "more kinetic operations in a month than we had in Baghdad in three months." Shaffer was in Iraq for six months in 2008. Hannabass agreed that simply by moving a short distance from a quiet district you can find yourself in a Taliban stronghold. When his unit went into Malajat, for example, on a follow-up sweep from the original mission, they brought a larger national police contingent as a way of training and showing them by example.

Excited after a first IED exploded, killing one policeman, they then set off a second. Some policemen withdrew across an open field, predictably setting off a third. Finally, in order to get control restored, Hannabass called in A-10s for an airstrike, resulting in thirty dead Taliban. Though it may have been an inauspicious beginning, as Hannabass observed, "The Afghanis learned from it."

In war the learning curve is a constant: steep, cruel, and bloody.

For the 615th, 504th, 630th, and others the war continues. Back at Fort Leonard Wood the 92nd MP Battalion—including Sergeant First Class Abigail Vantichelt—prepared to deploy. In January 2011 they replaced the 95th MP Battalion at FOB Justice.

The deployment wheel—seemingly endless to many of these soldiers—continues to grind. The men and women of the Military Police Regiment answer the call.

Ready to serve, prepared for sacrifice and hardship—the Army's Warrior Police in action.

25

CONCLUSIONS

Our first black bear visited that morning, a yearling who eyeballed me curiously from behind a laurel hedge, then casually ducked back into the brush and disappeared. We were still laughing about him as we sat on the deck of our rented cabin in the woods in the Great Smoky foothills in Murphy, North Carolina, and played gin rummy.

It was good to be back in the U.S., occasionally slapping mosquitoes without worrying about catching malaria anymore. The warm, clean summer air, profusions of multicolored butterflies, and the nighttime buzzing of cicadas contrasted starkly with the foul, dusty air of Afghanistan villages, openly hostile stares from the Pashtu population, and constant danger lurking in the background.

Chris made a seemingly innocent comment. "I wish Fallon was here with us right now." She meant Sergeant First Class Teresa Fallon, the medic assigned to the 95th MP Battalion who'd become her closest friend on FOB Lightning. "And I sure miss Watford, the way he always seems to make horrible true stories into black comedies. It would be great if Dailey and Manning were here, just smelling this forest air and relaxing here in such a private little natural habitat having fun without a care in the world for a change. So many of them. And Sparks too, he was a real piece of work!"

"All the soldiers would enjoy it," I replied, playing a card. I recalled the time that after many hours in an Afghani general's office in

Khost Chris suddenly got fed up with excessive formalities. Near the end of a fancy luncheon she got a little stir-crazy. Politely, she left to have a quiet after-lunch cigarette up on the roof by herself. Forget any lurking Taliban snipers or possible traitors, the nicotine pull and desire for just basic peace after hearing so many chattering voices in too many different languages over many hours was definitely strong.

Watching her leave, First Sergeant Larry Sparks from Bravo 151st discreetly extracted himself from the luncheon and raced hot on her heels to protect a wayward tourist in a war zone. She wanted to be left alone and he wasn't thrilled to babysit a "reporter" either, yet by the time I'd arrived on the roof some 30 minutes later to smoke my cigar they were happily chatting away.

Later Sparks graciously had his soldiers show us what his National Guard unit had built out of little more than scavenged lumber: a palace by local standards that neither one of us has forgotten. What soldiers could build by themselves after hours on their own initiative—marvelous miniapartments, stone headquarters facilities, and spacious decks built around native trees in the middle of hell—stayed with us.

In beautiful North Carolina months later, lightning struck.

"Let's make it real for all of them too, then. A permanent, beautiful place like this to go when they want or need it, a place of their very own, forever," Chris said. She had already given it a lot of thought. Rapidly she outlined a plan: We would set up a nonprofit for the benefit of post-9/11 soldiers, partially fund it to purchase a large tract of rural land in the mountains, and set up a place where soldiers could relax, work, heal, and learn in security and mutual comfort.

Some of the civilian contractors—professional tradesmen including electricians, plumbers, and construction experts—who worked around and alongside the soldiers in the combat zones might want to volunteer their time to teach and oversee building projects in exchange for also having access to such a refuge. Equally weary from years working in war zones under extremely dangerous conditions, this underserved and generally ignored population needs a special place to decompress and heal, too.

For the past three years we had traveled among soldiers while researching this book. By conservative estimates we probably interviewed close to a thousand. We had seen numerous cases of stress varying from extreme to barely manageable. We'd met many soldiers who were dissatisfied with the somewhat stock response of military and VA psychologists and psychiatrists who were too quick to medicate and too removed from the life of a combat soldier to be of real assistance to these particular individuals. Likewise, we saw similar issues with civilian contractors who do not have access to even basic support programs after retiring or otherwise leaving their corporate employers.

Traditional counseling and mental health processes seemed to be effective with some, but in too many cases the usual methods came up far short. We sensed a large gap in what soldiers needed and what was available through military, Veterans Administration, and existing nonprofit programs. At that moment we made a commitment to do what we could to fill that need.

The old *Field of Dreams* theme of "If you build it, they will come" seemed to apply. With help from professional tradesmen who have shared experiences in Iraq and Afghanistan, the soldiers—not just MPs, but other combat soldiers as well—would in fact be the actual builders, learning new skills and working hard for a facility that would in the end remain their own to enjoy, not to be abandoned like the unforgettable COPs and FOBs they previously knew as their (temporary) homes. And there they would grow, heal, and regain at least some degree of the camaraderie that is very rare outside combat zones, while having the chance to have fun in the process.

But first we needed to address a more mundane but equally germane issue: How are we going to pay for this place? The answer seemed simple: We'll donate from our personal funds to get it kick-started, then donate all profits from *Warrior Police* into the project.

After what these soldiers had done for us, their fellow countrymen, and for the pittance of support they asked in return, we thought that we could do no less. In effect we would be saying to them: "Now it's our turn to help you."

We began to discuss the project a lot. Aside from our work drafting the manuscript, conversations about this soldiers' retreat—a place for growing things, working farm animals, construction, innovative power generation, outdoor recreation, and more—began to occupy all our free time. Where would we get the land? What kinds of activities would be offered? How would we let them know that it was available? Who would get to visit, for how long, and specifically why on a case-by-case basis? Once these things start the questions multiply exponentially.

And another basic question remained: What are we going to call it?

By now we had shifted location up to Maggie Valley, closer to Asheville. Our rental house had a great balcony overlooking the spreading valley and adjacent mountains. We rigged three hummingbird feeders and watched the tiny birds battle to establish their personal territory within an environment where there was more than enough for all. Their antics over claiming "turf" over those three strategically placed feeders around the deck were delightful—and instructive, as we contemplated how to juggle the realities of a critically needed project within the restrictions of severely limited means.

As usual Chris pressed for fresh ideas. This unique special retreat project had to have a name, a very special one, what would it be? "How about 'Valhalla,' " I suggested. Bingo. Revive the old Norse legend of a home for warriors, this time for living ones, and give them a secure place to mend, refit, and get back into the world. That name resonated, worked and transformed and focused our ideas into what is now boldly called the Valhalla Project, an IRS 501(c)(3) nonprofit organization.

As we left North Carolina on our way to the 69th Military Police Regimental week celebration at Fort Leonard Wood, Missouri, we naturally discussed location. A mountain locale with a four-season climate and affordable land became our goal. Certain otherwise desirable places, such as western North Carolina, had become too popular with vacationers, and therefore land prices—even if one could find the two-hundred-acre-plus tract we sought—were budget-busters.

Tennessee definitely made the short list. Sections near the Great

Smokies seemed ideal, but we needed to explore a lot more before we made a decision. On the way out we stopped at Indianapolis, Indiana, on September 11 where Bravo Company 151st Infantry Regiment was meeting. While renewing friendships we sprang the Valhalla concept on several soldiers and were a bit stunned by the reaction.

"Tell me where it is," one sergeant said earnestly, "and I'll be there tomorrow." Others echoed his sentiments. "I definitely want to be a part of this," Sergeant Rick Dornick said, "please include me as you develop your plan." At Fort Leonard Wood we received equally enthusiastic responses.

Meanwhile, the Ozarks—four-season climate, mountains, clear air and water, good land, covered by wildlife, and affordable large spaces— invaded our imaginations for an extra-special haven from North central Arkansas. A largely undiscovered gem in the center of the country, accessible from everywhere. We began the search for suitable land in earnest.

What, we wondered, would the soldiers currently downrange think about Valhalla? We were quick to find out, when we returned to Afghanistan and our 95th MP Battalion hosts and friends in mid-October 2010. After listening to Chris make her very informal on-the-fly presentation, Specialist Jarid Matthews spoke up right away. "I'll shovel lots of shit if I can go there!" Farm animals tend to generate a lot of manure so such activities will naturally be on the regular Valhalla agenda. His nonetheless enthusiastic response seemed to encapsulate the reaction from all we spoke with.

Sergeant Nick "Ski" Olsiewski immediately decided to replicate the simple yet beloved plywood "smoke shack" at FOB Justice, where we all retired in the evening to puff cigars and tell stories, later at Valhalla. "You tell me where it is," he promised, "and I'm gonna go there and build this shack exactly like it is right here!" Months later we learned via Facebook that before leaving Afghanistan he had in fact ended up recording very detailed measurements and photographs (including pictures of the somewhat eerie, haphazardly spray-painted happy face on the interior back wall) to make sure the re-creation will someday be precisely accurate according to the combined memories of those who frequented that cheerful little hut.

Not exactly what we ourselves envision in a space mostly filled with Antonio Gaudi–inspired spaces and buildings, but there will always be room for "special projects" of historic value that remain particularly important to those who served. That's what it is all about. A plywood smoke shack with a floppy door or other seemingly odd structures of memorable note for the soldiers will be constructed and cherished in addition to more stately buildings.

Soldiers immediately perceive Valhalla as it is intended to be: a secure rural environment where they work for soldiers today—including themselves—as well as for the next generation of soldiers, and the next after them. "This is a one-hundred-year project," Chris explained to listeners downrange. "We want this to outlive us all."

Everyone works at Valhalla—and everyone has fun. Price of admission is a proven combat-zone background plus twenty-hour minimum work week and a positive attitude. The rest of the time can be spent in recreation and classes covering such topics as personal financial management and investing for their personal futures, living well but inexpensively, translating military service for potential civilian employers, and the many issues that are going to arise while reintegrating into an often detached civilian society.

Recreation includes many group and individual activities designed to address the needs and desires of each individual and to open up paths that some soldiers might never have thought about pursuing. Construction alone will expose soldiers to endlessly creative possibilities as they can shape and mold with elastic materials such as straw bales, concrete, and earthen plaster buildings, and design and create garden and pond spaces.

Carpentry and woodworking, wildlife and wildlands management, livestock husbandry, intensive yet still organic gardening, and a myriad of activities—many proposed by the soldiers themselves—will unlock many creative urges very far removed from frustrations and nightmares. Healthy outdoor activities such as hiking, camping, mapping and surveying, managing wildlife food plots, hunting, fishing, astronomy, meteorology, and orchard care will offer chances both to work and play simultaneously—an excellent, healthy combination.

Most of all the soldier-residents will have plenty of time to bond with their fellows, share experiences, and discuss any personal issues. They will form new friendships, in some cases for a lifetime, and quietly and informally help one another adjust, decompress, and relieve the stresses of multiple combat deployments, family separations, and readjustment to civilian society. At times Valhalla will host soldiers and spouses, and occasionally a "spouses-only" group to give them a chance to get away for a stress-relieving period of time.

We know already that we will never be able to meet the overall need that exists nationally. Even if we have fifty or more soldiers at a time at Valhalla, many more will seek a similar refuge. As of this writing there are an estimated nine thousand post-9/11 soldiers who are homeless, many taken by surprise by the realities of the ongoing economic crisis when they returned home, and tens of thousands more who are scraping by or simply struggling to readjust. Therefore we decided from the outset to construct a "franchise book"—a compendium of successes, failures, and lessons learned—that will be passed on to anyone who wants to replicate the Valhalla facility without having to reinvent the wheel. Pick it up and run with it!

Meanwhile, we are working concomitantly on building and funding the facility. Naturally we are in the business now of seeking support—financial or in-kind—where we can find it: from the public that overwhelmingly supports these soldiers, to military-friendly corporations of which there are many, and from foundations and organizations who recognize the need.

The Valhalla Project, we hope, will become a template for assisting combat-stressed soldiers and their families now and in future, inevitable wars. We urge all interested to get involved in any way that works for you.

Fewer than 1 percent of the U.S. population serves in the military. It only makes sense that the other 99 percent of us ought to dig deep to help them back into the society that they protected with their health and, in far too many instances, with their lives.

Our conclusion, formed after spending three years researching this book, is somewhat mundane: In the end, politics happen. Domestically the pendulum between left and right swings and policies morph, largely irrespective of downrange realities and often contradicting stated ideological beliefs. Missions creep into unforeseen areas and purported allies are irresolute, ungrateful, and dismally corrupt. Even high-level decision-makers of both parties appear unable or unwilling to recognize the nature of the enemy and the truth from the ground.

Many Americans appear to be wedded to sound bite analysis and bumper sticker proclamations. We desperately seek simplistic solutions to complex issues. "Nuke Afghanistan"—a vast, empty tribal country—makes no more sense than the muddle-headed desire to "Coexist" with an opponent who defines the "C" as capitulation of the Western world.

While there is hope for eventual success in Iraq—despite the corruption and sectarianism, we fumble with nation-building in Afghanistan where no nation has ever existed, save for meaningless lines on maps. But those issues are far beyond the scope and intent of this book.

What we're focusing on is something that matters: We can't influence policy, but we can assist those who attempt to carry it out with sacrifice and dedication. We take enormous pride in the American military and applaud their best efforts to carry out what at many times appears to be "mission impossible" without whining or complaint.

Regardless of your politics or thoughts on war, when all is said and done, all that really matters over the long haul is the willingness of the American people to recognize and give back what has already been freely given by our own soldiers. Interested readers can learn more about Valhalla at www.valhalla-project.com.

NOTES ON SOURCES AND ACKNOWLEDGMENTS

To the extent possible we relied on primary sources for *Warrior Police*: personal interviews, diaries of events, military "story boards," unit journals, and official after-action reports. When necessary we augmented sources by using contemporary news accounts and unit histories. In addition we joined units on three occasions—once in Iraq and twice in Afghanistan—as embedded media in order to see firsthand what conditions are like and experience living in a combat environment with soldiers.

This book started, as many do, almost by accident. A good MP friend—Colonel Michael Bumgarner—suggested that I come to Iraq to see what military police were doing. With assistance from public affairs officer Colonel Rivers Johnson I managed to get through the bureaucratic wickets required for an embed and spend a month with units around Baghdad. When I returned I knew there was a story that needed telling. My researcher Chris insisted that we also needed to go to Afghanistan and that she would coauthor the book—but only if she came along, too!

Consequently we met Lieutenant Colonel Duane Miller and invited ourselves to accompany his 95th MP Battalion to Afghanistan when they deployed. He graciously agreed, and along with his Command Sergeant Major Henry Stearns, proved to be excellent hosts.

We owe the entire 95th MP Battalion a great debt for the incredible care, oversight, and friendship the officers, noncommissioned officers, and soldiers showed us. We know we are "high maintenance" but they accepted us without reservation.

From start to finish we received incredible support for the *Warrior Police* project from Military Police Corps leadership. Since we first formed a friendship in Baghdad in spring 2008, Brigadier General David Phillips has been an unflagging supporter of this book. We received great encouragement from Major General David Quantock and top NCO leadership including Command Sergeant Major Charles Kirkland.

Our interview process was conducted primarily at Fort Leonard Wood during multiple visits. Each visit was made more pleasant than the last by the planning and flexibility of the Schoolhouse staff, particularly Diane Bailey, who met all of our requests—regardless of how last-minute or off-the-wall they were, with a constant smile and a positive attitude. Chiefs of staff during our visits—Colonels Wade Dennis and John "Mack" Huey—went out of their way to ensure that we met people and visited key training sites. From the Military Police Regimental Association retired Master Sergeant Rick Harne put the weight of this excellent nonprofit organization behind the project. We were escorted by Captain Tobias Clark and our driver on multiple occasions, Specialist Josh Thielen. Both made sure we got where we needed to go and saw as much as possible.

We were pleased at Fort Leonard Wood to interview Melissa Quantock, Dawn Phillips, and Melissa Lombardo. Their perspectives were a very important contribution.

Interviews at the Schoolhouse included COL Wade Dennis, COL John "Mack" Huey, 1SG Christopher Lalonde, 1SG James Sanguins, SGT Kiet Christensen, MSG Willie Bowman, 1SG Michael King, SFC Abigail Vantichelt, SSG Timothy Chiasson, MSG James Eakin, SGT Benjamin Allen, CPT Neal Green, historian Andy Watson, SGM (ret) Rick Morris, CPT Laura Weimer, MAJ Jason Avery, CPT Chase Crabtree, CPT Lance Fountain, CPT John Petkovich, SSG Jesse Hernandez, CW5 T. L. Williams, CPT Nathan Brookshire, CPT Ben Feicht,

CPT Byron Greene, SFC Clifton "Mike" Stillwell, 2LT Allen Rich, CPT Cassandra Facciponti, SSG James Runner, LTC Randall Thrash, and SSG Michael Murphy.

We met military working dogs Dak (who took us down on command), Bodo, Storm, Spaulding, Hatos, Falco, Frank, and Eva, plus their excellent handlers, SSG Lee McCoy, SPC Chris Bond, SPC Reed, SGT Jason Alber, SGT David Ricks, and SSG Michael Pierce.

In our two visits to MP units in Germany we were aided by CPT Martyn Crighton and his team from the 18th MP Brigade, headed by COL Thomas Evans and whose deputy, LTC Lance Stratton, flew with us to Afghanistan and became a great friend. CSM Brenda Curfman, whom I met in Iraq when she was sergeant major of the 95th MP Battalion, had moved to NCO in the 18th MP Brigade by that time. The visits to Germany afforded us the opportunity to meet soldiers and watch their predeployment training. We do not hold them responsible for frozen feet at the Mannheim Christmas market—next time we'll dress warmer!

While at Grafenwoehr we also met MAJ Stephen Gabavics and MSG Fredrick Moore, of the 709th MP Battalion, then preparing to leave Gardez, Afghanistan, and assisting the 95th MP Battalion with their mission readiness exercise (MRE). While there, retired USAF MAJ Ed Rykard exposed us to some of the incredibly realistic simulation training available to today's soldiers.

Coincidentally, we had more ground-time with the 95th MP Battalion than any other unit. I rolled with them in Iraq and we both spent three months with the unit in Afghanistan. When not deployed, the battalion nickname is "Superstars" and they demonstrated it during our time together.

In Iraq while with the 95th I interviewed LTC John Bogdon, CPT Elizabeth Cain, SSG Moses Santana, SGT Kristin Loeffler, SPC Evelyn Rodriguez, LTC Frank Nagel, LTC Michael Blahovec, MSG Todd Busch, CPT Josh Campbell, CPT Keith Edwards, SGT Andrew Utz ("Warlord 61, hot an' jammin'!"), and 2LT Geneva Arnold.

In western Baghdad with the 716th MP Battalion I was warmly received (the commander shared his two-person trailer with me), and had interviews with LTC Daryl Johnson, CSM Jeffery Palmer, CPT Byron Greene, CPT Scott Fredrick, CPT Katie Graves, CPT Nate Brookshire, and CPT Rebecca Beard.

North at Camp Speicher I was hosted by the 728th MP Battalion, commanded by LTC Brian Bisacre. Interviews included CPT Frank Pescatello, SSG Christina Huerta, SSG Ronald "Doc" Cardey.

Interviews at the 18th MP Brigade, then located at Camp Liberty, Iraq, included some among them who would become lifetime friends: LTC Thomas Lombardo, LTC Michael Inovina (the world's best brigade public affairs officer), COL Mark Spindler, SFC Jones, LTC and (CH) Peter Batkis.

At Phoenix Base in the Green Zone I met and interviewed Colonel Rivers Johnson (PAO par excellence), COL Lars Braun, COL James Coffman, and MAJ Ryan Milloy.

At Kabul, Afghanistan, we were hosted by LTC Lance Stratton (a super friend), COL David Palgutt, and COL Scott Jones. Our embed was smoothed considerably by the efforts of the Public Affairs Office personnel, especially SGT Christina Dion and CPT Regina Gillis.

With the 95th MP Battalion, Task Force Sheriff, Afghanistan, we also interviewed MAJ Michelle Goyette, MSG Andrew Chesser, MAJ John Tessman, 1LT Michael Murrell, SFC Raphael Fabian-Diaz (excellent friend and manic Dominican barbeque specialist), 1LT Timothy Kesselem, CPT Ryan Goltz, CPT Jeff Sprunger, my cigar buddies CPT Zach Pfannenstiel and SGT Nick Olsiewski (PSD squad leader and future builder of smoke shacks), CPT Claudia Harris, CPT Thomas Harris, CPT (Chaplain) Drew Arrington, MAJ Samuel Harvill (rear detachment commander), 1LT Lanika Van Borkula, SPC Dariana Baric, PFC "Radar" Lyle, SFC Timothy McKay, SFC Teresa Fallon, SGT Villalobos, SPC Frank Vale, SPC C. J. Rich, SPC Clayton Crowther, SGT Matt Kuntz, SFC Christopher Smoak, SSG Paul Royer, SPC Jarid Matthews, SPC Antwarnard Massey, PFC Arin Mitchell, CPL Curtis Kimball, SPC Danielle Dudley-Martin, SPC David Ackland, SPC Dontrell Dailey, SGT Jason Jethro Strickland, SPC Joseph Miles, SPC Joseph Talarico, SPC Joshua Eastep, SPC Kyle Norman, SGT Ryan Hoover, SPC Ryan Killoran, SPC David Ackland, PFC Miles, SPC Massey, and

SGT Stanley Douglas, SPC Kyle Norman, and SGT Dustin Lierly, who always took care of wandering writers in BAF.

At FOB Lightning, in Gardez, Afghanistan, we became fast friends with civilian electrician and former Navy Vietnam vet Gary "Memphis" Lunsford, John Coletta, and "Jim," a civilian special operator Pashtu-speaker who wore a giant Santa Claus beard, a Taliban scarf, and drove anywhere he pleased in a beat-up Ford pickup.

With the 92nd MP Company at FOB Gardez, CPT Marcus Perez, CPT Michael Barnhart, SFC Tony Rosado, SPC Jennifer Manning, SFC Gary Watford, SSG Mike Williams, SSG Donald Lowery, SGT Edward Dillard, SGT Joshua Turner, SPC Bobby Kah, SSG Philip Huestis, SPC Jeremiah Cope, SPC Jackson Shepherd, SGT Eli Hugera, SPC Lenzie Mangrum, SGT Michael Mannara, SGT "K", SGT Michael Legrand, SFC David Ronje, SSG James Prather, PFC Eric Ater, SPC Shawn Potts, SSG Reginald Howard, SPC Cody Warnaken, and SPC Jimmy Salazar.

On a brief visit to Khost we met members of Bravo Company, 151st Infantry, an Indiana National Guard unit performing an "in lieu of" mission for military policemen. Though not trained on the mission they quickly learned and were performing an exemplary job in a tough AO. Interviews included company commander CPT Chris Crawford, 1SG Larry Sparks, SFC Rick Dornich (who can build anything from scraps), SPC Johnson, and SSG Steven Ward (who gave a brilliant précis of the Afghani situation).

Others we interviewed included COL Viet Luong, commander of 1st Brigade, 101st Airborne Division (Air Assault), the famous Rakkasans, at FOB Salerno and his PAO section, MAJ Justin Platt and SSG Jimmy Norris. LTC Michael Chandler and LTC James Hayes in Kandahar city. By e-mail SSG Jesse James Shambo, COL James Freeman, and LTC Dennis Zink. Law-enforcement personnel Tom Anderson. Members of the Vermont Army National Guard's 86th Mountain Infantry Brigade including LTC Charlesworth and his PAO CPT Mark Steskal.

Embedded with the 504th MP Battalion (Dragon Fighters) in Kandahar we interviewed LTC John Voorhees, CPT Ben Bridon, 1LT

John Baum, CPT Chad Froehlich, CPT Neal Dyson, SFC Gregory Jones, SFC Michael Duque, SSG Scott Greene, 1LT Daniel Durkin, CPT Andrea Acosta, CPT Andrew Sergent, CPT Christopher Nogle, CPT James Hannabass, and CPT James Shaffer.

With the 630th MP Company at FOB Hughie, Jalalabad, Afghanistan: CPT Maria Perez, 1SG Thomas Buettner, SGT Michael Delong, SPC Benjamin Barttlett, SPC Nathanial Scott, SGT Chandra Hinton, SGT Christopher Logan, 1LT Cory French, and SFC Daniel Sturges.

Our final embed was with the 615th MP Company ("Wardawgs" while deployed), the unit that replaced the 92nd MP Company at FOB Gardez. The entire unit reflected the positive, aggressive, can-do attitudes of the commander, CPT Bryan Anderson, and 1SG Kimberly Forgione. Having spent a brief time with them almost a year prior in Germany it was a homecoming. Interviews included 1LT Kimberly DiFiori, 1LT Brittany Ray, SGT Daniel Micek, 1LT Patrick Jeffrey, SSG Ken Schoonover, 1LT Nathanael Higgins, CPL William Oppenheimer, CPT Zachary Enko, SSG Dennis Gurney, SPC Caleb Currie, and SPC Cory Gage.

Warrior Police is only possible because of the assistance we received from these and many other soldiers. We are extremely grateful for their help and thank them all for their service to our country.

Without the strong support of our agent Scott Miller of Trident (hat tip to our pal Ralph Peters for the introduction) *Warrior Police* would not have seen daylight. Scott searched hard and found an interested editor in the indefatigable Marc Resnick who treats every suggestion with respect, answers all questions promptly, and offers solid, substantive improvements to the work—qualities that make him the gold standard of editors. This manuscript is as smooth as it is today thanks to the keen eye and incredible attention to detail of Christina MacDonald our copy editor nonpareil.

While we were completing the last moment corrections to the manuscript we were aggressively searching for a home for the Valhalla Project. Thanks to the incredible support and efforts of the team at Rocking Chair Realty in Flippin, Arkansas, led by Dianna Marquis,

Vern Meents, and broker Kenneth Jefferson—all of whom were initially very puzzled over the long list of must-haves coming from two out-of-state strangers e-mailing them from a foreign country, but who all quickly came to understand and appreciate the entire Valhalla vision. We first walked with them onto the 200 incredibly beautiful Ozark acres that we have since acquired to bring the project to fruition.

We have relied heavily on the soldiers, civilians, friends, and professionals both to bring *Warrior Police* to publication and to turn Valhalla from concept to reality. All credit goes to these kind supporters for their invaluable assistance. Regardless, any mistakes in the text are strictly our responsibility.

List of Casualties

This list includes only those soldiers who held the military police occupational specialty. Names of other soldiers who were attached to MP units or who died in accidents with them are unfortunately not available to be provided by authorities.

LIST OF CASUALTIES

Last_Name	First_Name	Middle	Rank	Age	Date of Death	Compo	Unit	Theater	GWOT	Status	Fiscal Year
Tompkins	Travis	M.	SSG	31	16-Mar-11	AC	Brigade Special Troops Battalion, 4th Brigade Combat Team	Afghanistan	Yes	KIA	FY11
Weaver	Jason	M.	SGT	22	03-Mar-11	AC	504th Military Police Battalion	Afghanistan	Yes	KIA	FY11
Fahey	David	R.	PFC	23	28-Feb-11	AC	504th Military Police Battalion,	Afghanistan	Yes	KIA	FY11
Wilfahrt	Andrew	C.	SPC	31	27-Feb-11	AC	504th Military Police Battalion, 8th Military Police Brigade	Afghanistan	Yes	KIA	FY11
Creamer	Zainah	C.	SGT	28	12-Jan-11	AC	212th Military Police Detachment	Afghanistan	Yes	KIA	FY11
Hutchins	Andrew	L.	SPC	20	08-Nov-10	AC	3rd Special Troops Battalion	Afghanistan	Yes	KIA	FY11
Vieyra	Barbara		PFC	22	18-Sep-10	AC	720th Military Police Battalion	Afghanistan	Yes	KIA	FY10
Montoya	Diego	M.	PFC	20	02-Sep-10	AC	720th Military Police Battalion	Afghanistan	Yes	KIA	FY10
Ide V	James	R.	SSG	29	29-Aug-10	AC	230th Military Police Company, 95th Military Police Battalion	Afghanistan	Yes	KIA	FY10
Raver	Bryn	T.	SPC	20	29-Aug-10	AC	1st Brigade Special Troop Battalion, 1st Brigade Combat Team	Afghanistan	Yes	KIA	FY10
Fike	Robert	J.	SFC	38	11-Jun-10	NG	1st Battalion, 110th Infantry Regiment	Afghanistan	Yes	KIA	FY10
Hoover	Bryan	A.	SSG	29	11-Jun-10	NG	1st Battalion, 110th Infantry Regiment	Afghanistan	Yes	KIA	FY10
Merriweather	Daniel	D.	SSG	25	13-Jan-10	AC	118th MP Co, 503rd MP BN	Afghanistan	Yes	KIA	FY10
Whitsitt	Geoffrey	A.	SPC	21	13-Jan-10	AC	118th MP Co, 503rd MP BN	Afghanistan	Yes	KIA	FY10
Steffey	Brandon	K.	SPC	23	25-Oct-09	AC	178th MP Det	Afghanistan	Yes	KIA	FY10
Rudzinski	Christopher	M.	SSG	28	16-Oct-09	AC	293rd MP Co	Afghanistan	Yes	KIA	FY10
Owens	Brandon	A.	SPC	21	02-Oct-09	AC	118th MP Co, 503rd MP BN	Afghanistan	Yes	KIA	FY10
Smith	Shannon	M.	SSG	31	08-Sep-09	AC	545th MP Co	Iraq	Yes	KIA	FY09
Lyons	Thomas	F.	SPC	20	08-Sep-09	AC	545th MP Co	Iraq	Yes	KIA	FY09
Myers	Zachary	T.	SPC	21	08-Sep-09	AC	545th MP Co	Iraq	Yes	KIA	FY09

LIST OF CASUALTIES

Last	First	MI	Rank	Age	Date	Comp	Unit	Country			FY
Haney	Randy	M.	SSG	27	06-Sep-09	AC	HHC, 2nd STB	Afghanistan	Yes	KIA	FY09
Wertish	James	D.	SPC	20	16-Jul-09	NG	34th MP Co	Iraq	Yes	KIA	FY09
Wilcox	Carlos	E.	SPC	27	16-Jul-09	NG	34th MP Co	Iraq	Yes	KIA	FY09
Drevnick	Daniel	P.	SPC	22	16-Jul-09	NG	34th MP Co	Iraq	Yes	KIA	FY09
O'Neill	Jonathan	C.	SPC	22	15-Jun-09	AC	549th MP Co	Afghanistan	Yes	KIA	FY09
Hernandez	Roberto	A.	SPC	21	02-Jun-09	AC	549th MP Co	Afghanistan	Yes	KIA	FY09
Moncada	Raul		SGT	29	13-Apr-09	AC	563rd MP Co, 91st MP BN	Iraq	Yes	KIA	FY09
Moore	Gary	L.	SPC	25	16-Mar-09	AC	978th MP Co	Iraq	Yes	KIA	FY09
Reed	Jeffrey	A.	SPC	23	02-Mar-09	AC	411th MP Co	Iraq	Yes	KIA	FY09
Thompson	Daniel	J.	SGT	24	24-Feb-09	NG	715th MP Co	Afghanistan	Yes	KIA	FY09
Emmert	William	E.	1LT	36	24-Feb-09	NG	265 MP Co	Iraq	Yes	KIA	FY09
Pollini	Matthew	M.	SPC	21	22-Jan-09	NG	772nd MP Co	Iraq	Yes	KIA	FY09
Hernandez	Joseph	M.	CPL	24	09-Jan-09	AC	C Co, 1st BN	Afghanistan	Yes	KIA	FY09
Rodriguez	Gregory	A.	SFC	35	02-Sep-08	AC	527th MP Co	Afghanistan	Yes	KIA	FY08
Gonzalez	Michael	L.	SPC	20	28-Aug-08	RC	340th MP Co	Iraq	Yes	KIA	FY08
Hale	James	M.	CPL	23	13-Aug-08	AC	978th MP Co	Iraq	Yes	KIA	FY08
Menke	Jonathan	D.	SPC	22	04-Aug-08	NG	38th MP Co	Iraq	Yes	KIA	FY08
Henry	Gary	M.	SGT	34	04-Aug-08	NG	38th MP Co	Iraq	Yes	KIA	FY08
Finley	James	M.	SPC	21	31-May-08	AC	MF PLT, HHC, STB	Afghanistan	Yes	KIA	FY08
Ward	Aaron	J.	PFC	19	06-May-08	AC	170th MP CO, 504th MP BN	Iraq	Yes	KIA	FY08
Eakes	Lance	O.	SPC	25	18-Apr-08	NG	1132 MP CO	Iraq	Yes	KIA	FY08
Pickett	Emanuel		SSG	34	06-Apr-08	NG	1132 MP CO	Iraq	Yes	KIA	FY08
Ray II	Thomas	C.	SGT	40	22-Mar-08	NG	1132 MP CO	Iraq	Yes	KIA	FY08
Williams	David	B.	SGT	26	22-Mar-08	NG	1132 MP CO	Iraq	Yes	KIA	FY08
Stelmat	David	S.	SPC	27	22-Mar-08	NG	1132 MP CO	Iraq	Yes	KIA	FY08
Tabb	Donald	T.	SSG	29	05-Feb-08	AC	6th MP Det	Afghanistan	Yes	KIA	FY08
Emery	Blair	W.	SGT	24	30-Nov-07	AC	571st MP CO	Iraq	Yes	KIA	FY08

LIST OF CASUALTIES

Last_Name	First_Name	Middle	Rank	Age	Date of Death	Compo	Unit	Theater	GWOT	Status	Fiscal Year
Mason	Casey	P.	PFC	22	14-Nov-07	AC	552nd MP CO	Iraq	Yes	KIA	FY08
Muller	Adam	J.	PFC	21	05-Nov-07	AC	1st BDE STB	Iraq	Yes	KIA	FY08
Linde	John	D.	SSG	30	05-Nov-07	AC	1st BDE STB	Iraq	Yes	KIA	FY08
Stenroos	Derek	T.	SGT	24	05-Nov-07	AC	1st BDE STB	Iraq	Yes	KIA	FY08
Town Sr.	Robin	L	SSG	52	24-Oct-07	NG	275th MP CO	Iraq	Yes	KIA	FY08
Munn	Donald	L.	SSG	25	11-Oct-07	AC	Special Troops BN	Iraq	Yes	KIA	FY08
Duckworth	Eric	T.	SSG	26	10-Oct-07	AC	HHC, 759th MP BN	Iraq	Yes	KIA	FY08
Collins	James	S.	SGT	35	28-Aug-07	AC	303rd MP CO, 87th MP BN	Iraq	Yes	KIA	FY07
Witham	Donovan	D.	PFC	20	21-Aug-07	AC	1st Squadron,73rd Cav Reg	Iraq	Yes.	KIA	FY07
Bohannon	Jeremy	S.	PFC	18	05-Aug-07	AC	59th MP CO	Iraq	Yes	KIA	FY07
Blackwell	Justin	R.	SPC	27	05-Aug-07	AC	59th MP CO	Iraq	Yes	KIA	FY07
Murchison	Matthew	M.	SPC	21	04-Aug-07	AC	127th MP CO, 709th MP BN	Iraq	Yes	KIA	FY07
Coffelt	Ronald	L.	SGT	36	19-Jul-07	AC	503rd MP BN	Iraq	Yes	KIA	FY07
Joshua	Ron	J.	PV2	19	17-Jul-07	AC	401st MP Co	Iraq	Yes	KIA	FY07
Bobb	Brandon	K.	PV2	20	17-Jul-07	AC	401st MP Co	Iraq	Yes	KIA	FY07
McGee	Thomas	P.	SGT	23	06-Jul-07	AC	546th MP Co	Afghanistan	Yes	KIA	FY07
Clifton	Karen	N.	SPC	22	21-Jun-07	AC	554th MP Co	Iraq	Yes	KIA	FY07
Legrand	Glenn	D.	SPC	27	12-Jun-07	AC	571st MP Co, 504th MP BN	Iraq	Yes	KIA	FY07
Horner	Bruce		SGT	43	01-Jun-07	NG	127th MP Co, 708th MP BN	Iraq	Yes	KIA	FY07
Rosa Jr.	Alexander		PFC	22	25-May-07	AC	239th MP Co	Iraq	Yes	KIA	FY07
Farrar	William	A.	PFC	20	11-May-07	AC	127th MP Co	Iraq	Yes	KIA	FY07
Jones III	Roy	L.	PFC	21	10-May-07	AC	984th MP Co	Iraq	Yes	KIA	FY07
Sabalu Jr.	Wilberto		MSG	37	06-May-07	AC	TASS-RCE	Afghanistan	Yes	KIA	FY07
Harrison Jr.	James	W.	COL	47	06-May-07	AC	USA CGSC	Afghanistan	Yes	KIA	FY07

LIST OF CASUALTIES

Last Name	First	MI	Rank	Age	Date	Comp	Unit	Country		KIA	FY
Soenksen	Katie	M.	PFC	19	02-May-07	AC	410th MP Co, 720th MP BN	Iraq	Yes	KIA	FY07
Avery	Jeffrey	A.	PFC	19	23-Apr-07	AC	571st MP Co, 504th MP BN	Iraq	Yes	KIA	FY07
Ritzberg	Brian	E.	SPC	24	02-Apr-07	AC	577th MP Co, 97th MP BN	Iraq	Yes	KIA	FY07
Bowling	William	G.	SGT	24	01-Apr-07	AC	2nd BSTB	Iraq	Yes	KIA	FY07
Mejias	David	A.	SSG	26	01-Apr-07	AC	2nd BSTB	Iraq	Yes	KIA	FY07
Mcdowell	Robert	M.	SGT	30	01-Apr-07	AC	2nd BSTB	Iraq	Yes	KIA	FY07
Vick	Eric	R.	SSG	25	01-Apr-07	AC	2nd BSTB	Iraq	Yes	KIA	FY07
Kaiser	Anthony	A.	SPC	27	17-Mar-07	AC	504th MP BN	Iraq	Yes	KIA	FY07
Parr	Brandon	A.	SGT	30	03-Mar-07	AC	630th MP Co, 759th MP BN	Iraq	Yes	KIA	FY07
Moyer	Ashly	L.	SGT	21	03-Mar-07	AC	630th MP Co, 759th MP BN	Iraq	Yes	KIA	FY07
Peek	Michael	C.	SGT	23	03-Mar-07	AC	630th MP Co, 759th MP BN	Iraq	Yes	KIA	FY07
Armstrong	David	C.	PFC	21	01-Feb-07	AC	57th MP Co, 8th MP BDE	Iraq	Yes	KIA	FY07
Butler	Kenneth	T.	PFC	21	01-Feb-07	AC	57th MP Co, 8th MP BDE	Iraq	Yes	KIA	FY07
Garrigus	Mickel	D.	SGT	24	27-Jan-07	AC	543rd MP Co	Iraq	Yes	KIA	FY07
Stout	Brandon	L.	SPC	23	22-Jan-07	NG	45th MP Co, 210th MP BN	Iraq	Yes	KIA	FY07
Sanchez	Paul	T.	SGT	32	14-Jan-07	AC	543rd MP Co, 91st MP BN	Iraq	Yes	KIA	FY07
Roberson	Jeffrey	G.	CPL	22	28-Nov-06	AC	230th MP Co, 95th MP BN	Afghanistan	Yes	KIA	FY07
Shank	Michael	A.	SSG	31	28-Nov-06	AC	230th MP Co, 95th MP BN	Afghanistan	Yes	KIA	FY07
Preistap	James	D.	SFC	39	23-Nov-06	NG	45th MP Co, 210th MP BN	Iraq	Yes	KIA	FY07
McCoy	Gregory	W.	SSG	26	09-Nov-06	AC	410th MP Co, 720th MP BN	Iraq	Yes	KIA	FY07
Kennard	Courtland	A.	SGT	22	09-Nov-06	AC	410th MP Co, 720th MP BN	Iraq	Yes	KIA	FY07
Bostic	Kenneth	E.	SGT	21	30-Oct-06	AC	204th MP Co	Iraq	Yes	KIA	FY07
Stanton Jr.	Kenny	F.	PFC	20	13-Oct-06	AC	57th MP Co, 718th MP BN	Iraq	Yes	KIA	FY07
Williams	Phillip	B.	SPC	21	09-Oct-06	AC	4th BCT	Iraq	Yes	KIA	FY07
Oremus	Michael	K.	PFC	21	02-Oct-06	AC	57th MP Co, 718th MP BN	Iraq	Yes	KIA	FY07
Perry	Joseph	W.	SGT	23	02-Oct-06	AC	21st MP Co, 503rd MP BN	Iraq	Yes	KIA	FY07
Huff (Henderson)	Ashley	L.	1LT	23	19-Sep-06	AC	549th MP CO	Iraq	Yes	KIA	FY06

LIST OF CASUALTIES

Last_Name	First_Name	Middle	Rank	Age	Date of Death	Compo	Unit	Theater	GWOT	Status	Fiscal Year
Seig	Anthony	P.	PFC	19	09-Sep-06	AC	118th MP CO, 519th MP BN	Iraq	Yes	KIA	FY06
Graves	Joseph	A.	SPC	21	25-Jul-06	AC	110th MP Co, 720th MP BN	Iraq	Yes	KIA	FY06
Contreras	Andres	J.	SGT	23	15-Jul-06	AC	519th MP BN	Iraq	Yes	KIA	FY06
Lawson	Isaac	S.	SPC	35	05-Jun-06	NG	49th MP BDE	Iraq	Yes	KIA	FY06
Lewis	Bryan	A.	SSG	32	13-May-06	RC	258th MP BN	Iraq	Yes	KIA	FY06
Hernandez	Robert		SSG	48	28-Mar-06	RC	3rd BN, 318th REG	Iraq	Yes	KIA	FY06
Dudkiewicz	Kasper	A.	SPC	22	15-Jan-06	AC	511th MP CO	Iraq	Yes	KIA	FY06
Johnson	Robert	T.	SPC	20	07-Jan-06	RC	805th MP CO	Iraq	Yes	KIA	FY06
UpChurch	Clinton	R.	SPC	31	07-Jan-06	AC	3rd BCT	Iraq	Yes	KIA	FY06
Field	Nathan	R.	SGT	23	07-Jan-06	RC	4249th MP CO	Iraq	Yes	KIA	FY06
Bennet	Keith		SSG	32	11-Dec-05	NG	28th MP Co	Iraq	Yes	KIA	FY06
Atkins	Julia		SGT	22	10-Dec-05	AC	64th MP CO	Iraq	Yes	KIA	FY06
Delgado	Marc	A.	PFC	21	24-Nov-05	AC	170th MP Co, 504th MP BN	Iraq	Yes	KIA	FY06
Reynolds	Steven	C.	SSG	32	24-Nov-05	AC	170th MP Co, 504th MP BN	Iraq	Yes	KIA	FY06
Lightner	Daniel	R.	SSG	28	27-Oct-05	RC	28th MP Co	Iraq	Yes	KIA	FY06
Robinson	Jeremiah	W.	SPC	20	06-Oct-05	NG	860th MP Co	Iraq	Yes	KIA	FY06
Westbrook	Marshall	A.	SGT	43	01-Oct-05	NG	126th MP Co, NM	Iraq	Yes	KIA	FY06
Allen	Howard	P	SGT	31	26-Sep-05	NG	860th MP Co, AZ	Iraq	Yes	KIA	FY05
Derrick	Andrew	J.	SGT	25	23-Sep-05	AC	411th MP Co, 720th MP BN	Iraq	Yes	KIA	FY05
Allers	William		SGT	28	20-Sep-05	NG	198th MP BN	Iraq	Yes	KIA	FY05
Campbell	Jeremy	M.	SPC	21	11-Sep-05	AC	108th MP Co (ABN)	Iraq	Yes	KIA	FY05
Partridge	Todd	Willard	SGT	35	20-Aug-05	AC	170th MP Co, 504th MP BN	Iraq	Yes	KIA	FY05
McNaughton	James	D.	SSG	27	02-Aug-05	RC	306th MP BN	Iraq	Yes	KIA	FY05
Butler	Adrian	J.	SPC	28	27-Jul-05	AC	411th MP Co, 720th MP BN	Iraq	Yes	KIA	FY05

LIST OF CASUALTIES

Last Name	First Name	MI	Rank	Age	Date	Comp	Unit	Country		KIA	FY
Tollefson	John	O.	SPC	22	27-Jul-05	AC	411th MP Co, 720th MP BN	Iraq	Yes	KIA	FY05
Hines	Timothy	J.	PFC	21	14-Jul-05	AC	64th MP Co, 720th MP BN	Iraq	Yes	KIA	FY05
Coutu	Matthew	S.	2LT	23	27-Jun-05	AC	64th MP Co, 720th MP BN	Iraq	Yes	KIA	FY05
Hayes	Michael	R.	PFC	29	24-Jun-05	NG	6-7th MP Co	Iraq	Yes	KIA	FY05
Huff	Sam	W.	PFC	28	18-Apr-05	AC	170th MP Co, 504th MP BN	Iraq	Yes	KIA	FY05
Hudson	Aaron	M.	PV2	20	16-Apr-05	AC	401st MP Co, 720th MP BN	Iraq	Yes	KIA	FY05
Ramirez-Gonzalez	Aleina		SPC	33	15-Apr-05	AC	STB, 3rd BDE	Iraq		KIA	FY05
Bruce	Travis	R.	SPC	22	23-Mar-05	AC	504th MP BN	Iraq	Yes	KIA	FY05
Koele	Shane	M.	SSG	25	16-Mar-05	AC	2-2th MP Co	Iraq	Yes	KIA	FY05
Harrison	George	D.	PFC	22	02-Dec-04	AC	293rd MP Co	Iraq	Yes	KIA	FY05
Larsen	Cole	W.	PFC	19	13-Nov-04	AC	272nd MP Co	Iraq	Yes	KIA	FY05
Cunningham	Darren	J.	SSG	40	30-Sep-04	AC	89th MP BDE	Iraq	Yes	KIA	FY04
Price	Timothy	E.	1LT	25	07-Sep-04	AC	127th MP Co, 709th MP BN	Iraq	Yes	KIA	FY04
Daniels	Danny	R.	SPC	23	20-Jul-04	AC	630th MP Co	Iraq	Yes	KIA	FY04
Frank	Craig	S.	SPC	24	17-Jul-04	NG	1775th MP Co	Iraq	Yes	KIA	FY04
Martin	Stephen	G.	SSG	39	01-Jul-04	RC	330th MP Det	Iraq	Yes	KIA	FY04
Kiser	Charles	A.	SSG	37	24-Jun-04	RC	330th MP Co	Iraq	Yes	KIA	FY04
Mastrapa	Arthur	S.	SGT	25	16-Jun-04	NG	351st MP Co	Iraq	Yes	KIA	FY04
Tuazon	Andrew	L.	PFC	21	10-May-04	AC	293rd MP Co, 3rd MP BN	Iraq	Yes	KIA	FY04
Murray	Rodney	A.	SGT	28	09-May-04	NG	351st MP Co	Iraq	Yes	KIA	FY04
Buryj	Jesse	R.	PFC	21	05-May-04	AC	66th MP Co	Iraq	Yes	KIA	FY04
Garrison	Landis	W.	SGT	23	29-Apr-04	NG	333rd MP Co	Iraq	Yes	KIA	FY04
Witmer	Michelle	M.	SPC	20	09-Apr-04	NG	32nd MP Co	Iraq	Yes	KIA	FY04
Kephart	Jonathan	R.	SPC	21	09-Apr-04	AC	230th MP Co	Iraq	Yes	KIA	FY04
Shanberger III	Wentz	J.	SSG	33	24-Mar-04	AC	2-st MP Co	Iraq	Yes	KIA	FY04
Mowris	James	D.	SSG	37	29-Jan-04	RC	805th MP Co	Afghanistan	Yes	KIA	FY04
Mihalakis	Michael	G.	SPC	18	25-Dec-03	NG	270th Mp Co, 49th MP BN	Iraq	Yes	KIA	FY04

LIST OF CASUALTIES

Last_Name	First_Name	Middle	Rank	Age	Date of Death	Compo	Unit	Theater	GWOT	Status	Fiscal Year
Reese	Aaron	T.	SSG	31	10-Dec-03	NG	135th MP Co	Iraq	Yes	KIA	FY04
Tomko	Nicholas	A.	SGT	24	09-Nov-03	RC	307th MP Co	Iraq	Yes	KIA	FY04
Bell	Aubrey	D.	SGT	33	27-Oct-03	NG	214th MP Co	Iraq	Yes	KIA	FY04
Williams	Michael	L.	SPC	46	17-Oct-03	NG	105th MP Co	Iraq	Yes	KIA	FY04
Bellavia	Joseph	P.	SSG	28	16-Oct-03	AC	716th MP BN	Iraq	Yes	KIA	FY04
Bosveld	Rachel	K.	PFC	19	16-Oct-03	AC	527th Mp Co	Iraq	Yes	KIA	FY04
Grilley	Sean	R.	CPL	24	16-Oct-03	AC	716th MP BN	Iraq	Yes	KIA	FY04
Orlando	Kim	S.	LTC	43	16-Oct-03	AC	716th MP BN	Iraq	Yes	KIA	FY04
Potter	Darrin	K.	SGT	24	29-Sep-03	NG	223rd MP Co	Iraq	Yes	KIA	FY03
Andrade	Michael		SPC	28	14-Sep-03	NG	115th MP Co	Iraq	Yes	KIA	FY03
Caldwell	Charles	T.	SGT	38	01-Sep-03	NG	115th MP Co	Iraq	Yes	KIA	FY03
Camara	Joseph		SSG	40	01-Sep-03	NG	115th MP Co	Iraq	Yes	KIA	FY03
Franklin	Bobby	C.	SSG	38	20-Aug-03	NG	210th Mp Co	Iraq	Yes	KIA	FY03
Perry	David	S.	SSG	36	10-Aug-03	NG	649th MP Co	Iraq	Yes	KIA	FY03
Ramsey	Brandon		PFC	21	08-Aug-03	NG	933rd MP Co	Iraq	Yes	KIA	FY03
McMillin	Heath	A.	SGT	29	27-Jul-03	NG	105th MP Co	Iraq	Yes	KIA	FY03
Puello-Coronado	Jaror	C.	SGT	36	13-Jul-03	RC	310th MP BN	Iraq	Yes	KIA	FY03
Orengo	Richard	P.	SPC	32	26-Jun-03	NG	755th MP Co	Iraq	Yes	KIA	FY03
Burkhardt	Travis	L.	SGT	26	06-Jun-03	AC	170th MP Co	Iraq	Yes	KIA	FY03
Nalley	Kenneth	A.	PVT	19	26-May-03	AC	501st MP Co	Iraq	Yes	KIA	FY03
Petriken	Brett	J.	SSG	30	26-May-03	AC	501st MP Co	Iraq	Yes	KIA	FY03
Evans Jr.	David		PVT	18	25-May-03	AC	977th MP Co	Iraq	Yes	KIA	FY03

ENDNOTES

PART I: TESTING THE REGIMENT

3: FINDING A ROLE FOR THE MILITARY POLICE: OPERATION ENDURING FREEDOM

1 Gregg Jones, "Forces Search Caves: Efforts Fail to Yield Osama bin Laden," Knight Ridder News Service, December 19, 2001.

2 Two detainee deaths were reported up the chain of command and an Army criminal investigation initiated as a result. Subsequently this led to courts-martial of those involved, which were completed by early 2005. The deaths were ruled to be homicides carried out by military police and military intelligence soldiers: one on December 4 and the other on December 10, 2002. It is important that these actions are noted, but this is not place for a detailed review. Our objective is to discuss the role and daily works of professional MPs, not murderers or criminal cases.

5: TOPPLING SADDAM: OPERATION IRAQI FREEDOM BEGINS

1 Only Iraqi convicts; the units for non-Iraqi prisoners were not included. Also exempted from the deal were murderers who had not been forgiven by the families of their victims and those who owed money to the state; see "Jailbirds Fly Free in Iraq," Cameron W. Barr, *Christian Science Monitor,* October 22, 2002; "Saddam

Empties Iraq's Jails," David Blair, *UK Telegraph,* October 21, 2002.

2 Associated Press, "Saddam's Amnesty Blamed for Iraq's Crime," May 16, 2003.

3 John F. Burns, "How Many People Has Hussein Killed?" *The New York Times,* January 26, 2003.

4 *Helena Independent Record,* "The War's Long End Game," March 11, 2003.

5 Steven Kraytak, "1,100 More Fort Hood Troops Will Be Sent Overseas," *Austin American-Statesman,* March 18, 2003.

6 Anna Mulrine, "Former POW Jessica Lynch Recalls Her Captivity in Iraq," *U.S. News & World Report,* March 18, 2008; John W. Gonzalez, "Ex-POWs Get Hero's Welcome / Thousands Cheer Return of 7 to Texas," *Houston Chronicle,* April 20, 2003; Michael Luo and Chris Roberts, "Soldiers of Ambushed 507th Maintenance Company Finally Tell Their Story," Associated Press, August 26, 2003.

7 ABC News Online, "Pentagon Confirms Nine U.S. Bodies Retrieved," May 5, 2003; "Lynch Rescue Team Dug up Bodies with Bare Hands," Reuters, April 6, 2003.

8 *CBS News,* Bootie Cosgrove-Mather, "On the Scene: Looting in Baghdad," April 8, 2003.

9 Reuters, "Rampant Looting Across Iraq," April 19, 2003.

10 CNN, "Saddam Statue Toppled in Central Baghdad," April 9, 2003; CCTV.com, "Saddam Statue Toppled in Baghdad amid Looting, Anarchy," April 10, 2003.

11 Associated Press, "Looters Plunder Iraq National Museum, Smashing and Stealing Artifacts," April 12, 2003; Maria Puente, "The Looting of Iraq's Past," *USA Today,* April 15, 2003.

12 Associated Press, "Looters Storm Baghdad Palace: Rest of City Quiets Down," April 13, 2003; Jaime Holguin, "Looters Taking the Kitchen Sink, Too" *CBS News,* April 10, 2003.

13 Associated Press, "China: Looters Attack Embassy in Baghdad," April 13, 2003.

14 BBC UK, "Animals Looted from Baghdad Zoo," April 17, 2003.

15 *The Washington Post,* "U.S. Foresaw Chaos, but Was Unprepared for Baghdad's Quick Fall," April 15, 2003.

16 Alan Sipress, "Military P.R. Force Wages a Battle to Stay on Message" *The Washington Post,* March 29, 2003.

17 Paul Harris, "Children Run Cheering as Troops Roll In," *UK Guardian,* March 23, 2003; Gregg Zoroya, "At Last, Smiles Greet U.S. Troops as They Enter Holy City in Iraq" *USA Today,* April 3, 2003.

18 Associated Press, "U.S. Sending Up to 4,000 to Baghdad for Looting Patrol," April 29, 2003.

19 AFP, "Graves of Nearly 1000 Iraqi Political Prisoners Found," April 22, 2003; Andrew Buncombe, "Iraq's Secret Prison of Horror and Death Unveiled," *New Zealand Herald,* April 15, 2003.

20 Ian Fisher, "As Hussein Faded, Prisoners Were Executed," *The New York Times,* April 28, 2003; *The Age Australia,* "Into the Regime's Death Machine," April 16, 2003.

6: CUL-DE-SAC OF DEATH

1 *The New York Times,* "President Bush's Remarks Declaring an End to Major Combat in Iraq," May 2, 2003; David Paul Kuhn, "'Mission Accomplished' Revisited" *CBS News,* April 30, 2004.

2 Spc. Kristopher Joseph, "18th Military Police Brigade Helps Iraqis Restore Law and Order," USAREUR News Release, May 16, 2003.

3 John Mintz and Vernon Loeb, "Americans Release 3500 Prisoners of War on Parole" *Sydney Morning Herald,* May 10, 2003.

4 Patrick E. Tyler, "New Policy in Iraq to Authorize GI's to Shoot Looters," *The New York Times,* April 14, 2003.

5 AFP, "U.S. Takes Aim at Baathists," May 18, 2003.

6 Rory McCarthy, "U.S. Police to Be Boosted by 6,000" *UK Guardian,* May 16, 2003.

7 Spc. Kristopher Joseph, "V Corps and Iraqi Police Reopen Baghdad Jail," V Corps News Release, May 21, 2003.

8 Mary Dejevsky, "U.S. Disbands Saddam Army and Bans Ba'athists" *UK Independent,* May 24, 2003; AFP, "Iraqi Security Bodies, Army Dissolved: U.S. Move to Consolidate Control," April 24, 2003; Joel Roberts, "U.S. Dismisses Saddam's Troops" *CBS News,* May 23, 2003; Rory McCarthy, "Saddam's Army and Apparatus Sacked" by *UK Guardian,* May 24, 2003.

9 Associated Press, "Saddam's Amnesty Blamed for Iraq's Crime," May 16, 2003.

10 Michael R. Gordon, "Debate Lingering on Decision to Dissolve the Iraqi Military," *The New York Times,* October 21, 2004.

11 Associated Press, "One U.S. Soldier Killed, Five Injured in Fallujah Rocket Attack," June 5, 2003.

12 Michael R. Gordon, "G.I.'s in Iraqi City Are Stalked by Faceless Enemies at Night," *The New York Times,* June 11, 2003.

13 William Booth and Daniel Williams, "U.S. Soldiers Face Growing Resistance," *The Washington Post,* June 10, 2003.

14 Associated Press, "FBI: U.N. Bomb Made from Materials from Saddam's Old Arsenal," August 19, 2003; Vivienne Walt, "Military Munitions Used in UN Blast, FBI Says" *The Boston Globe,* August 21, 2003.

15 *Fox News,* "Envoy Dead as Blast Shatters UN's Baghdad HQ," August 20, 2003; *Fox News,* "Bombing at U.N. HQ in Baghdad Raises Terror Concerns," August 20, 2003; Vivienne Walt, "UN Workers Feared Security Was Too Lax," *The Boston Globe,* August 31, 2008.

16 Vivienne Walt, "Military Munitions Used in UN Blast, FBI Says," *The Boston Globe,* August 21, 2003; BBC, "FBI Search for UN Bomb Clues," August 21, 2003.

17 *Newsweek*, "Countdown to Mayhem," September 1, 2003.

18 *Fox News,* "U.N. Blast Probe Focuses on Security Guards," August 23, 2003.

19 "U.S. Reacted Slowly to Looting of Ammunition," *Times of India,* November 1, 2004.

7: THE YEAR FROM HELL BEGINS

1 Leo Shane III, "All I Thought Was 'Shoot back!' " *Stars and Stripes,* June 14, 2005.

2 Identified in part by a note written by Yi and posted to the fallen, heroesmemorial.com Web site.

8: FUELING THE FLAME

1 Judy Pointon, "New Day Dawns for Iraq's Press" BBC, June 24, 2003.

10: COALITION UNDER SIEGE

1 While we have not had the pleasure of meeting Alvin Shell in person, we learned about his valor during an interview with MG Quantock and were able to reconstruct his story using the following materials: Ellen N. Woods, "Badly Burned After Rescuing His Sergeant, His Long Recovery Typifies Perseverance, Courage" Stephens Media; Navy Lt. Jennifer Cragg, "Army Family Heals Together, Stays Together" American Forces Press Service, July 1, 2009; Department of Defense Wounded Warrior Diaries, video interview (http://www.defense.gov/home/features/2008/0908_wwd/index_ Shell.html).

13: NATIONAL GUARD WEEKEND

1 "After Action Report: Raven 42 action in Salman Pak," blackfive .net.

2 Steve Fainaru, "Silver Stars Affirm One Unit's Mettle," *The Washington Post,* June 26, 2005.

3 McQ, "Project Hero: SSG Timothy Nein, Distinguished Service Cross," Project Hero Web site, posted February 23, 2008.

4 Michael D. Doubler, "The National Guard and the War on Terror: Operation Iraqi Freedom," Defense Department, Army National Guard Bureau.

5 Steve Fainaru, "Silver Stars Affirm One Unit's Mettle," *The Washington Post,* June 26, 2005.

6 Video interview: "America's Army Real Heroes: Jason Mike" (YouTube.com).

7 McQ, "Project Hero: SSG Timothy Nein, Distinguished Service Cross," posted February 23, 2008.

8 "After Action Report: Raven 42 Action in Salman Pak."

9 Steve Fainaru, "Battle Knows No Gender Lines," *The Washington Post,* June 26, 2005.

10 We did not have the opportunity to interview personally any participants in this action. In addition to the previously referenced citations, the following materials were used to reconstruct Raven 42's Palm Sunday Ambush: Leo Shane III, "Bullets Pinging All over the Place" *Stars and Stripes,* June 14, 2006; Martha Raddatz, "Small Guard Unit Fends Off Dozens of Iraqi Insurgents" *ABC World News Tonight*; "Kentucky Guardsmen Decorated for Gallantry," United States Forces—Iraq press release, June 15, 2005.

14: DEPLOYMENT CYCLES

1 Interview with Command Sergeant Major Henry Stearns, April 2010, at FOB Lightning, Gardez, Afghanistan.

16: BETRAYAL IN KARBALA

1 Suleiman al-Khalidi and Luke Baker, "Muslim Holy Day Ends in Karbala Bloodshed," *Independent Online* [South Africa], March 2, 2004.

2 James Conachy, "Who Benefits from the Karbala and Baghdad Bombings?" World Socialist Web Site news, March 5, 2004.

3 Suleiman al-Khalidi and Luke Baker, "Muslim Holy Day Bloodshed," *Independent Online* [South Africa], March 2, 2004.

4 *BBC News,* "Iraq Suicide Bomb Blasts Kill 120," January 5, 2006.

5 Mark Kukis, "Ambush in Karbala," *Time,* July 26, 2007.

6 "Qods (Jerusalem) Force—Iranian Revolutionary Guard Corps (IRGC - Pasdaran-e Inqilab)" Federation of American Scientists Web page, August 21, 1998.

7 Bill Roggio, "Iraqi Forces Search for Qods Force Agents," *The Long War Journal,* November 7, 2009.

8 CNN, "U.S. General: Iraqi Militants Trained in Iran," May 25, 2007.

9 Sergeant Sara Wood, "Petraeus: Interrogations Reveal Iranian Influence in Iraq," American Forces Press Service, April 26, 2007.

10 Press briefing with Brig. Gen. Kevin Bergner, spokesman, Multi-National Force—Iraq, July 2, 2007.

11 Michael R. Gordon, "U.S. Ties Iran to Deadly Iraq Attack," *The New York Times,* July 2, 2007.

12 BBC News, "U.S. Troops Kill Iraq Raid 'Leader,' " May 21, 2007; John Ward Anderson and Sudarsan Raghavan, "Roadside Bombs Kill 7 Soldiers, Interpreter," *The Washington Post,* May 21, 2007.

13 Alissa J. Rubin and Michael R. Gordon, "U.S. Frees Suspect in Killing of 5 G.I.'s," *The New York Times,* June 8, 2009.

14 David Williams, "Evidence Grows That British Hostage Peter Moore WAS Held by the Iranians," *UK Daily Mail,* January 1, 2010; Jack Bremer, "Hostage Peter Moore Has to Defend Torture Claims," *UK First Post,* March 16, 2010 .

PART II: GOBSMACKED: A DOWNRANGE REALITY CHECK

21: GRINDING IT OUT

1 Lisa Zyga, "Huachuca Biometrics Device Separates Friends from Foes," March 17, 2008.

2 "Biometric Automated Toolset (BAT) and Handheld Interagency Identity Detection Equipment (HIIDE) Overview for NIST XML & Mobile ID Workshop," September 19, 2007.

INDEX